£10

1997

National Service was one of the great dividing lines for Britain's post-war generations. For 2.3 million youngsters born before or during the Second World War conscription was a necessary rite of passage. For those born thereafter it was a narrow escape, something gratefully avoided following the government's decision in 1957 to concentrate on all-volunteer forces backed by the nuclear deterrent. For later generations it became an historical curiosity which only surfaced whenever Blimps suggested that a dose of conscription would sort out juvenile crime.

Looking back, it is curious to find only brief references to National Service in the books dealing with that period. Partly this is due to the reluctance of historians to integrate social with military history; partly, too, it reflects an absence of primary sources and a small and selective literature. But there is another reason. Few of the young men completing their National Service recorded their experiences at the time. Only later did they look back – sometimes in anger, more often nostalgically – at their youthful lives when they wore uniform as sailors, soldiers or airmen.

It was a time when Britain was changing rapidly as the old certainties gave way to the euphoria of rock and roll which presaged the emergence of a new youth culture. By the late 1950s conscription was markedly unpopular and the strong public approval which had accompanied its introduction in 1947 had given way to distaste. The Korean War of 1950–3 was one reason, the counter-insurgency campaigns in Malaya, Kenya and Cyprus another. Neither the conscripts nor their families could understand what they were about. Nearly 400 National Servicemen were killed on active service and hundreds more were recklessly exposed to radiation in nuclear bomb tests in Australia and the Pacific.

And yet, for most conscripts the experience appears to have been only mildly negative. So various were the opportunities offered by the armed forces that National Servicemen did benefit. They were taught trades; there were opportunities to see the world at a time when air travel was the preserve of the wealthy; and exposure to responsibility turned young men into mature adults.

Since National Service came to an end in 1963 Britain's armed forces have undergone radical change. Smaller, professional, well equipped and technologically minded, it is impossible to imagine conscripts ever serving with them again. National Service is one of the great untold stories of 20th-century military history: I hope this book will redress the balance.

D1081270

The Best Years of Their Lives
The National Service Experience 1945–63

TREVOR ROYLE

JOHN MURRAY
Albemarle Street, London

A catalogue record for this book is available from the British Library

ISBN 0 7195 5688 0

Printed and bound in Great Britain by The University Press, Cambridge

*The inset cover illustrations are reproduced courtesy of (clockwise from top) John
Inglis; James H. Austin; Regimental Headquarters, King's Own Scottish Borderers;
and Mike Burdge. The background illustration is reproduced courtesy of Regimental
Headquarters, Duke of Wellington's Regiment.*

CONTENTS

LIST OF ILLUSTRATIONS

I would like to thank the following for permission to reproduce illustrations: James H. Austin (18); British Aerospace (24); BBC Hulton Picture Library (4); Mike Burdge (15, 34); Peter Davies (12, 22, 28); Regimental Headquarters, Duke of Wellington's Regiment (30, 31); Ian Duncan (21); John Inglis (14, 19); Regimental Headquarters, King's Own Scottish Borderers (1, 3, 9, 32); John G. McIlvean (11); David McMurray (6); David McNeill (10); Navy, Army and Air Force Institutes (25, 26, 29); Derek Pilkington (20); RAOC Museum (2); George Savage (13, 23); *Soldier* (5, 7, 8, 16, 17, 27, 33).

LIST OF ABBREVIATIONS

AA: Anti-Aircraft
AB: Able-bodied Seaman
AC: Aircraftman
AER: Army Emergency Reserve
ARP: Air Raid Precautions
ATC: Air Training Corps
ATDU: Aircraft Torpedo Development Unit
AWOL: Absent Without Leave
BAOR: British Army of the Rhine
BEF: British Expeditionary Force
BOAC: British Overseas Airways Corporation
BTA: British Troops Austria
CB: Confined to Barracks
CCF: Combined Cadet Force
CIGS: Chief of the Imperial General Staff
CND: Campaign for Nuclear Disarmament
CO: Commanding Officer
CPO: Chief Petty Officer
CQMS: Company Quartermaster-Sergeant
CSM: Company Sergeant-Major
CT: Captured Terrorist
DCIGS: Deputy Chief of the Imperial General Staff
DSO: Distinguished Service Order
EOKA: National Organisation of Cyprus Fighters
FarELF: Far East Land Forces
FEAF: Far East Air Force
GD: General Duty
GHQ: General Headquarters
GOC: General Officer Commanding

HLI: Highland Light Infantry
HMTT: Her Majesty's Troop Transport
HNC: Higher National Certificate
IRA: Irish Republican Army
KOSB: King's Own Scottish Borderers
KSLI: King's Shropshire Light Infantry
LAC: Leading Aircraftman
LSE: London School of Economics
MASH: Mobile Army Surgical Hospital
MC: Military Cross
MCP: Malayan Communist Party
MEAF: Middle East Air Force
MELF: Middle East Land Forces
MIO: Military Interviewing Officer
MO: Medical Officer
MP: Military Police; Member of Parliament
MPAJA: Malayan Peoples Anti-Japanese Army
MRLA: Malayan Races Liberation Army
MTB: Motor Torpedo Boat
NAAFI: Navy, Army and Air Force Institutes
NATO: North Atlantic Treaty Organisation
NCO: Non-Commissioned Officer
OCS: Officer Cadet School
OCTU: Officer Cadets Training Unit
OR: Other Ranks
PO: Petty Officer; Potential Officer
POM: Potential Officer Material
POW: Prisoner of War
PSO: Personnel Selection Officer
PT: Physical Training
PTI: Physical Training Instructor
RA: Royal Artillery
RAC: Royal Armoured Corps
RAEC: Royal Army Educational Corps
RAF: Royal Air Force
RAFVR: Royal Air Force Volunteer Reserve
RAMC: Royal Army Medical Corps
RAOC: Royal Army Ordnance Corps
RAPC: Royal Army Pay Corps
RASC: Royal Army Service Corps
RE: Royal Engineers
REME: Royal Electrical and Mechanical Engineers
RNAS: Royal Naval Air Station

RNVR: Royal Naval Volunteer Reserve
RP: Regimental Police
RSM: Regimental Sergeant-Major
RTU: Returned to Unit
RUR: Royal Ulster Rifles
SAC: Senior Aircraftman
SAS: Special Air Service
SBS: Special Boat Service
SEATO: South-East Asian Treaty Organisation
SHAPE: Supreme Headquarters Allied Powers Europe
SNP: Scottish National Party
SOE: Special Operations Executive
SP: Special Policeman
SSG: Summed Selection Group
TA: Territorial Army
TAF: Tactical Air Force
TEWT: Tactical Exercise Without Troops
TR: Training Regiment
TRREME: Training Regiment Royal Electrical and
   Mechanical Engineers
TRRS: Training Regiment Royal Signals
TUC: Trades Union Congress
UN: United Nations
USAF: United States Air Force
USAMC: United States Army Medical Corps
USB: Unit Selection Board
WAAF: Women's Auxiliary Air Force
WOSB: War Office Selection Board
WRNS: Women's Royal Naval Service
WRVS: Women's Royal Voluntary Service

PREFACE

I did not do National Service. By the time I was 19 – the usual age of call up – the last National Servicemen had been discharged and the armed forces were becoming once more societies apart. Nevertheless, National Service cast a long shadow over my earlier schooldays in the 1950s: like the steam train, the Teddy Boy and Mrs Dale's Diary, it was simply a part of the fabric of everyday life. The purpose of this book, therefore, is to tell the story of National Service through the memories of the men who were called up into the nation's armed forces during the post-war period of conscription – that is, between 1945 and 1963. Many of these I interviewed, others provided written accounts in answer to questions; others still allowed me to see diaries and letters written by them at the time of their National Service, or generously lent me photographs and other treasured souvenirs. All the services are represented, the majority coming from the Army: for every Royal Navy National Serviceman, the Royal Air Force claimed twelve and the Army thirty-three. This proportion is reflected in the numbers of men who agreed to provide me with the plethora of first-hand accounts, stories and viewpoints which make up this book.

For the military historian to adopt this approach, though, is to enter a minefield of hidden critical traps. While it is hardly a disqualification to write about events of which he has no direct personal experience, reliance on first-hand accounts only can produce distortions. Was it really possible for so many piles of coal to have been whitewashed? Did thousands of National Servicemen waste their time weeding lawns armed only with their eating irons? Or has one case become a universal example, the creation of a nation of Kilroys? Myth-making was not unique to National Service, but it was a powerful element in the lives of young men plunged at an impressionable age into the harsh hurly-burly of service life. It surprised me how potent were many of those myths and how frequently they recurred in accounts of National Service life. Equally surprising were the number of absurd or comic incidents which turned out to have a solid foundation in fact. Both provided a useful lesson – that however useful personal experience is as evidence, it is dangerous to present it as a universal truth.

Much of the evidence in this book comes from 'oral history', the area of historical research which A. J. P. Taylor condemned as 'old men drooling over their youth'. Certainly, there are obvious pitfalls in being hypnotised by one man's account of an event in his past, but at one time all history was oral and it is only in fairly modern times that it has been reduced to 'hearsay', valuable only when it has been analysed and then committed to paper. This is to disregard the nature of oral evidence which provides a different and human standpoint to an event. It was one thing, for example, to read the official history of the war in Korea and of the part played in it by the National Servicemen: it was another to listen to the story of a conscript corporal seriously wounded at the Third Battle of the Hook. One provided an overall, detached analysis of the war; the other, one man's account of a cataclysmic event in his life. Both perspectives are equally valid in understanding the multi-dimensional reality of life in the services.

In each case, where direct experience is quoted, the account was shown to the National Serviceman for his comments, both to check for accuracy and to ensure that the evidence had been presented in its correct context. I am grateful for all the patience, humour and enthusiasm generated by this task, for it was one of the unwritten codes of National Service life that a man should never volunteer for anything. Ever. This book could not have been written without the unflagging and generous help of all those ex-National Servicemen who chose to break that rule and who allowed themselves to be interviewed or who provided written accounts. Some have preferred to remain anonymous and I have honoured that condition. The others who contributed directly are listed at the back, but they all have my special thanks.

In particular, I would like to thank Robin Morgan, Principal of Daniel Stewart's and Melville College, Edinburgh, who suggested the idea in the first place and who then made many valuable comments and suggestions to improve the completed manuscript. I should also like to thank those ex-National

Servicemen who read and commented upon sections of the book, although I hasten to add that all errors of fact and judgement remain my responsibility alone.

Two Regular Army soldiers assisted with my research. General Sir Anthony Farrar-Hockley, GBE, KCB, DSO, MC, allowed me to read his unpublished thesis on National Service and British Society which he completed during 1968–1970 while holding a defence fellowship at Exeter College, Oxford. Major-General Frank Richardson, CB, DSO, OBE, who has helped me greatly with other ploys in the past, offered advice and encouragement and provided useful information about youth training schemes. I am grateful to them both.

At a critical stage in my research, Professor J. M. Lee, Professor of Politics in the University of Bristol, informed me of the existence of his archive of letters dealing with National Service, which he had given to the Nottingham Record Office for safe-keeping. He then extended that help by providing me with background information and in helping to make contact with his erstwhile correspondents. Having been determined unfit for National Service, Professor Lee acted as a 'link-man' in the correspondence of his fellow sixth-formers at the Henry Mellish Grammar School in Nottingham who were called up. Adrian Henstock and his staff in Nottingham then made the task of researching the archive a relaxed and enjoyable experience. They all have my thanks.

For their help or advice in researching the many different facets of National Service life and the social and military background, I would like to thank the following individuals and organisations:

David Alton, MP, for information about the British Nuclear Tests Veterans Association.

G. H. Bolsover, formerly Director of the School of Slavonic and East European Studies in the University of London, for advice on the arrangements for teaching Russian to selected National Servicemen.

David Cullum, formerly 3rd Officer on HMTT *Empire Wansbeck*, for information about trooping arrangements on the Harwich to Hook of Holland run.

The Campaign for Nuclear Disarmament, for information and evidence about the British nuclear tests series of the 1950s.

The Defence Begins at Home Committee and its Secretary Michael Hickey, for papers relating to home defence.

Michael Grieve, for the loan of papers dealing with his prison sentence as a Conscientious Objector.

The Imperial War Museum, especially T. C. Charman of the Department of Printed Books and Dr Christopher Dowling, Keeper of the Department of Education and Publications.

The Ministry of Defence, Army Historical Branch, for providing a bibliography of National Service material.

The Racial Equality Commission, for advice on the recruiting of coloured Commonwealth citizens.

The Royal British Legion and the Royal British Legion, Scotland, for help in contacting ex-National Servicemen.

N. E. Trowell, Hon. Curator, NAAFI Historical Collection, for assistance with the location of photographs.

Lt. Col. D. C. R. Ward, King's Own Scottish Borderers, for assistance with the location of photographs.

For information about their parties' current and past attitudes towards conscription, I wish to thank the staffs of the Conservative, Labour, Liberal, Scottish Conservative, Scottish National and Social Democrats parties.

For their understanding toleration of the bizarre financial conditions faced by authors, grateful thanks are due to my bankers, The Royal Bank of Scotland.

No book of this kind could have been researched without the willing help of the press and the broadcasting media. I am especially grateful to the following editors and producers who assisted me by publishing requests for information from ex-National Servicemen: Elaine Maclean, BBC Radio Scotland; the AM Programme, BBC Radio Wales; Bill McStay, editor of *Claymore*; William Deedes, editor of *The Daily Telegraph*; Rennie McOwan of the *Edinburgh Evening News*; Maurice Fleming, editor of *The Scots Magazine*; Anthony Troon of *The Scotsman*; Peter M. Howard, editor of *Soldier*; the editor of *The Times Literary Supplement*; Denis Gane of the *Western Mail*.

For their customary patient help and encouragement I wish to thank the staffs of the National Library of Scotland, Edinburgh and the Public Record Office, Kew.

I acknowledge with thanks permission to include in this volume quotations from: George Coppard, *With a Machine Gun to Cambrai* (HMSO); Sir Rupert Hart-Davis (ed.), *Siegfried Sassoon Diaries 1915–1918* (Faber and Faber); Richard Hillary, *The Last Enemy* (Macmillan Ltd, London and Basingstoke); Edmund Ions, *A Call to Arms: Interlude with the Military* (David & Charles); Rudyard Kipling, 'Tommy', from *The Definitive*

Edition of Rudyard Kipling's Verse (The National Trust for Places of Historic Interest or Natural Beauty); Eric Linklater, *Our Men in Korea* (HMSO); David Lodge, *Ginger, You're Barmy* (Martin Secker and Warburg); Compton Mackenzie, *On Moral Courage* (The Society of Authors); William Moore, *The Durham Light Infantry* (Leo Cooper); Alan Sillitoe, *The Key to the Door* (W. H. Allen), Copyright © Alan Sillitoe 1961; Andrew Sinclair, *The Breaking of Bumbo* (Faber and Faber); Christopher Sinclair-Stevenson, *The Life of a Regiment: The History of the Gordon Highlanders, 1945–1970*, vol. VI, (Leo Cooper); John Tucker, *Johnny Get Your Gun* (William Kimber). Every effort has been made to trace the holders of copyright in the quotations included. For any errors or omissions I naturally and formally apologise.

Chapter One

OUR GUARDS AND GARRISONS

Traditionally, the people of Great Britain have entertained a profound revulsion toward the idea of maintaining large conscript armed forces. Yet on three occasions this century, in 1916, 1939 and 1947, parliament has resorted to compulsory military service, passing acts which required men over the age of 18 to serve in one of the nation's three armed services. Twice, war in Europe, or the threat of it, demanded that Britain raise a mass army to fight the huge conscript forces of her enemies. On the third occasion, in 1947, wartime conscription was continued as peacetime National Service, a measure forced on a Labour government confronted by a deteriorating international situation and by the need to cover the retreat from Empire. Altogether, some 14 million men have been called up to serve in the colours this century, the last conscript soldier being demobbed in May 1963 when the armed forces went back to what they always had been: a small corps of highly trained professionals, a society apart.

The reasons for a widespread distrust of a standing army are long embedded in the nation's history. For centuries, the defence of Britain was delegated to the ships of the Royal Navy: when there was a war on the continent, armies could be hurriedly raised and then just as quickly disbanded once peace had been secured. The safety of the kingdom and the means of internal security lay in the hands of the militia, a compromise between the demands for compulsory or voluntary military service, which in theory provided for a nation in arms, should the need ever arise. Based on the historical principle that every man in Britain had an obligation to defend his country, the Militia had been in existence since Anglo-Saxon times (as the *fyrd*) and continued in being in one form or another until well into the nineteenth century. During the Tudor and Elizabethan periods it had been an effective instrument, but by the time of the Restoration it was a debased and useless military force, capable only of minor police duties. The experience of the seventeenth-century civil war, and of the ensuing Commonwealth with its 40,000-strong professional army, had further convinced most responsible citizens that the presence of a standing army was an evil to be avoided at all costs. When King Charles II returned to the throne in 1660 it was agreed by Parliament that, with the exception of a personal bodyguard for the monarch, the army should be disbanded. A minor insurrection led by a lunatic called Venner changed all that. Dispersement of the armed forces was halted and two of General Monck's regiments were kept in being for the protection of the King's person. In addition, two regiments of foot-guards and two troops of horse-guards were raised, and the *Royal Ecossais*, Scots troops in French service, were recalled to Britain. (These live on today as, respectively, the Grenadier Guards, the Life Guards, the Royal Horse Guards and the Royal Scots.) It is from that date, 1661, that the first regular regiments of the British Army boast their origins, and it can be argued, too, that it is from their foundation that the problem of recruitment began on a large scale.

It was a precarious enough beginning. Parliament refused to call the new forces an 'army' and the country's annual estimates for military expenditure referred only to 'our guards and garrisons', in deference to the public abhorrence of a professional army. The word 'army' did not appear officially until 1755, when the first Army Lists were published. For the soldiers, conditions mirrored the lack of interest taken in them by the country's political leaders. Pay was bad and frequently in arrears, clothing and food lay within the purlieu of the colonel of the regiment and was all too often second-rate, living conditions were primitive and punishments barbaric. During the eighteenth and nineteenth centuries the army was an extremely unpopular institution, and it was widely observed that only the most worthless young men would 'go for a soldier'. Those who did volunteer did so for reasons which were hardly idealistic. Poverty, unemployment, crime, sexual misdemeanours, boredom, all offered an impetus for a young man to change his lot for a way of life which at the very least offered some security, a modicum of pay, clothing and food, and a certain position in the world. Once they had joined up, they were in for life, thus widening further the gap between civilian and military society.

Recruiting was done by 'Beat of Drum'. Regiments were

empowered to raise sufficient recruits by the voluntary principle of offering the sovereign's shilling, but the method was grossly abused. Recruiting parties became little more than press gangs, and thousands of able-bodied men were kidnapped or duped into joining the army throughout the eighteenth century. It was a routine which continued into the nineteenth century, too, when Britain was again involved in a major European war. Rifleman John Harris had been conscripted into the 66th Regiment (2nd Berkshire) in 1803 but two years later he fell in with a recruiting party of the 2nd battalion, 95th Rifles, while serving in Ireland. Their green jackets and devil-may-care appearance, plus the presence of seemingly unlimited whiskey, convinced him that nothing would do until he, too, was a Rifleman.

> We started on our journey, one beautiful morning, in tip-top spirits from the Royal Oak at Cashel; the whole lot of us (early as it was) being three sheets in the wind. When we paraded before the door of the Royal Oak, the landlord and landlady of the inn, who were quite as lively, came reeling forth, with two decanters of whisky, which they thrust into the fists of the sergeants, making them a present of decanters and all to carry along with them, and refresh themselves on the march. The piper then struck up, the sergeants flourished their decanters, and the whole route commenced a terrific yell. We then all began to dance, and danced through the town, every now and then stopping for another pull at the whisky decanters. Thus we kept it up till we had danced, drank, shouted and piped thirteen Irish miles, from Cashel to Clonmel. Such a day, I think, I never spent, as I enjoyed with these fellows; and on arriving at Clonmel we were as glorious as any soldiers in all Christendom need wish to be. In about ten days after this, our sergeants had collected a good batch of recruits, and we started for England.[1]

In such manner, with music and whiskey, did Harris and his fellow recruits become Riflemen and soldiers of the King, but before they could board their ship they met with a detachment of Irish mothers determined to prevent their sons from being empressed into British service. Their tearful protests were to no avail and the Irish recruits set out, drunk as lords, for Bristol where they 'roamed about the town, staring at and admiring everything they saw, as if they had just been taken wild in the woods.'

It was a scene which was depressingly familiar at the time. Another highly literate recruit, and contemporary of Harris, Bombardier Alexander, remembered being tricked into joining up in Glasgow by a sergeant of artillery who plied him with drink and painted a rosy picture of bounties, sergeant's stripes, eager women and riding to war on a charger. The reality, Alexander quickly discovered, was quite different, but his experience was probably no worse than that suffered by one of his fellow countrymen in Edinburgh. This unfortunate fellow ran away from home to try his luck as an actor but on his first appearance on stage dried completely. So taken aback was he, and so deranged by the incident, that he rushed out of the theatre and took refuge in drink in the neighbouring port of Leith. The following morning he awoke to ashes aboard a southbound troopship, having taken the King's Shilling while in his cups from a sergeant in the 71st Regiment (Highland Light Infantry). Others could be more fortunate, like John Shipp of Winchester who was inveigled into the army at the age of ten and who rose in time to the commissioned rank of Ensign, but for most recruits, whether empressed or volunteers, the army was a dead end. Thomas Jackson ended his service with the Coldstream Guards after losing a leg and was awarded a pension of a shilling a day, 'a might poor recompense,' he thought, 'for having spent twelve years of the prime of [my] manhood in the service of [my] country'.

Because the government feared a standing army run by professionals, commissions were usually only awarded to those who could afford to purchase them. Thus, high-ranking officers were only promoted because they were gentlemen or aristocrats who could afford not only the purchase of their commissions, but also their upkeep. As a result, most of them had little clue what they were supposed to do: at the beginning of the Napoleonic Wars the Adjutant-General complained that of the twenty-six regiments at his disposal, twenty-one were 'commanded literally by boys or idiots'. Private means, not brains, were an essential requirement of any officer who wanted to rise, and gradually the army became a dumping ground for dull-witted young gentlemen whose fathers could not place them in any other profession. Certain corps like the Royal Artillery and the Royal Engineers promoted their officers according to their proficiency, and careerist officers gravitated towards the Indian Army, but for much of the nineteenth century officers remained a caste apart, conditioned by their private wealth and their public school educations.

For all those drawbacks – an officer corps which did not know what it was doing and a rank and file composed of layabouts and men forced into service – the British Army was not without its virtues as a fighting force. Bolstered by mercenary forces it triumphed in Marlborough's wars and, in spite of the

Adjutant-General's misgivings, performed well against the professional armies of France, eventually defeating Napoleon's seemingly impregnable battalions at Waterloo. That it did so was no thanks to the recruiting system. In 1802 the government passed the Ballot Act which laid down that all men between the ages of 18 and 40 were liable for military service by dint of lottery, but this attempt at conscription foundered on the escape clause which allowed those drafted to pay a substitute to take their places. After Waterloo, Britain began to disengage from European affairs and the army became an instrument of colonial expansion and policing, fighting wars far away from home and helping to extend Britain's world empire. It would take the disaster of the Crimean War before the mould could be broken and the army begin its long route-march towards acceptance by the public and, more importantly, by its political masters.

Things fared little better in the Royal Navy, where few landlubbers would have disagreed with Dr Johnson's dictum that 'no man will be a sailor who has contrivance enough to get himself into a jail; for being in a ship is being in jail with the chance of being drowned'. The navy had good reason to treat its seamen as prisoners, for it knew that most of them would desert their ships were regular shore-leave to be granted as a right. Below decks – the haunt of 'The People' as the crew were known – common sailors lived in cramped, crowded and filthy conditions where disease was endemic. More sailors died of illness or perished in accidents than were killed in action and only the daily dose of grog, a half pint of rum mixed with water, kept crews semi-comatose and relatively happy. Recruitment was carried out by the press gang, a horrible and violent method of forcible conscription by which groups of sailors roamed major ports clubbing their victims into service. During the Napoleonic Wars the gangs gained a measure of official respectability through the Admiralty's Impress Service, but the horror and violence did not lessen. Five out of six sailors served their country during this period only because they had been caught by the press gang, and for them it was a loathsome experience.

> We had pressed him [William Skill] out of the India fleet, just on a return from a three-year voyage, pleasing himself with the idea of beholding those he held most dear (a mother and sister) for whom he had brought presents many a long mile: and although in his spare time aboard us he had made away with most of his apparel for grog, which he was fond of, yet the presents remained untouched, hoping one day to take them home himself.[2]

The unfortunate William Skill did not live to give his presents
to those he held most dear: like some 80,000 other anonymous
sailors in King George III's navy he died in an accident, falling
overboard during a storm.

Only in the contribution of its officers was the navy better
served than the army. During the reign of Samuel Pepys, one of
the most sensible and forthright naval administrators of all time,
it was ruled that no officer could become a lieutenant without
passing a professional examination and without serving several
years at sea. Entry to the naval officer corps might have been by
wealth and social standing, but promotion depended on skill,
intelligence and energy – so much so that most sailors were happy
to put up with an autocratic captain provided he was also
efficient. (A business-like captain was more likely to capture an
enemy ship, and the subsequent prize money meant booty for
everyone who had taken part in the action.)

As happened with the army, the old order was changed by the
Crimean War. From mid-century onwards the Royal Navy was
reformed as the ages of first, the ironclad, and then of the big-gun
battleship, were introduced. In a world which saw the
development of screw propulsion, the triple expansion steam
engine, the mine and the submarine, the Royal Navy could no
longer rely on the press gang and the lash to maintain its ships'
crews: improvements in the technology of ships were matched by
wide-ranging reforms in the men's conditions of service. Sailors
were given proper uniforms, life below decks became more
hygienic and humane, decent rates of pay were introduced and
pensions awarded on retirement. As British dreadnoughts and
gunboats gradually became the embodiment of the Victorian *Pax
Britannica* and the symbol of Britain's right to world dominion,
the Royal Navy became a self-contained society, willing and able
to look after those who served it. Consequently, recruiting
became less of a problem and by 1897, the year of Queen
Victoria's Jubilee Review at Spithead, the Royal Navy was able
to pick and choose from the healthiest and best-educated young
men wanting to join its ranks. The Admiralty might have
remained conservative and cautious, and technological advances
might have been frequently haphazard, but the late Victorian
navy offered its men the chance to learn a trade and to see the
world; and in the era of the gunboat, young officers who had
previously had to wait for dead men's shoes for a chance of
promotion were given independent commands while still in their
twenties. At the dawn of the twentieth century it was no bad thing

to be a sailor: as the music hall song said, didn't all the nice girls love them?

In the army the change was less dramatic, reflecting perhaps the government's view that it was only the second shield of defence, and dyed-in-the-wool conservatism at the War Office meant that old habits died hard. The purchase of commissions was abolished in 1871, a move which was not universally welcomed in military circles: the Gordon Highlanders' historian noted that it was 'a boon to the officers but a great cost to the country', and in one of the smart cavalry regiments a young subaltern was heard to remark, on being told that the War Office had credited his account with one hundred pounds, 'Good God, do they actually pay us?'

Responsibility for the wind of change rested in the capable hands of Edward Cardwell, Gladstone's Secretary of State for War and the man most closely linked with the great Liberal reforms of the Victorian army. Although many of his reforms were built on previous changes in the administration of the War Office and on the reorganisation of the Militia in 1852, Cardwell's term of office forced the army hierarchy to correct some of its more obvious defects and anomalies. Under his Army Enlistment Act of 1870 the period of a soldier's service was reduced to twelve years, six with the colours and six on reserve, and closer links were developed between the regular regiments and the Militia and the Volunteers, thus providing the army with a reserve pool of trained men. Some living conditions were improved as new barracks were built and rates of pay became less miserly, but in spite of the reforms the army was still considered to be the home of rascals, drunks and other social misfits. 'There are plenty of things Steady Young Men can do when they can read and write as you can,' his mother told young Wullie Robertson when he joined the 16th Lancers in 1877. 'I would rather bury you than see you in a red coat.' Robertson went on to become a commissioned officer and one of the army's greatest administrators, crowning his career with a Field Marshal's baton, but Mrs Robertson was not alone in showing such maternal concern at her son's choice of career. Countless other mothers fretted when their sons joined up, and until the Boer War the army remained largely out of sight, though firmly in mind, fighting Queen Victoria's little wars of empire. The army's rank and file found its poet laureate in Rudyard Kipling, whose *Barrack-Room Ballads* seemed to most soldiers to echo their own private sentiments and values.

You talk o' better food for us, an' schools an' fires, an' all:
We'll wait for extry rations if you treat us rational.
Don't mess about the cook-room slops, but prove it to our face
The Widow's Uniform is not the soldier-man's disgrace.
For it's Tommy this, an' Tommy that, an' 'Chuck him out, the
* brute!'*
But it's 'Saviour of 'is country' when the guns begin to shoot;
An' it's Tommy this, an' Tommy that, an' anything you please;
An' Tommy ain't a bloomin' fool – you bet that Tommy sees!

In fact, Tommy Atkins and his brother Jock were not really to find acceptance with the great British public until the Boer War of 1899–1902 brought home the unmistakable truth that, however competent the army had been at fighting ill-equipped and primitively armed natives in bushfire wars, it could be held by the superior weapons and tactics of the white Boer farmers. At the end of the Boer War the British volunteer army in South Africa numbered a quarter of a million, and few British families had not been brought into contact with it and with the realities of warfare and high losses. Certainly, most Britons could not avoid learning the lesson that their army was not the power it had seemed to be and that radical reforms were needed. Between 1902 and 1909 a succession of Secretaries of State for War – St John Brodrick, Arnold-Foster and Haldane – helped to drag the army into the twentieth century. Under Haldane – the most visionary of the three – the Territorial forces came into being as a first line of home defence, based on the old Volunteer and Yeomanry forces; the Militia was transformed into a Special Reserve; and from the Regular Army a small and well equipped Expeditionary Force (BEF) was formed as a highly mobile fire brigade for action overseas.

The problems facing Haldane were formidable. With limited manpower he had to construct an army to garrison India, based largely on long-service troops, and he had to reorganise the home field army and the reserve system so as to provide a constant pool of first-class fighting soldiers. Throughout his reforms it was made perfectly clear to him by his fellow Liberals that conscription was a non-starter, that public opinion would not smile on any politician who advocated the notion that the defence of his country was the responsibility of every capable male citizen. By 1913 recruitment into the army had fallen to a new low – only 35,000 men joined up that year – and, if questioned on the subject, most people would have gladly echoed Swift's sentiments, written almost two hundred years earlier in his cynical pamphlet, *Of Public Absurdities in England*: 'A standing army in England, whether in time of Peace or War, is a direct absurdity for it is no part of our business to be a warlike nation, otherwise than by our fleets. In foreign wars we have no concern, further than in conjunction with allies, whom we may either assist by sea, or by foreign troops paid with our money.'

Although most right-thinking Britons would have abhorred the notion of employing mercenaries, it was still generally considered that Britain's first line of defence was provided by the ships of the Royal Navy. When Britain went to war in August 1914 its army was still some 50,000 short of its official complement: nevertheless, through Haldane's reforms, the BEF, which sailed to France shortly after war had been declared, was the best organised and best equipped army ever to leave Britain's shores. It acquitted itself with honour at the Battles of Mons and the Marne, though at great cost to men and equipment, and by Christmas it was obvious to everyone that the war would not be quickly won. One man had foreseen that eventuality: Field Marshal Horatio Herbert Kitchener, Secretary of State for War and the Empire's greatest soldier. It was at his behest that Britain's first mass army, 70 divisions strong, was called into being, and it was under his rule at the War Office that the battle for conscription reached its climax.

At the outbreak of the First World War, Britain's regular army numbered 247,432 troops, of which half had been earmarked for service with the six divisions of the BEF. The reserves and Haldane's Territorial forces added a further half-million men liable for service, but these had been pencilled in for home defence and for the defence of the great imperial garrisons. Not that such paucity of men worried Britain's war leaders, whose strategy argued that the war would be won at sea by the weight of numbers and superior quality of the ships of the Royal Navy. Meanwhile, in France, the small but highly efficient BEF would stand on the left of the French army to repulse the Germans, holding them up long enough to be crushed by the Russian steamroller from the east. That, too, was the strategic scenario favoured by most professional soldiers: few envisaged that the conflict would become a war of entrenchment, and it was an indication of British optimism that volunteers were originally invited to sign on for six months or for the duration of the war, whichever proved to be longer.

Kitchener, who had been called in by Asquith to be the first soldier since General Monck to sit in the Cabinet, refused to fall in with his colleagues' wishful thinking. His military career had been built on his great victory at Omdurman in 1898, when, by dint of careful planning and superior firepower, he had crushed completely a native army, and in the Boer War where his ponderous military juggernaut had broken the mobile Boer farmers' will to win. No other British military commander in modern times had ever used his men in such large numbers in order to achieve his objectives. All his military instincts, therefore, suggested that Britain could not win the war without an army which was the numerical superior of her enemies. At his first meeting of the Cabinet he astonished his colleagues by telling them that the war would last three years and that Britain would require one million men in arms. The race was then on to find that number.

The story of the building of Kitchener's volunteer armies is one of the great tales of British improvisation. By the end of 1914, 1,186,000 men had enlisted. In August, on one day alone, 35,000 men joined up – as many as had been recruited during the whole of 1913. For some, the early weeks of the war had an unreal quality, creating a feeling that it was all a glorious adventure and that man had been transformed and liberated from the doldrums of everyday existence. Ordinary people felt ennobled by the exhilaration of war and chivalry; self-sacrifice and heroism were the watchwords of those first weeks. There were few who did not respond to their call.

> Glossing over my childhood, I merely state that in 1914 I was just an ordinary boy of elementary education and slender prospects. Rumours of war broke out and I began to be interested in the Territorials tramping the streets in their big strong boots. Although I seldom saw a newspaper, I knew about the assassination of Archduke Ferdinand at Sarajevo. News placards screamed out at every street corner, and military bands blared out their martial music in the mainstreets of Croydon. This was too much for me to resist, and as if drawn by a magnet, I knew I had to enlist straightaway. [3]

George Coppard, the nephew of the distinguished English short story writer A. E. Coppard, served from 1914 to 1919, first with the Royal West Surrey Regiment and then with the newly-formed Machine Gun Corps; he enlisted when he was little over sixteen and his attitude towards volunteering was fairly typical of his generation. (His memoirs, *With a Machine Gun to Cambrai*, are also amongst the best from the World War I period.)

Patriotism and a fear that they might miss out on a glorious adventure were the main reasons for the men of 1914 flocking to join the colours, but there were other impulses. War had not come as a bolt from the blue. German re-armament and continuing unrest in the Balkans and the near east, plus the formation of the major power blocs, had alerted the informed to the possibility of conflict, a prospect which the Liberals had sought to avoid by appeasement. Now that appeasement had failed it was the turn of the younger men to put a stop to the arms race and to international aggression: for those idealists the war in 1914 was a war to end wars. There was, too, a sense of honour that if Britain were to remain a first-class power, a world leader worthy of the right to control its Empire, then the only way to uphold that privilege was to fight. 'Morale and patriotism were marvellously high. The great majority of the British public was tremendously proud of our heritage and of our enormous world-wide Empire. The greatest incentive was, of course, the determination to protect our families and homes from foreign invasion. The possibility of defeat was not for one moment entertained, so great was our faith and trust in the nation.'[4] That testimony of Johnny Tucker, a volunteer who fought on the western front at the Battles of the Somme, Ypres and Arras, was echoed by over two million of his generation.

The country went recruitment mad. Posters appeared everywhere, cajoling young men to enlist – the most famous and the most telling being Alfred Leete's depiction of Lord Kitchener as a messianic recruiting sergeant with his pointed command, 'Your Country Needs YOU!' Mass meetings, addressed by the great and good, were held all over the country, popular artists like Harry Lauder offered their services free of charge, and the movement spawned Phyllis Dane's famous call to arms in her music hall song 'We don't want to lose you, but we think you ought to go.' Other patriotic flag-waving innovations included the notorious all-female Order of the White Feather, whose members made it their business to roam the towns of Britain distributing white feathers to those not in uniform; and the Women of England's Active Service League, who called upon patriotic women to refuse to be seen in the company of men who had not enlisted. Soon men of service age were saying that the chance of meeting such bloodthirsty Amazons was worse than the prospect of a dawn attack on the German lines.

The press, too, played its part in raising Kitchener's armies, and by the beginning of 1915 the all-party Parliamentary Recruiting Committee was confident that it could raise a continuous supply of ready recruits for the armed services. The first volunteer divisions were in action by the Spring, but that year was destined to bring a bitter harvest in terms of casualties and with it a drastic fall-off in the number of recruits. For the Conservative opposition this could only mean one thing – the introduction of compulsory service. Although it had been toyed with in 1906 when Haldane had begun his military reforms, the Liberal ministers had turned their faces against any form of conscription, arguing that it would infringe individual liberties and offend the trades union movement with its inbuilt distrust of any legislation which would erode workers' rights.

Nevertheless, the notion of Britain's young manhood serving a term in the colours refused to go away: in 1905 Lord Roberts, one of the country's best-respected soldiers, took up the cause of the National Service League which advocated a period of service in the armed forces for all young men. It rested its case primarily on the need for a strong army for home defence, arguing that Germany was preparing for a war of invasion and that the Royal Navy would not be able to prevent it happening. As late as 1912, Roberts was claiming that once Germany had achieved naval and military superiority over Great Britain it would make a lethal strike across the North Sea and that Britain would be powerless to resist, a claim which caused an uproar. A motion was raised in the House of Commons for the old Field Marshal's pension to be reduced and the Liberal press roundly condemned him for uninformed scaremongering. While Roberts was correct in his assessment that Germany was re-arming with war in mind, he was stretching a point in suggesting that Britain's naval and military defences were so weak that any invasion could not be repelled. The other weakness in the League's argument was that the conscripts would only be used in home defence, whereas any future war would be fought overseas. But what had killed off any hope of the League's succeeding in its aims was the overwhelming dislike most people felt for compulsory military service.

From the beginning of the war Kitchener, too, had been convinced that compulsory service was not necessary to raise the men he required to defeat the Central Powers. Rather, his solution preferred an arrangement whereby volunteers would be assimilated quickly into the army without the need to assemble new bureaucratic machinery to deal with conscription. To confirm the logic of his thinking he pointed out that it had taken France and Germany some thirty years to perfect the administration of their conscript armies; how could Britain equal that in the space of a few months? Besides, he was not unaware of the magic of his personal magnetism in gaining new recruits. 'I have held up my finger and the men are flocking to me in thousands,' he was often heard to remark in the War Office whenever compulsory service was suggested by his colleagues. He might have added, too, that voluntary service seemed to be both fair and virtuous to those who joined up, or to those who allowed their employees to enlist. 'The employer allowed a percentage of his men to go,' noted General C. R. Ballard. 'Instead of grumbling about compulsion, he felt a glow of virtue over doing his bit. The rich merchant, whose chauffeur had enlisted, sweated virtue as he walked to the office. Everybody felt the uplift which comes from voluntary service.'

However, by the summer of 1915 the voluntary recruitment figures were low enough to send alarm bells ringing in the Cabinet, by then a coalition administration under Prime Minister Asquith. The heady days of a popular rush to the colours being a thing of the past, the government introduced in July 1915 the compromise measure of the National Registration Bill, whereby a register would be compiled of all persons, male or female, aged between 15 and 65. Out of it came the Derby Scheme, administered by Lord Derby, under-secretary for War and – especially in the north of England – a popular political orator.

The basis of the scheme was that men from the register aged between 18 and 41 would sign up, or 'attest', but would only be called up as and when they were needed, depending on such factors as the importance of their jobs to the war effort or whether or not they were married: the object of the exercise being first of all to enlist all young bachelors in unskilled jobs. Attesting the recruits was left in the hands of local tribunals, who were not always the best judges of a man's suitability, and the scheme frequently fell foul of corrupt practices. Nevertheless, the principle of voluntary recruiting, so dear to most Liberals, remained intact until the beginning of 1916 when the Military Service Bill was passed, automatically transferring all attested single men on the register to the Army Reserve. Even that draconian measure failed to bring in the desired numbers, and conscription became law in May 1916 with the passing of the National Military Service Act. Thus, at one stroke, compulsory service, so long resisted in Britain, became the law of the land at a time when the country was facing its greatest hour of need.

Over five million men served their country during World War I and the introduction of conscription meant that almost every available man was put into uniform of one kind or another. Even the incapacitated had room found for them in labour battalions, and women, too, were called up to serve in the auxiliary services. War on that scale had never been experienced by the British people and by its end, in November 1918, it had created a feeling of relief added to numb despair. Scarcely a family in the country had failed to be affected by it, the mood at Armistice being captured in his diary by the poet Siegfried Sassoon:

> I was walking in the water meadows by the river below Cuddesdon this morning – a quiet grey day. A jolly peal of bells was ringing from the village church, and the villagers were hanging little flags out of the windows of their thatched houses. The war is ended. It is impossible to realise. Oxford has much flag-waving also, and signs of demonstration.
>
> I got to London about 6.30 and found masses of people in streets and congested Tubes, all waving flags and making fools of themselves – an outburst of relief and mob patriotism. It was a wretched wet night, and very mild. It is a loathsome ending to the loathsome tragedy of the last four years.[5]

For most of the volunteers and conscripts who were demobbed in 1919, the watchword for post-war Britain was 'Never again!' Within twenty years their pious hopes were to be dashed as once more Britain had to rebuild a mass army for service beyond her shores.

When the men of Kitchener's armies went off to war in France they sang such cheerful songs as 'Tipperary' and 'Mademoiselle from Armentieres', or hopeful sentimental ditties like 'The Roses of Picardy'. In 1939 their sons, called to the ranks by peacetime conscription, were more likely to give vent to their feelings of disillusionment when they burst into song:

> *We had to join, we had to join, we had to join Belisha's army.*
> *Fourteen bob a week,*
> *Fuck all to eat,*
> *Marching round the square with bloody great blisters on our feet;*
> *We had to join, we had to join, we had to join Belisha's army.*
> *If it wasn't for the war,*
> *We'd have fucked off long before,*
> *Hore-Belisha – you're barmy!*

Not that the men of 1914 were any purer in mind than their successors – 'Mademoiselle from Armentieres' spawned a host of outrageously crude variations – but there was a sense of shared experience in the songs they sang. Battalions going up to the line were encouraged to sing by their commanding officers, both to keep up their spirits and to take their minds off the coming ordeal. Soldiers in World War II were more likely to sing sad songs of pessimism and despondency with their lot. While the Australians were cooped up in Tobruk during the North African campaign, their thoughts strayed not to patriotism but to a self-mocking contemplation of the sheer awfulness of their plight:

> *All bloody fleas, no bloody beer,*
> *No bloody booze since we've been here,*
> *And will it come? No bloody fear,*
> *Oh Bloody! Bloody! Bloody!*
> *The bloody rumours make me smile,*
> *The bloody wogs are bloody vile,*
> *The bloody Tommies cramp your style,*
> *Oh Bloody! Bloody! Bloody!*

Later, the verses – with some variations – were taken up by the soldiers of the Orkney garrison during the same war.

They had good reason to be down-hearted. Their fathers had told them about the horrors of the trenches on the Western Front, and during the early 1930s especially there had been a strong antipathy to the armed forces and conscription. Although Britain had been 'victorious' in 1918, the general post-war public reaction was that the army had won in spite of the mistakes made by its senior battlefield commanders, who had recklessly allowed British blood to run freely in senseless frontal attacks on the German lines. To make matters worse, soldiers returning from the front found not the land fit for heroes promised by Lloyd George, but conditions of poverty and neglect. Men who had been conscripted between 1916 and 1918 found themselves unemployed and forced to beg while their red-tabbed senior officers won handsome gratuities from a grateful parliament. Politics, too, had begun to change. The Liberals went into a permanent decline while the Labour Party became stronger, taking its support from the trades union movement and channelling it into political power. Pacifism became an acceptable ideology as people recoiled from the butchery of war. Britain had had enough of her armed forces for the time being, and the new mood of the people was distinctly anti-military.

'No-one who is so placed as I am,' said military theorist Basil

Liddell Hart in a radio broadcast in 1936, 'to hear the views of all sorts and classes of people can help realising what lasting harm the memory of the Somme and Passchendaele has done to the cause of defence and the attitude of people towards it.' He was not far wrong. These were also the views of the sons of infantrymen who had fought in Flanders, and they were determined not to undergo the same experience.

The consequences for the army were far-reaching. Just as had happened so often in the past, the mass army needed to fight a war in Europe was quickly disbanded. The National Military Service Act was rescinded, thereby bringing conscription to an end, and the army became something of a backwater, far removed from the mainstream of British life. Expenditure on it and the Royal Navy was reduced in 1919 by the so-called 'Ten Year Rule', by which defence estimates were controlled on the philosophy that no major war could be expected within ten years of drawing up the figures. (In 1932 this was reduced to five years.) Only the fledgeling RAF, founded upon the army's Royal Flying Corps in April 1918, was to receive funds for expansion in the belief that any future war could not be won without a large fleet of bomber aircraft. In turn, the army reverted to its imperial police-keeping role and stagnation crept into its strategic and tactical thinking: ironically, the tank, the major British military innovation of World War I, was largely ignored by the military planners, and the army was not properly mechanised until the latter years of the 1930s.

By then the failure of appeasement, the revelation of the League of Nations as a broken reed, and the rise of Hitler's Nazi Germany culminating in Chamberlain's climb-down at Munich, had convinced most politicians that Britain's military house had to be put in order. Under the new Secretary of State for War, Leslie Hore-Belisha, the Conservative government abandoned the concept of Britain's limited liability in a future war and belatedly began to rebuild and re-equip her army. The first step was taken at the beginning of January 1939 when a National Service Appeal was launched, calling on able-bodied citizens to volunteer for service in the country's armed forces. As Chamberlain explained in a wireless broadcast, the appeal had been made by the government to prevent the introduction of compulsory service.

Compulsion is not in accordance with the democratic system under which we live, or consistent with the tradition of freedom which we have always striven to maintain. We are confident that we shall get all the volunteers we want without recourse to compulsion.

The initiative had the support of the Labour and Liberal parties because it seemed to avoid the dreaded concept of conscription, but within two months it was obvious to service chiefs that a little more coercion might be necessary. Partly in response to French taunts that in the event of war the British would fight to the last drop of French blood, Hore-Belisha was persuaded to double the size of the Territorial Army, a move which was announced to universal approval in the House of Commons on 29 March. A fortnight earlier, units of the German Army had occupied Prague: even the most ardent optimist could not fail to ignore that war in Europe was just around the next corner.

In fact, the increase in the size of the Territorial Army achieved little in putting Britain on a war footing. The only way for the army to make any impact on European strategy, as it had done in Wellington's and Kitchener's time, was as a mass fighting force – and that meant the re-introduction of conscription. Against a background of continuing German aggression in eastern Europe and Anglo-French guarantees of support to Poland and Roumania, Chamberlain was forced to come to terms with the fact that some kind of compulsory military service would have to be imposed upon the country. Until then he had endorsed the promise made by his predecessor, Baldwin, that conscription would not be introduced in peacetime, but the tenor of the times demanded a desperate solution. With the British press baying for action, Chamberlain reluctantly gave way to Hore-Belisha's proposals for limited national military service. On 26 April he rose in the House of Commons to announce his plans for conscription which were contained in the Military Training Bill. This gave the government the power to call up for military training all men between the ages of 20 and 21. Training would last six months; thereafter conscripts would serve for three-and-a-half years in the Territorial Army, but their service was to be limited to home defence in the United Kingdom. Provision was to be made for those in reserved occupations and for conscientious objectors; a later amendment excluded men from Northern Ireland from being called up. In addition, a Royal Naval Special Reserve was created to train men for the navy, and the bill was passed by parliament a month later with limited support from the Labour and Liberal opposition.

Hore-Belisha had maintained that the Act would provide the

army with 200,000 extra men in the first year and 800,000 within three years (in consequence of the higher birth rates of 1920 and 1921), but within three months of the declaration of war in September 1939, 727,000 men had registered for service. They were known as militia men. By the end of 1941 that number had swollen to 4,320,000 conscripts, the legislation being regularised by subsequent National Service (Armed Forces) Acts which adjusted the age-range of potential recruits to those between 18 and 41 (extended to 51 in 1941). Other emergency measures introduced by the government included provision for national service in industry, as ARP (Air-Raid Precautions) wardens, firemen, ambulance drivers, etc., and 21,800 young men worked as 'Bevin Boys' in Britain's coalmines. In all, 16,416,000 men and women registered for non-military national service during World War II.

Given the dislike and suspicion most young men had entertained for the armed services, it may well be asked why they flocked to join up. There was none of the raw patriotism of 1914, nor did society feel inclined to offer white feathers to those not wearing uniform; men joined up with little enthusiasm, it is true, but they did want to get the job done, to bring war to an end and defeat Hitler's Germany. In World War I blind obedience had been enough, but the traditional rebuke to any serviceman showing initiative – 'You're not paid to think!' – found no place in World War II. Instead, the armed forces organised lessons and lectures explaining the reasons for the war, and commanding officers were encouraged, whenever possible, to take their men into their confidence before going into action. In that respect, the conscripts of World War II were probably better informed than their predecessors, and less likely, too, to be taken in by calls to King and Country.

Of course, there were those who joined up to prove a point, to show that they were not the dilettantes a hostile press had painted them. In February 1933 the Oxford Union had caused great offence by debating, and then supporting, a motion 'that this House will in no circumstances fight for its King and Country.' When war broke out, Oxford men of a slightly later vintage like Richard Hillary were not slow in volunteering their services.

> We were disillusioned and spoiled. The press referred to us as the Lost Generation and we were not displeased. Superficially we were selfish and egocentric without any Holy Grail in which we could lose ourselves. The war provided it, and in a delightfully palatable form. It demanded no heroics, but gave us the

opportunity to demonstrate in action our dislike of organised
emotion and patriotism, the opportunity to prove to ourselves and
to the world that our effete veneer was not as deep as our dislike of
interference, the opportunity to prove that, undisciplined though
we might be, we were a match for Hitler's dogmafed youth.[6]

By his own admission, Hillary's experience was unusual in that
he had enjoyed a gilded youth far removed from the economic
pressures of the 1930s but his hatred of Nazism was probably little
different from that felt by others of his generation. By 1939
awareness of the Nazi menace was palpable; not a few, too,
remembered 'the crystal spirit' of the Spanish Civil War and the
dream of a popular front to unite the opponents of Fascism.

At the outbreak of war the British Army was in a position to
put four divisions into the field in France, plus seven divisions in
the Middle East, a field division and a brigade in India and two
brigades in Malaya. The Royal Navy had started rebuilding in
1936 and entered the war with a numerical superiority over the
Germans, but it was still woefully short of escorts for convoy
duty. Only the RAF had prospered with the introduction of radar
and the huge fighter programme resulting in adequate supplies of
Spitfire and Hurricane aircraft for home defence. Once again it
seemed that Britain was going to war with the mentality and
equipment of the previous conflict. After two years of muddle she
re-adjusted her war aims but still Britain could not play the
commanding role of World War I. Russia bore the brunt in the
defeat of Germany, and America took the leading role in the
operations against the Japanese; only in North Africa and Italy
did the British armed forces take the major initiative.
Nevertheless, by 1945 the men in uniform were better equipped,
fitter and numerically stronger than any who had fought before. It
had been a long slog, and now they were fed up with war and with
the armed forces: to a man they were browned off and wanted to
get back to civilian life. As they had been told they were fighting
for freedom, they now wanted it themselves.

Their attitudes had altered in other, more fundamental ways.
Many of the old shibboleths of drill and bull had gradually
disappeared during the war itself. Only a minority of men,
especially in the army, saw active service, and those who fought
not only had a good conceit of themselves but also a clear idea of
where discipline ended and common sense began. In many
fighting units after D-Day, officers and NCOs refused to wear
badges of rank, were on Christian name terms with their men,
and while in combat allowed themselves to come under the orders

of men in better tactical positions, whatever their rank. Many of
those innovations were introduced to confuse enemy snipers but
there was, too, a new sense of democracy in the forward fighting
units in 1944 and 1945. Typical of their sense of *amour propre* was
an incident recorded in his memoirs by R. M. Wingfield, a
conscript in 1/6th Queen's Royal Regiment, attached to the 7th
Armoured Division in northern France in 1944. While waiting to
board the ship taking them to Normandy, his unit gave vent to
their frustration at being treated in a high-handed manner by
displaying the same insolent tactics used by mutinous French
troops in 1917.

> Some wag in the first file let out a quavering 'Ba-a-a-a-a.' Soon the
> noise spread throughout the ship and on to the waiting lines on the
> quay. A Brigadier, purple and frothing, stormed up and down the
> line screaming at us. The sheep stopped in his immediate vicinity
> and resumed their frenzied bleating when he passed. Having
> demonstrated our Infantry superiority and defied official threats,
> we shut up when we became bored. The Brigadier nearly burst
> into flames.[7]

Eventually Wingfield and his mates got aboard the troop-ship
and settled down, but not before they had been forced to
'requisition' deck space from an Artillery unit whose officer had
sneered, 'You bastards are expendable!' The squaddies' reaction
was predictable – here were no sacrificial lambs being prepared
for slaughter on a new Western Front: when the Gunner officer
tried to pull rank, it was suggested to him that he mind his own
business. 'You can fetch Monty! We won't even move for him. So
— off!' Men of that calibre were hardly likely to be enamoured
when it became known in 1945 that Britain still required a large
army, navy and air force to meet her vastly increased global
responsibilities, and to concentrate resources in key areas in
Europe and her increasingly brittle Empire.

It took two years for the Labour government under Prime
Minister Clement Attlee – a critic of conscription in 1939 – to
come to terms with the problems of wartime conscription. During
that time many far-reaching civilian reforms had been introduced
to British society – a vast re-housing programme had been
instituted, a National Health Service had come into being in 1946,
the coal industry was nationalised that same year, the railways a
year later. Little attention, however, had been paid to the armed
forces, many of whose men were still in the firing line in far-flung

parts of the world. The difficulty facing Attlee's government was that, having been elected largely on the strength of the 'khaki' vote, it was now honour-bound to try to speed up demobilisation. If compulsory service were to come into being – as was increasingly likely – then it would have to be handled carefully. By educating the army, the sergeants of the Army Education Corps had encouraged the men to think about what they had been fighting for and to apply those lessons to their own lives. The post-war soldier was inclined, therefore, to be more critical, more questioning of orders. Many service chiefs, in turn, doubted the wisdom of retaining half-hearted wartime recruits in peacetime and understood that their men, having served their country, were now anxious to return to civilian life. In several units of the Army and the RAF indiscipline was rife, and there were cases of near-mutiny by men no longer prepared to accept wartime conditions of discomfort.

The most serious of these involved 258 men of the 13th Bn. The Parachute Regiment who mutinied at Muar Camp near Kuala Lumpur in Malaya. When they refused to return to their lines on 14 May 1946, expressing dissatisfaction with their living conditions, their Commanding Officer had them all arrested and put under the armed guard of the 1st Bn. The Devonshire Regiment. Most of the paratroopers were still in their early twenties and had fought at D-Day, the Ardennes and the Rhine Crossing, but their posting to South East Asia Command proved to be the last straw when they found that their camp was little more than a slum with inadequate sanitation and insect-ridden living accommodation. At the trial, held at Kluang in September, their defending officer referred to the action as a 'strike', to which the Judge-Advocate responded: 'The word "strike" is not in Army vocabulary. It is mutiny or nothing else.' The sentences were predictably severe. Three men were admonished but eight were given five years' imprisonment with hard labour and 247 received two years' similar punishment. By showing a strong hand the military court was no doubt attempting to discourage other attempts at mutiny, but the punishment was out of keeping with the times and the sentences were later quashed on the grounds of technical irregularities during the trial. Mutiny of another kind had erupted in 1945 when an unsuccessful attempt was made to establish a Soviet in a British infantry regiment stationed in Egypt: although these were both minor enough incidents, they did prove a point that there were good political reasons for speeding up demobilisation and replacing the wartime army with peacetime recruits.

Faced by the twin evils of a deteriorating international situation and the possibility of unrest in the ranks, the Labour government, against all previous practice, was forced to introduce a National Service Bill in March 1947, making every male citizen between the ages of 18 and 26 liable for eighteen months' compulsory military service. The measure was due to remain effective at least until 1954 although the Labour Secretary of State for War, Mannie Shinwell, hoped that he would be able to soothe backbench critics by rescinding it an early date. The Conservatives supported the Bill but some seventy Labour MPs sided with the Liberals in opposing it. So vociferous was their challenge that the government compromised by reducing the length of service to twelve months, the amended Act becoming law in May. Within a year, a National Service (Amendment) Act had been passed, extending the period of enlistment to eighteen months, with four years in the reserves; and in 1950 the war in Korea produced a further amendment increasing the period to two years with three-and-a-half in the reserves.

Opposition to the measure was mainly confined to those who thought that, *ipso facto*, conscription was a bad thing, and to those who believed that compulsory service would weaken the effectiveness of the armed forces. Others feared that the Act heralded industrial conscription, or that the exodus of large numbers of fit young men would wreck Britain's chances of an early post-war economic revival; but even those politicians who had qualms about National Service were forced to agree that, as it applied to every section of the community, it was a fair system.*
From a strategic point of view, National Service was justified by a desire to maintain large reserve forces, but by 1951 Regular recruiting had fallen to such a low ebb that National Servicemen made up fifty percent of the Army's total manpower.

Most of the young men called up in the first years of National Service had memories of the war, and these no doubt helped them to adjust to the idea of military service. In turn, the armed forces were used to dealing with conscripts, and for many young National Servicemen the transition from peacetime civilian life to the post-war army turned out to be an easy enough passage.

*Exemption was granted without qualification to British subjects in government posts abroad, to mental defectives, to the blind and to clergymen. As long as they stayed in their jobs, indefinite deferment – amounting to exemption – was also granted to coalminers, oil shale underground workers, merchant sailors and seagoing fishermen, agricultural workers in essential food production, graduate science teachers and police cadets.

We went to Colchester to some old barracks. We did strict training but it didn't seem to be brutal. I had had plenty of experience of playing soccer at school – from 14 years of age to 18 years of age I played for the first team. Hence I was not afraid of a few 'knocks'.

The food was first class and I cannot say we were overcrowded in the barrack rooms. I believe there was hot and cold water available. No corporal or sergeant stands out in my memory.

Then I was sent to Catterick to train in the Royal Signals. I was on an NCO course and it was pretty tough, but necessary. I could use a rifle, a Bren gun and a Sten with some confidence eventually. One sergeant stands out in my memory – a Sergeant Baldwin. He said he'd had some experience of active service but he was not boastful. We disliked him intensely at first, but he was always immaculately dressed. Then we noticed that he was always out with us in all sorts of weather conditions! His relationship with us improved as we realised that he wouldn't ask anyone to try an exercise that he couldn't accomplish!

(Corporal D. M. Williams, Royal Corps of Signals)

Williams joined up in December 1945 when he was nineteen, just after completing his Higher School Certificate examinations in Chemistry, Physics and Biology. After training at Catterick he served in Italy and Germany until May 1948, leaving the Royal Signals with the rank of corporal, feeling that 'in a strange way' he had enjoyed his military service. Less fortunate in his experience was Thomas Varty who was called in June 1946 at the age of twenty-three, following his pharmacy apprenticeship. At school he had been a member of the ATC, but it proved to be a very different kind of training than the one which awaited him at the Maidstone Barracks of the Royal West Kent Regiment.

At Maidstone boots had to be polished with dubbin; the use of boot polish was a punishable offence, yet the shine had to be comparable with that produced by moderate application of polish. Hence many recruits used boot polish secretly, then dulled it by a light application of dubbin. Rifles had to be cleaned so that even a speck the size of a full-stop left on a non-critical part such as the butt would be punished with fatigue duty. There was such a rush in the morning to get dressed at breakfast before 7 a.m. drill that one had to polish the rifle the previous evening or very early in the morning. The rifle parked beside the bed would then acquire the odd strand of wool (maybe one eighth of an inch long) which would involve censure. I found that if the outside and tip of the barrel were cleaned completely free of oil the fibres did not stick. This worked very well and passed the morning inspections, until one morning the parade was extended. During this period light rain developed, and by the time the officer came around rust had developed on the barrel. The officer told the sergeant to put me on a charge. Fortunately the sergeant ignored the instruction, which was just as well, for I had resolved to face a court martial rather than accept a punishment.

(Sergeant-Dispenser III Thomas Varty, RAMC)

Later, he transferred to the Royal Army Medical Corps, becoming a Sergeant-Dispenser, and ended up with the 48th British General Hospital in Graz, Austria. He was demobbed in August 1948 after an experience he had thought 'a waste of time' though 'always interesting', and returned to Britain and a career with Boots the Chemist. D. M. Williams also picked up the strands of his academic career, taking a BA and Dip.Ed. at University College, Swansea, prior to a career in teaching.

Both men had widely differing service experiences and their reactions to immediate post-war National Service are poles apart; but they present a spectrum of opinion with which a new generation of young men were becoming increasingly familiar. Like it, or not, compulsory military service in peacetime had become a British institution by 1948: it was then simply a fact of life.

Chapter Two

YOU'RE IN THE ARMY NOW

Of the three services, the Army gained most from National Service. For the first time in its history it was provided with large and regular peacetime intakes of reasonably nourished, well educated and malleable young men as recruits. In all, 1,132,872 National Service conscripts served in its ranks or as commissioned officers. It, therefore, looked on National Service as a godsend and used its annual consumption of around 160,000 men to bring its strength from 380,000 in 1949 to 440,000 by 1953: these were used to meet the country's home defence requirements, to fortify the British Army of the Rhine (BAOR) and to garrison the remaining outposts in the receding Empire. During the period of National Service the Army was also involved in fifty-seven officially recognised actions of varying severity and between 1945 and 1963 not a year passed without British soldiers, many of them conscripts, seeing action of one kind or another.

It was the largest army that Britain had ever possessed in peacetime, larger even than the army of September 1939, but its composition and shape would hardly have been recognised by the fathers of the National Service generation. Whereas the infantry had taken up half the Army's strength in pre-war years, by 1951 it had shrunk to one fifth, 88,100 out of a total manpower of 417,800. Now the greater bulk of the Army was committed to serve in the back-up, supplies and administrative corps. To reflect those changes, the government reorganised the infantry and the Foot Guards into fifteen groups, and with the exception of the Grenadier, Coldstream and Scots Guards and the Parachute Regiment the same legislation of 1946 reduced all infantry regiments to a single battalion. By the end of 1947 the Army had 77 infantry battalions as well as 8 Gurkha battalions, 69 artillery regiments and 30 armoured regiments – 184 combat units in all.

The specialist corps, the Royal Engineers, the Royal Electrical and Mechanical Engineers, the Royal Army Service Corps, the Royal Army Ordnance Corps and the Royal Army Medical Corps, had all expanded during the war and were destined to provide solid careers for the professional soldiers who wanted to learn a trade or master a new skill. As evidence of that shift towards harnessing modern technology, in 1949 those corps employed more lieutenant-colonels on their complement than the whole of the infantry put together.

In the Royal Navy the contraction and reorganisation had been even more pronounced. At the end of 1945 the Royal Navy was larger than it had ever been in its history, numbering 929 capital ships, 137 submarines and 6,485 patrol boats, landing craft and other auxiliary vessels. Its personnel consisted of 790,000 officers and men and 74,000 WRNs, and to meet the changing needs of naval warfare it possessed 70 Fleet Air Arm squadrons consisting of 1,336 aircraft. Within two years the greater part of the fleet was in mothballs with older vessels being broken up and a rapid and successful process of demobilisation had whittled down the service to parlous peacetime levels. The Home Fleet had been reduced to a token force and the Mediterranean Fleet, so vital to Britain's post-war strategy, consisted of two aircraft carriers, four cruisers, two flotillas of destroyers, seven frigates and sloops and eight submarines. Elsewhere, in the Far East, the West Indies and the South Atlantic, the diminution of naval strength had been equally drastic, and by 1947 the British battle fleet was as small as it had been after the Napoleonic wars. Large capital ships, now obsolescent, like the battleships *Queen Elizabeth* and the *Renown*, were scrapped and greater emphasis began to be placed on naval aviation and on submarine and anti-submarine warfare. As this was the territory of the specialist, the Royal Navy never looked on National Service as a solution to its manpower problems, preferring instead to concentrate on providing better terms of service for volunteers interested in long-term engagements.

The post-war years had also been difficult for the RAF. It had ended the war with its prestige unimpaired; of its 55,469 aircraft, 9,200 were in front-line service, and its personnel amounted to 1.1 million men and women. Now, in the name of economy, all that was to change. Under the Air Estimates of 1946 three-quarters of a million men were earmarked for demob and a brake was put on aircraft development. Bomber Command would continue to depend on ageing piston-engined Lancaster and

Lincoln bombers, and Fighter Command would not be totally re-equipped with jet fighters like the Meteor and Vampire until 1950 for day fighter squadrons, and 1952 for night fighter squadrons. In turn the peacetime complement of front-line aircraft was to be contracted to one thousand. By the time the new generation of aircraft did arrive – Canberra and Valiant bombers, Hunter day fighters and Javelin all-weather fighters – the RAF was no longer prepared to train National Servicemen as aircrew; consequently, a good many RAF conscripts found themselves relegated for the most part to fairly run-of-the-mill duties.

Those necessary reductions came about largely because the country could no longer afford to maintain armed forces on a large scale. Fighting World War II had drained Britain financially, and Attlee's post-war Labour government found itself having to grapple with the problems of recession, shortages and financial restrictions imposed by the shattered economy. In a world which saw Britain negotiating a loan of $3,750 million from the United States, followed by harsh measures of domestic economic restriction, massive expenditure on the armed forces was a luxury the nation could ill afford. Between 1946 and 1948 the RAF Estimates shrank from £255.5 million to £173 million. The Naval Estimates for 1949 totalled £153 million, a decrease on the previous year of £44 million, and on both services the government urged further economies in manpower and materiel. Expenditure on the Army was reduced, too, to £270 million, and World War II equipment was not replaced in any quantity until well into the 1950s, allowing Field Marshal Viscount Montgomery of Alamein, Chief of the Imperial General Staff between 1946 and 1948, to remark that 'the Army was in a parlous condition, and was in a complete state of unreadiness and unpreparedness for war.'

Despite the financial difficulties, however, strategic considerations argued that Britain could not dismantle completely the might of the forces which had triumphed in 1945. Three years after the war had finished in Europe, Britain ended her centuries-old continental isolation by committing herself to a military alliance with France and the Benelux countries through the Treaty of Brussels, signed in March 1948. This led to the creation of Uniforce, an attempt at allied military cohesion in the event of war, and paved the way for the establishment of a larger western alliance enshrined in NATO, the North Atlantic Treaty Organisation which embraced Belgium, Canada, Denmark,

France, Iceland, Italy, Luxembourg and the Netherlands in a mutual defence treaty, followed by Greece and Turkey in 1951 and the Federal Republic of Germany in 1954. Under its terms Britain contributed the 2nd Tactical Air Force and the 77,000-strong BAOR to guard the northern flank of western Europe, as Germany became the buffer in the Cold War between the Red Army in the east and NATO forces in the west.

Although the granting of independence to India and Pakistan in 1947 had helped to cut back the Army's overseas commitments, British troops were still needed to guard the traditional imperial trade routes through the Mediterranean and the Middle East. The reasons for their deployment might have ended with the surrender of British rule in India, but both the Labour government and Churchill's Conservative government after 1951 refused to consider giving up the large, expensive and strategically important bases in Cyprus, Libya, Palestine, Egypt and Aden. In due course the presence of British forces in those countries was to spur the local population into armed revolt; but in 1947, in pursuit of an obsolete global strategy, those garrisons had to be manned, armed and equipped. The overseas deployment of the Army's infantry forces that year indicates the importance the British still placed on maintaining its pre-war imperial pretensions.

> Egypt: 3 infantry battalions, 2 armoured regiments
> Libya: 3 infantry battalions, 2 armoured regiments
> Cyprus: 1 infantry brigade
> Somaliland: 2 infantry battalions
> Sudan: 1 infantry battalion
> Far East: 13 infantry battalions
> Jamaica: 1 infantry battalion
> West Germany: 18 infantry battalions, 8 armoured regiments

In Britain and Northern Ireland the quota was 30 infantry battalions and 17 armoured regiments, most of which were earmarked for depot duties and training the new generation of recruits. For all those commitments the Army needed men.

To get them, it became the law of the land under the National Service Acts for every male citizen to register at his local branch of the Ministry of Labour and National Service as soon as he became eighteen. Information about the relevant age-groups and clear-cut instructions were placed in the national newspapers and broadcast on BBC radio, and schools and employers also played their part in passing on the relevant official information to their young charges. Short of deliberately refusing to register there was no way the method of call-up could be ignored, and those who did were always traced through their National Health records. Within a short time of registering – usually no longer than two or three weeks – a notice would arrive ordering the potential recruit to attend a medical examination, normally in the same branch of the Ministry of Labour and National Service at which registration had taken place. Numerous apocryphal stories have emerged from this process, mostly involving the substitution of a cow's or other animal's urine for the necessary sample, or feigning mental instability by turning up exhausted with a hangover, but there is little evidence of many recruits trying to fail the medical examination on purpose. In any case, it was notoriously difficult to fail, designed as it was to place the recruit in one of three grades for military service, the fourth grade being reserved for those who were physically or mentally incapacitated and who would be refused permission to serve. Some fifteen per cent of each annual intake regularly fell into that latter grade. Most eighteen-year-olds, conditioned not to question routine discipline and rules, were anxious to be graded A1 even if in some cases it meant covering up minor physical ailments.

> When I went for the medical my own family doctor was on the examination panel. I had been suffering quite a lot from asthma and it would have been no problem to be declared unfit. However, I told him that it was under control and that I would be all right. The other point about the medical which remains particularly clear in my memory is going to have my hearing tested. On entering the room I stood at the end of a line of men, the doctor said, 'Can you hear my watch ticking?' I replied that I could and he told me not to be so stupid because he was talking to the person at the other end of the line.
>
> (Signalman R. G. Jones, Royal Corps of Signals)

At his medical in 1951 it was noted that Anthony Faucheux was suffering from a pilonidal sinus which required surgical attention. His service was deferred until 1954 to enable him to complete his training as an articled clerk, but when he advised the authorities that he was available for service three years later he was told that he could not be called up until the cyst had been removed.

> This left me with an open-ended liability because the National Health Service was in no position to deal quickly with non-urgent surgery. Since I wished to undertake my National Service as soon

as possible and pursue my career, I indulged in a little blackmail. I advised the authorities that since there was likely to be some delay in my receiving medical attention I intended to obtain a job overseas and accordingly would not be available. To my surprise the bluff worked, in that I was called to a local hospital within four weeks for the required surgery.

(2nd Lieutenant A. A. Faucheux, Royal Army Pay Corps)

After the medical the recruit was then interviewed by a Military Interviewing Officer (MIO) in the same building. This was usually an officer on the retired list or an NCO whose duty it was to explain to the youth the possibilities which existed for him in the services. Because Royal Navy recruits were accepted on the basis of their earlier experience they were excused this ritual, which in many offices was left in the hands of harassed warrant officers of the Army and the RAF.

Entrance to the RAF was by intelligence test, and I duly reported to a Ministry of Labour wooden hut in Dumbarton Road. Usually only one in ten or so passed, since the whole thing was geared to the much smaller number of recruits needed. In the event, of the 20–30 youths there, almost half passed, including myself, so there must have been a larger number needed that week. I also got my first practical lesson in the difference between the two services. After the result of the test, our half was asked to go into an adjoining room by a very pleasant RAF corporal who began to give us a lecture, painting a glowing picture of the interesting trades, exotic postings and generally sybaritic life-style available to the average recruit (at the price of signing on, of course). As he rambled on, a fearsome bellow came from the room we had just left. Through the doorway, I could see an enormous sergeant-major wearing a red sash. It was the familiar figure (to anyone from Glasgow at the time) of the recruiting sergeant from the Sauchiehall Street office and he was giving the poor wretches next door a vivid picture of what they were to expect over the next two years, at the top of his very loud voice. The corporal asked, very politely, if someone would mind closing the door, after which he continued with his holiday brochure.

(SAC David McNeill, RAF Coastal Command)

The majority of the recruits found themselves thrust upon the tender mercies of men like the HLI sergeant-major or upon the unhurried concern of an elderly major, and for them the period of initial selection could be an unnerving experience. Men who had served apprenticeships as engineers and who expressed a preference for a service corps could find themselves marked down for the infantry; others who had accounting experience useful to the

Royal Army Pay Corps ended up as orderlies in the Royal Army Medical Corps and so on. Partly, the reason for such mistakes lay within the organisation itself which had been evolved in World War II and had not been changed to meet the calmer needs of peacetime. Very often, a request for service in a specialist arm would be met with the dusty response: 'No, you can't do that. I've got enough electricians for one day.'

Obviously, there were men who were given the postings of their choice – Post Office apprentices who joined the Royal Signals, builders who found their way into the Royal Engineers, trained nurses who became medical orderlies – but one of the great gripes of the ex-National Servicemen today was the Army's inability to make any use of the skills they felt they could offer. In many cases, even when the recruit found himself in a unit which could use his civilian abilities, he was still only given menial tasks to perform. This was particularly true in the early days of National Service when the Army was still grappling with the need to evolve a peacetime administration to cope with its short-service recruits.

Sharing our billet was a cascade of Royal Signals troops, all from BAOR, Germany, who were to have a brief two week course at Longmoor, the better to understand its mysterious geography and baffling customs, its flora and fauna and the habits of its inmates, so that when they returned with the AER from the fortnight's camp they would know all about it. As these fellows drifted through, pissing and moaning, complaining about Germany to all of us who pined to travel abroad, I slowly grasped the non-technical meaning of entropy. They were substantially tradesmen, and one of them, a Cockney, engendered the thought by asking, 'Look at all of us! A painter, four plumbers, a carpenter, two motor mechanics, a platelayer, two shipbuilders . . . (I forget all the others) . . . And what do we do? March about the square, stand in queues for kit all day, obey orders from stupid bastards who couldn't get by in civvy street . . . walk round that rope, don't hop over it, stamp your number on the lower left hand brace of your braces, not the right hand . . . And look around any town in Britain – slums, broken-down buildings, chaotic railways and buses, and where are we, who could fix it all up into a decent country? We're here, saluting snivelling idiots who don't know whether their arsehole's bored or punched!' So, in general, here's the youth of the country, dissipating their energies in utterly non-productive wasted activity, while the country, badly needing their labour, moulders and stagnates. Even the Roman Empire didn't have it that bad before its decline and fall.

(Corporal Iain Colquhoun, Corps of Royal Engineers)

Iain Colquhoun paints a somewhat extreme picture of the high wastage rate of technicians in the Royal Engineers in the early 1950s, but anyone who doubts the Army's ability to abuse the expertise of those who could serve it best should look again at its attitude to combined service amphibious landings. Having mastered the art at D-Day, it dismantled the organisation with the result that the landings at Suez twelve years later were botched affairs with landing craft being loaded non-technically – that is, with essential equipment packed first instead of last. Similar blunders haunted the 1982 Falklands campaign when it became obvious to planners that equipment needed for amphibious operations had not been replaced since being scrapped after 1945. After the campaign, Brigadier Julian Thompson, the commanding officer of 3 Commando Brigade, admitted that this was 'potentially the most hazardous phase of the war'[8] and that men died during the landings as a result of a lack of tactical and technical foresight.

It was during this period of limbo between registration and call-up that decisions were taken about deferment and about conscientious objection to military service. Deferment was generally given without question to youths completing their apprenticeships or to students who had begun university or college courses. Into this category came medical students, who were encouraged to complete their training and were commissioned subsequently as medical officers. They supplied the forces with a ready supply of much-needed doctors, and most 'medicos' found National Service a useful and enjoyable experience. Less fortunate were those school-leavers who decided to apply for deferment and went on to complete other degree courses before being called up. It was one thing to put up with drill and bull at the age of eighteen, but it was quite another three or four years later when the recruit had experienced the freedom of a university course or the higher rates of pay offered to apprentices in civilian occupations. Most of the younger National Servicemen tended to pity those colleagues in their twenties who found it difficult to adapt to service life and were more prone to be upset by the NCOs during basic training.

In the case of the Conscientious Objectors, they followed the same procedure as the recruits for military service. When their number came up they registered at the same branch of the Ministry of Labour and National Service, but instead of putting

down their names for military service they would register as
Conscientious Objectors, giving their reasons on an official form.
In time their cases would be heard by a Local Tribunal made up
of local worthies and chaired by a County Judge in England and
Wales, and in Scotland by a Sheriff or Sheriff-Substitute. In front
of them the appellant would enlarge on his reasons for objecting
to military service, but those arguments had to be sound if his
appeal were to succeed. A plea such as 'no person has the right to
kill or to use force against another person' was unlikely to move
the Tribunal, who would take the view that it was too specious or
ill-defined, but a fundamentalist objection based on religious
principles and backed by a minister of the church was usually well
received. The system of registering conscientious objection had
been evolved in 1916 with the first introduction of conscription
and had been continued during World War II. When peacetime
compulsory service came into force, Hugh Dalton, Chancellor of
the Exchequer, had assured Victor Yates, Labour MP for
Birmingham, Ladywood, and a long-standing critic of conscription, that objection to military service on grounds of conscience
was to be part of the new National Service Acts.

> There will be provision for Conscientious Objectors as has long
> been the case in our law [he told Parliament on 18 November
> 1947], but not in the form to give a Conscientious Objector an
> advantage over a person who does his service. The Conscientious
> Objector will be excused military service, but will not be excused
> from some alternative form of peaceful service for the community,
> details of which we will work out.

The local Tribunal had three options open to them in reaching
a decision. The appellant could be registered as a Conscientious
Objector without any conditions; he could be registered conditionally on agreeing to undertake work of a civilian character; or
he could register as a Conscientious Objector liable for military
service in a non-combatant unit such as the RAMC or the Non-
Combatant Corps, which was commanded by NCOs and officers
from the Royal Pioneer Corps and generally given the most
menial and degrading tasks to perform. If he was not satisfied
with the decision he could take his case to an Appellate Tribunal
whose proceedings were held in public. Very few appellants had
their appeals upheld.

Once registered as a Conscientious Objector – on any of the
three grades – the youth then had to attend a military medical
examination, and it was on that point that most objectors, those

registered conditionally or liable for military service, came to grief. Every year a handful of men on the register of Conscientious Objectors refused to submit for service of any kind and therefore simply did not turn up for the medical examination. Inevitably a warrant would be issued for their arrests and just as inevitably they would be sentenced to a statutory six months in prison. In 1947 and 1948, 922 men applied for registration: of these 31 were registered unconditionally, 429 were registered conditionally, 187 were given non-combatant duties in the Army and 275 failed to be placed on the register. 28 were given prison sentences. It was a pattern which was to continue. Of the men registering as Conscientious Objectors in subsequent years the number never rose above 0.4%, and that percentage included men who were excused military service on grounds of hardship or for other pressing domestic reasons.

In fact, no objector, other than those who objected on religious or quasi-religious grounds, ever won his case and there were several notable examples which gained public notoriety because the objector made his appeal on political grounds. One of these involved Michael Grieve, the son of C. M. Grieve (better known by his pseudonym as the poet Hugh MacDiarmid). In December 1950 the Edinburgh Local Tribunal rejected Michael Grieve's application to be registered as a Conscientious Objector: he had based his objection on his opposition to an imperial war being waged in Kenya, and on his argument that conscription was a violation of clause XVIII of the Act of Union of 1707, which, according to interpretation, seemed to safeguard Scots from being sent abroad by a Westminster government. This stood or fell on the interpretation of the wording that 'no alteration be made to laws which concern private right, except for evident utility of the subjects within Scotland'; but there was no court in Scotland which would uphold the view that it allowed Scots to refuse to obey the government's call to conscription.

Grieve's argument had first been employed in 1942 by Douglas Young, poet, classicist and Chairman of the Scottish National Party, who had gone to jail in support of his party's resolution of 1937 – 'All male members of the Scottish National Party of military age hereby pledge themselves to refuse to serve with any section of the Crown forces until the programme of the Scottish National Party has been fulfilled.' During the war the SNP supported the government's aims, but also lent moral support to those who took an anti-war line. Two years later Young was in jail again for refusing to register for industrial work, an action which drew the admiration of Compton Mackenzie in his study, *On Moral Courage.*

> With a sad show of pusillanimity another set of Scots judges refused to hear the appeal and committed the appellant to gaol. Caledonia douce and mild is not fit nurse for a poetic child like Douglas Young, and anyway this is not the place to argue about the legal rights and wrongs of the case . . . The point is that . . . Douglas Young [was] prepared to carry [his] beliefs far beyond inconvenience, the acceptation of which Sir James Fitzroy Stephen recognised as a test of moral courage . . .[9]

Grieve had the support of several eminent men including Young himself, the veteran nationalist R. E. Muirhead, and a senior counsel, Gordon (later Lord) Stott, who had also been a Conscientious Objector; but his legal battle ended on 16 June 1952 when he was sentenced to six months' imprisonment at Glasgow Sheriff Court.

Throughout the period of National Service some nationalists in Scotland had advocated that young Scots should follow Grieve's example and go to jail rather than serve in an English army. 'Your conduct in tholing [suffering] this disagreeable experience will be acclaimed by all true Scots as honourable,' read one leaflet issued by the Scottish Secretariat, 'and by your example others will be encouraged to make a similar resistance.' Nationalist theory, however honourable, knew nothing of the fate awaiting Conscientious Objectors in Scottish prisons. 'My prison conditions were pretty frightful,' remembers Michael Grieve. 'My time in Barlinnie was spent amongst razor slashers, murderers, perverts; in the morning you slopped out by hurling the contents of your chamber pot five or six yards over a stinking sea. From sewing mailbags I finally graduated to become head of the sock-darning squad.' One of the difficulties Grieve had faced in arguing his case was that the National Service Act of 1948 was read in conjunction with the Criminal Justice (Scotland) Act of 1949. As a consequence, Scottish youths prosecuted in that way could be subjected to the indignity of visits and reports from probation officers, as if they were guilty of moral turpitude, and were liable to be sent to Borstal; whereas in England, under English law, the Lord Chief Justice, Lord Goddard, had made it clear that the same degrading treatment would not be meted out to English Conscientious Objectors. Not unnaturally, this legal anomaly caused a good deal of offence in Scottish nationalist circles.

The action was also cited of another Scotsman, the playwright

William Douglas-Home, who was court-martialled in 1944 rather
than take part in the attack on Le Havre because he knew that the
allied action would cause civilian casualties. Other leaflets
pointed to the comparison with Northern Ireland whose young
men had been exempted from both the wartime and the
peacetime National Service Acts. Similar protests were made in
Wales where several young men refused to complete their call-up
papers in any other language than Welsh.

During World War I the notion of the Conscientious Objector
had become almost a term of abuse. Around sixteen thousand
men had registered their objection to military service and most of
those were treated to a harsh code of discipline and deliberate
persecution. Seventy Conscientious Objectors are believed to
have died as a result of their experiences in prison or in Military
Detention Centres, and there was a theoretical possibility that
those on the register could face the death penalty (none did).
Things improved during the next war when 60,000 registered,
many of whom saw service on the land or with Civil Defence and
non-combatant units of the Army, and by the time of National
Service there was greater public sympathy for the lot of the
Conscientious Objector. Nevertheless, the procedure of appearing before a Local or an Appellate Tribunal could be a harrowing
business for the one objector amongst every six hundred recruits.
In most cases the appellants had not thought through their
arguments, so that the superior legal experience of the men on
the Tribunals easily ran rings around the callow pleas offered by
the objector. Only if he happened to be a Jehovah's Witness, a
Plymouth Brother or a Christadelphian did the appellant stand
any real chance of being granted the opportunity of registering
unconditionally as a Conscientious Objector.

For those – the vast majority – who were accepted for military
training, the next step was not long in coming. Within six weeks
of the interview a buff envelope would thunder through the
letter-box: in it would be an enlistment notice giving information
about when and where to report, a rail warrant for a ticket from
his home to the station nearest the reception camp, and – in the
early days of National Service – a postal order for four shillings,
being an advance on pay. This arrived two weeks before the
actual date of enlistment so that the conscript could arrange his
domestic affairs and where necessary give notice to his
employers. (The National Service Acts decreed that all such jobs

were to be kept open for their holders after they had completed their military training.)

Although the conditions were to improve the longer peacetime National Service continued, the process of enlistment and basic training, especially in the Army, was to change little. Enlistment always took place on a Thursday and all over the country trains would pull out of stations, taking their quotas of raw recruits to the Army's training centres – to Inverness for Fort George, to Darlington for the branch line to Richmond and Catterick, to Preston for Fulwood Barracks, to Worcester for Norton Camp, to Brookwood in Hampshire for North Frith Barracks. It came as a surprise to find that nearly all of the passengers were fellow recruits. 'Which unit are you?' '6th Training Regiment, Royal Engineers, Norton.' 'No. 29 Selection and Basic Training Unit, Whittington.' '7th Training Regiment, Royal Signals, Catterick.' 'Highland Brigade Training Depot, Fort George.' A new language was being learned.

The railway system had been modernised in 1947, with British Railways being formed a year later, but the war had drained the operation and left it miserably run-down. Rolling stock was often of questionable vintage, steam locomotives were elderly and prone to break down, timetables chaotic – it took over eight hours to travel from London to Edinburgh by even the fastest train. But whatever the drawbacks of rail travel and however crowded the trains, for most recruits the journey started out as an adventure. For many it was their first time alone away from home and on the trains they met other young men like themselves from different parts of the country and from different backgrounds, speaking in different accents but united by the common denominator of the Army.

> By the time of call-up I had met few people not from Swindon (exceptions being teachers and doctors) or from other social classes (because of the gulf between grammar schools and others). So, to be surrounded by so many different or new accents, expressions – Geordie, Scouse, Mancunian, Brummie, Jock, Cockney etc. – was an ear-opener. Then, to meet ex-Borstal Boys, Public Schoolboys, Graduates, Illiterates etc. was an even greater experience.
>
> (Corporal Tony Carter, REME)

Once at the designated station – few National Servicemen who were stationed at Catterick can ever forget the chaos in the station-yard at Richmond – NCOs were waiting to herd their charges into TCVs (trucks with wooden seats). Now they really were in the army.

We changed trains at Darlington and caught what later came to be known as the 'Catterick Flyer'. It turned out that most of us, myself included, had never been out of Scotland previously (one of the many 'firsts' which National Service gave me). The Catterick Flyer was packed with young men. On reflection we must have looked very similar to one another, even without uniform. Yet at that point we were still individuals.

We ceased to be individuals the moment our feet touched (or did they?) the platform at Richmond station. There may have been twenty to thirty NCOs in the 'welcome party' but they were more than capable of rounding up several hundred reluctant recruits. I was separated from my friends and did not see them again for several days. By that time I was '22947595 Signalman Findlay, W., Sir!'

(Signalman W. Findlay, Royal Corps of Signals)

Most intakes were timed to arrive around 3 o'clock in the afternoon, to allow the process of registration and kit issue to be completed before the evening meal at six o'clock: and for most recruits that first day came as a rude shock. Firstly, the unit clerks interviewed the conscripts, took down their personal particulars and issued them with their 'bibles' – their AB 64 part one (Soldier's Service Book) and part two (Pay Book), both of which had to remain in the soldier's possession throughout his army service. Then followed a haircut – a severe back and sides and no sideburns – a medical and a batch of inoculations. (With some intakes this took place the following day.) Kit came next: handed out in batches by corporals who read out each item from a list before pressing it into the hands of the recruit. 'Drawers, cellular, green, other ranks, two pairs; blouses, battledress, khaki, other ranks, one . . .': a dreary litany which continued until a pile of oddly assorted articles lay ready to be stuffed into a kitbag and taken along with the bedding to the barrack-hut which had been assigned on arrival. Sometimes this formality had its comic side, like the English recruit in a Highland regiment who could not understand that 'galluses' are braces in Scotland, but the majority were bewildered by the helter-skelter speed of the whole transaction. Everything now had to be done 'at the double'.

After being issued with things and examined at length (there was a strong superstition that when they made you bend over and straighten up they were not looking for scoliosis or spinal defects, they were 'looking up your arse for piles') and so on, our intake, dressed in horrid new ill-fitting denims, clumping boots, braces and football shirts, got to the mess about 6 p.m. for our first meal which was merely what had not yet been eaten, and consisted

solely of stewed leeks. Several lads threw up during the night,
several (like me) had diarrhoea, others were unaffected – all was
attributed to nerves. Our civilian clothes were taken and mailed,
parcel post, to our homes – to prevent or minimise desertion. One
heard rumours, but never knew, as in the theory of the bromide in
the tea, whether anyone really tried.

(Corporal Iain Colquhoun, Corps of Royal Engineers)

All around, corporals chivvied their new charges, shouting
orders, cajoling them into a new routine – from the Army's point
of view the idea was to give the recruits a short, sharp shock in
order to accustom them quickly to the disciplinary needs of the
military regime. From the recruits' point of view it was, for the
most part, a numbing and dislocating experience.

The transition from civilian to soldier was dramatic both in its
speed and its effect. The whirlwind of Day One left a patchwork of
recollections. Of Blanco and Brasso; of Does and Don'ts; of
disbelief and acceptance; of crude instruction on doing things the
Army way – from lacing boots to making a bed; of tyrannical
NCOs, all the time terrorising, menacing and bullying; of the
hopeless realisation that two sheets of simple brown wrapping
paper, in which civilian clothes were to be sent back home to
mother, represented the end of links with the outside world. The
effect of all this numbing and the prospect of another 729 days led
to more than one stifled sob as the newcomers to Barrack Room 22
reflected in the darkness on a day which had so rudely changed the
lives of them all.

(Corporal Denis Gane, Royal Corps of Signals)

Those who had been away to camp with the Boy Scouts or the
Boys Brigade or who had served in any of the military cadet
forces coped best with the first forty-eight hours of basic training;
so too did those who had worked in the three intervening years
since leaving school at fifteen; likewise, but at the other extreme,
boys who had been sent to boarding schools had little difficulty in
adapting to army life. The ones who suffered most were boys who
had never been away from home before or who had led fairly
sheltered lives. It was not uncommon for a hard-bitten lad, who
had worked previously in a factory or on a building site, to be
astonished by the sight of his grammar school-educated neighbour weeping silently in his bed at night – a classic image of social
collision between the stoicism of the working-class labourer and
the inadequacy of the middle-class pen-pusher.

Despite the egalitarian policies of the post-war Labour
government, class was still an all-absorbing topic in Britain and

boundaries between the different classes, far from being abolished, had simply been readjusted to meet the needs of a changing world. However, in the raw atmosphere of an army hut at a huge training centre like Catterick, class divisions did evaporate quickly, if only temporarily; and far from creating fresh schisms, basic training introduced a new form of solidarity. Suddenly, for every member of the sixteen-man squad, a whole new world had come into focus, circumscribed by a new vocabulary of screamed orders, personal humiliation and crude, belittling taunts.

> We lived with fear every moment of our waking lives at Catterick. Perhaps some had tormented dreams but I remember going out exhausted with the lights at ten o'clock and sleeping the deepest of sleeps until we were disturbed by the Orderly Corporal's obscenities at 6 a.m. From that moment onwards life was a dreadful thing. No matter what we were doing we felt vulnerable, afraid that one of the lurking bully boys who hounded us with their vile abuse would find some reason to put us on a charge which would lead to the misery of 'jankers'. Crop-haired and depersonalised in our shapeless, ill-fitting denims, we doubled hither and thither pursued by foul-mouthed fiends, most of them sporting as their regimental badge an all too appropriate skull and crossbones. The only relief from this purgatory was the extraordinary comradeship, solidarity and human warmth of the barrack-room. There was no other warmth in Waitwith Lines. The stove didn't work.
> (2nd Lieutenant R. M. Morgan, 1st Bn. Gordon Highlanders)

Each squad was put under the aegis of a corporal or lance-corporal whose task it was to instruct his recruits in army lore, to offer help and advice, and to keep order within the hut. Any mistakes made by his squad – dirty kit, untidy lockers, scuffing on the floor – reflected on him and so he was the first link in the chain of command. Above him were the sergeants, and at the apex the regimental sergeant-major, with a battery of degrading insults at his disposal. If the recruit were to survive these had to be taken with an extra large pinch of salt.

> One day, on RSM's muster parade, I was second man, front rank, first platoon. Having finished five years as an apprentice joiner working at a bench I was a bit round-shouldered. We were formed up. All of a sudden a voice rent the air. 'Sergeant Mills, second man, front rank looks like a vulture about to shit.' I almost died on the spot, but afterwards it was very funny. I will remember it to my dying day.
> (Private R. H. Burford, 1st Bn. The Duke of Edinburgh's Royal Regiment)

It was the task of the drill sergeants to get the squads to move as one man on parade by instilling in them the basic facts of the Army's drill book until each man could carry out every order precisely on the word of command. To accomplish this they threatened, then coaxed, then bullied again, normally using a stream of insults which had been carefully nurtured over the years.

> The Catterick snow gave way to a hint of coming Spring and it became possible to smile at the sadistic humour of the bully-boy NCOs, even during the seemingly endless hours of purgatory on the parade ground, learning by numbers drills which could not be forgotten in a lifetime. 'If you don't swing that arm, laddie, I'll tear it off, stick it up your arse and have you for a lollipop.'
> (Corporal Denis Gane, Royal Corps of Signals)

In most cases the bark of the sergeants was worse than their bite, but in almost every squad there was one victim who had to be picked on – the bespectacled grammar school boy with the polite accent, the clumsy recruit who could never get his brasses cleaned, the gormless squaddie who was always late on parade, the 'tick- tock' man who could not march properly. The presence of men who simply could not or would not conform mentally or physically to the Army's code of discipline reduced most sergeants to apoplexy, and life for the unwilling recruit could be made utterly miserable. Perversely, though, in many cases the more a sergeant would bully a hopeless recruit, the more his squad would rally to his aid.

> I can remember vividly the chat as we blancoed our webbing, polished our buckles and buttons, and rubbed endless circles on the toe-caps of our boots with spit and polish, the questioning as we discovered how differently we lived, and the surprise, too, at finding how very similar we were behind the accents. And how very unimportant accents are in a situation where survival, that is the avoidance of 'jankers', depended on cooperation and mutual support. Did someone have to 'show clean'? Then we all cleaned his boots or his small pack for him. If the room's total incompetent, and there always seemed to be one, even at OCS, could not lay out his kit in other than a jumble, we all rallied round to make sure he passed muster when our troop sergeant came prowling *quaerens quem devoret*.
> (2nd Lieutenant R. M. Morgan, 1st Bn. Gordon Highlanders)

There are horror stories of men being so inept that they had to be hidden in cupboards during inspections, but, for the most part,

squads were so terrified of being collectively punished – or, even
worse, 'back-squadded' (i.e., being made to repeat basic training)
– that they would make sure that the weakest of their number
got it right for inspection. (The most common way of ensuring
perfection was to lay out his kit the night before, make up his bed
and then force the unfortunate lad to sleep on the floor.) Far from
being frowned upon, this tradition – for so it soon became during
the National Service years – was encouraged tacitly as a means of
establishing an *esprit de corps* and cementing the squad into a
cohesive unit acting as one in the interests of military discipline.

The first difficulty was the uniform – the battledress, the rough
woollen khaki shirts, the gaiters, webbing, the shapeless blue
beret and hard unyielding boots. There was an Army saying; 'If it
fits, you must be deformed.' Therefore, very few National
Servicemen were happy with what was issued to them. After basic
training the battledress could normally be tailored, but for the
first eight weeks recruits had to make do with what had been
issued to them and to coax it into uniform acceptability.
    To begin with, the trousers had to be pressed to give them a
perfect crease. This task was usually performed with damp brown
paper and an iron hired from the barrack-room corporal and
returned at the end of basic training. Another variation was to
place the trousers carefully between mattress and bedstead,
although this practice was frowned upon – one RAF recruit at
Bridgnorth who was discovered doing it was put on a charge for
'being idle while asleep'. As thick worsted cannot take a
longlasting crease the wool had to be scalded or shaved off along
the crease, a precarious process which sometimes led to accidents. Then shirts, pants and other personal items went through
the same ritual and were folded to exact Army specifications: to
maintain the ensuing perfection some recruits would prefer to use
their own clothes rather than disturb such symmetry. To make
them look good, pouches would be stuffed with newspaper, and
cardboard squares would fill out small packs to uniform proportions. Next, webbing had to be attended to. Most of it had been
used before and had to be scrubbed clean so that the blancoing
process could begin all over again. Using Number 3 Green
Blanco and liberal amounts of water, the resultant paste would be
brushed vigorously into the webbing, layer by layer, until a
smooth surface built up. Too much blanco and it would crack; too
little and the result would be patchy. Brasses – badges, buttons

and insignia – had to be scoured with wire brushes until they could take Brasso and a final polishing, but the strangest ritual was reserved for the evolution of 'best boots' – those worn on parade.

When they were issued, all pairs of boots were standard issue, made of stout leather uppers and soles with tell-tale 'pimples' on the uppers. To make them fit for inspection and to get the mirror-like surface demanded by the sergeants, the recruits had to go through the never-to-be-forgotten process of scalding off the pimples, usually with a heated spoon, until bare leather had been reached. When that had been achieved – the more daring set fire to their boots, burning off the surface with meths – the second stage was to use heated polish and a good deal of elbow grease until the surface gleamed. As such, they were things of beauty, but their unsullied sheen made them useless as pieces of military equipment: if worn on parade in the rain the surface would quickly crack up and disintegrate. In all the preparations for inspection there was a fair helping of the illogical, but the bulling of boots was the most absurd part of the procedure.

> Trying to blanco kit outdoors, 50–60 under one lamp-post as there was no light in the blanco shed and it was more than our life was worth to blanco in the ablutions. The first two weeks: no hot water for shaving, no fires to warm our freezing bodies, windows kept wide open until evening, the feeling of finality and loss as we parcelled all our civvies to send back home. No NAAFI in the evening, orders for essential cleaning materials and cigs entrusted to one or two of the squad. Bulling floors – walking on blankets – polishing fireplace and bucket; scraping broomhandles and tables; learning the intricacy of kit layout; marching everywhere, even over a hill path in the dark to get to a regimental boxing match.
> (Lance-Corporal Bob Downie, Royal Army Ordnance Corps)

In addition to kit, the barrack-room had to be kept spotlessly clean, its floor polished and the stove blackened. In the newer barracks constructed after the rebuilding programme of 1955 the accommodation was good. Many were centrally heated, had modern furniture, covered floors and offered a reasonable living area. Those of earlier vintage – the wooden 'spider' huts dating back to World War I – were more dubious propositions. Built on an 'H' shape with ablutions in the centre section and the barrack-rooms branching off, these were often draughty, cold, dingy places with leaking windows, heated, if at all, by elderly coke-fired tortoise stoves. They were impossible to keep clean and the ablutions were usually crude and insanitary places devoid of either hot water with which to wash or shave, or plugs for the wash basins. The existence of the 'spiders' in many training camps was a monument to the lack of funds given to the Army in post-war years by successive governments, and to the absence of any coherent planning for a large peacetime army. Just as bad were the mess halls, which in the first years of National Service could equal the living accommodation in their levels of filth and neglect.

> One reason the men skipped meals was the washing up process. There were three sinks, each with a tap from which flowed a mere trickle of dirt-cold water. A tiny greasy tow mop was provided, and each man had to wash his plates, mug and eating irons with that arrangement. Long queues were there at all times and waits of twenty minutes were commonplace. One or two lads wiped their plates clean with stale bread, threw that in the huge bins swimming with the tasteless weak tea that everyone threw a pint of therein, and walked out. This stopped soon when the RPs were detailed to inspect the plates everyone carried when attempting to leave the place and to send recalcitrant ones back to the end of the queue . . . Every day, after the apology for lunch, all chairs and tables were stacked at one end of the dining hall and the rough pebbled stone floor was flooded with water and scrubbed by us, end to end. The discarded food was scrubbed along with the water, leaving behind its own dissolved traces.
>
> (Corporal Iain Colquhoun, Corps of Royal Engineers)

Such conditions – and they were not untypical – should be seen in perspective. Even in 1953 the country was still gripped by neglect and showing the signs of wartime damage and pre-war recession. There were still bomb-sites and slums in the main towns and cities, and industrial scars littered the landscape as the country attempted to get itself back into condition again. Although rebuilding programmes had been initiated and new housing estates had begun to appear, there was still a great deal of leeway to make up. The average number of new houses completed in any year between 1946 and 1951 never exceeded 200,000, largely because there was a severe shortage of raw materials. In those conditions the Army came well down the list, and the hated spider with its primitive conditions remained on many camps until well into the 1950s. Troops stationed with BAOR had the lesson of their homeland's post-war austerity rammed home in dramatic manner when they found themselves stationed at ex-Wehrmacht or ex-SS barracks. There, the accommodation, built in the 1930s, would be hygienic and welcoming – usually with three or four men to a room – in sharp

contrast to the twenty iron bedsteads in a cramped spider. It was
with good reason that one of the first warnings a National Serviceman learned was, 'Keep out of my bed space!'

Not all training was bull and drill. There was plenty of PT and
cross-country runs to raise standards of physical fitness, and basic
weapon training with the .303 rifle, the Bren and Sten guns was
given to everyone, even the most short-sighted or cack-handed. A
typical day during basic training might run to a timetable like this:

06.15 Reveille
07.00 Breakfast
07.45 Clean room and platoon area
08.15 Platoon Muster Parade
08.30–09.20 Drill
09.20–10.00 Lecture
10.00–10.20 NAAFI break
10.20–11.00 Weapons training
11.00–11.50 Fieldcraft
12.00–12.40 Physical training
12.40 Lunch
13.45–14.45 Education
15.00–16.15 Miniature range
17.30 Tea
22.30 Lights Out

That was very much an idealised view of the course an average
recruit's day should take. So nervous were most of them of the
08.15 muster parade that squads would get up before reveille and
queue outside the mess hall at an ungodly hour, in order to leave
more time for cleaning the barrack-room. Others stayed up half
the night cleaning brasses and polishing boots to the standard of
perfection demanded by the inspecting officer and his accompany-
ing sergeants the following morning. Even a speck of dust *behind* a
cap badge could give the hapless victim a term of 'jankers' –
peeling potatoes, washing out ablutions, storing coal or any other
task the sergeant could dream up at a moment's notice. Some
squads put on collective jankers could be made to cut lawns with
scissors or to weed officers' gardens with their eating irons. There
was usually no end to the inventiveness displayed by the NCOs.

We were treated like slaves almost, being sent to clean offices,
fireplaces at the Officers' Quarters, washing greasy pans in the
cookhouse without soap. These were referred to as fatigues. One
lad from my squad was told to move rice from one container to

another: when he asked what with, the Cook Sergeant said, please
yourself. So he used the coke shovel.
(Corporal Peter Davies, Royal Army Medical Corps)

Most of the punishments were ridiculous, designed to break a
man's spirit and to make him conform, so it is little wonder that
most recruits remember only the bull, the drill, the ordering about
and the constant humiliation.

> Basic training was all rush and bull. During the day we were rushed
> all over the place – shouted at and bullied all the time. Evenings
> were spent bulling kit and there was very little free time. Kit was
> inspected frequently, and I have seen men's kit tipped onto the floor
> and freshly blancoed webbing thrown through windows when not
> meeting the standards demanded by the inspecting NCOs.
> (Lance-Corporal R. Dulson, 1st Bn. The Cheshire Regiment)

Drill took up an inordinate time during basic training, roughly
one-third, its object being to emphasise the unimportance of the
individual. Added to the irrational demands of bull, the process –
in the Army at least – seems to have been designed to beat each
individual into a shape predetermined by the military authorities.
At the end of basic training each man wore an identical and
immaculate uniform and every minute of his day was ruled by the
Army's regulations. To the military mind this was the acme of
discipline, a concentrated process which turned out men trained to
be courageous, responsible, self-reliant and tolerant, and capable
of fighting should war ever break out. For, as Major T. B.
Beveridge explained in a training booklet of 1953, *A Guide for the
National Serviceman in the Army*, it had never to be forgotten that
the primary responsibility of the soldier was to be ready to fight.

> Discipline is the foundation of the Army, as it must be more or less
> in any organisation, but especially of a fighting machine. It must
> never be overlooked that the main duty of the Army is to prepare
> for war. In war the issuing of orders with the certainty that they will
> be obeyed is, of course, essential; without discipline we should get
> nowhere. Discipline starts with the individual and there is nothing
> debasing about it; in fact the very reverse.

It might have been difficult for the raw recruit, fresh from
civilian life, to understand that the ability to present arms in the
correct sequence had anything to do with warfare, or that mirror-
like boots made the complete combat soldier, but these were vital
first lessons in understanding the Army's psychology. A soldier
who cared about arms drill was less likely to be wayward when he
got to the next stage on the firing range. To begin with, rifles and

other weapons were handled empty, and it was only once the soldier had learned to strip them, reassemble them and use them correctly that they would be fired with live ammunition. The Army's theory was that a well-disciplined recruit would be less likely to do anything silly on the range – like pointing a jammed weapon armed with live ammunition at his instructor or playing with his rifle as if it were a toy. This made good sense: unfortunately the message was not always put across by the NCOs, and consequently recruits did not always see discipline in that light.

Men have always groused about discipline, especially when it is enforced without logic or applied by over-abrasive superiors. During World War II General Wavell remarked that 'The soldier does not mind a severe code of discipline provided it is administered fairly and reasonably'; and most senior commanders were anxious to avoid the use of discipline for discipline's sake, realising that insensitive bullying was bad for morale. At a time when a civilian army was being licked into shape to fight a ruthless enemy, most conscripts tended to accept the military code. In peacetime things should have been different but, faced by large annual intakes of potentially rebellious adolescents, NCOs tended to clamp down and exercise a crude and belittling form of discipline during the recruits' first weeks. There is little doubt that the period of basic training was designed to be tough and to acclimatise the troops to obey orders without questioning them. However, in the amorphous mass which the peacetime army became, many 'little Hitlers' in positions of petty authority became bullying NCOs who terrorised their charges simply because that was the only way they could keep order. Some older sergeants in particular thought that discipline had become too lax in the final days of World War II; remembering the rash of mutinies and near-mutinies, they were determined to enforce their authority in a manner which would have been easily understood by the recruits in Kitchener's armies, who had to be quickly and ruthlessly trained for the rigours of trench warfare. Not that every NCO adopted the ways of the senseless bawling bully. Some were firm and paternal, ready to offer help and advice, but not to suffer fools gladly. Others understood their men's predicament and won them round to the idea that basic training was finite – and that, as they had to do it, why not make a good fist of it?

> We had three super instructors, Sergeant Rennie, Corporal Le Page and Corporal Baker, who were very strict but fair to all. Sergeant Rennie told us that he had never had a squad win the passing out parade at the end of six weeks' training – at Redford Barracks in

Edinburgh there were six Highland Regiments, HLI, Argylls, Seaforths, Black Watch, Camerons and Gordons. As none of us had much money, around about £1 a week, Saturday was the only day any of us went out, either to Tynecastle or Easter Road to watch football, then a fish supper and stroll around the centre of Edinburgh before the tram back to Redford. We all decided we would try our best not to let Sergeant Rennie down. We used to practise what we had learned during the day in barrack-room at night after cleaning our kit. On the two passing out days we won the cross-country run, weapon training, PT, turn-out and drill, and came second in shooting. First overall. As we sat at our passing out meal – of course we were at the top table – it gave us all a great satisfaction to see Sergeant Rennie's face completely light up, as proud as Punch.

(Private Alexander Robb, 1st Bn. Seaforth Highlanders)

Generally speaking, NCOs and drill sergeants tended to adopt a more fatherly attitude in infantry regiments. Tough they might have been, with sharp tongues in their heads, but because they realised that the recruits were destined to stay in the same regiment, they were anxious to encourage them to succeed through their own efforts.

During my four months' training in Ballymena and Omagh, most of the National Service drafts were made up of Cockneys from south London, and some of us were rather cocky Teddy Boys so the Irish NCOs took a great delight in knocking us into shape . . . In a way we relished the bull-shit and were very proud of our glossy boots and smart turn-out. Our drill sergeant was a young Irish veteran from Korea who had been wounded in the Imjin battle; the tales he told us made what little hair we had left stand on end, but we would have done anything for him and won him the cup for the best drill squad. I recall the pride of the squad in getting our 160 paces per minute arms-drill so sharp we moved like a one-man machine.

After our training and transformation we went on two weeks embarkation leave, home to dear old London to show off our black-buttoned battledress to our velvet-collared mates who were still waiting to be called up.

(Rifleman George Savage, 1st Bn. Royal Ulster Rifles)

NCOs like the RUR drill sergeant and Sergeant Rennie were obviously exceptional men, leaders who could understand their men's point of view and instil pride and determination for the task ahead. All too often, though, by the end of basic training, the system had broken down, leaving men dispirited, ready to skive, unwilling to volunteer for anything and disenchanted by anomalies which encouraged common-sense on the one hand but frowned upon any display of initiative or intelligence.

> One corporal giving us a piece of weapon instruction said, 'You hold your arms to make what sort of triangle?'
> Intelligent soldier: 'Equilateral, Corporal.'
> Corporal: 'We're not all bloody educated ——. That —— is an equal-sided bastard. We don't know all these —— clever words. I left school at fourteen.'
> (Private A. J. Bayley, Royal Army Service Corps)

In the RAF the process of basic training was rather different, although many of the facets remained the same. On receiving their call-up papers most recruits were directed to one of the RAF's huge kitting-out camps at RAF Padgate near Warrington or RAF Cardington in Bedfordshire, before proceeding to a training camp. In much the same way that no soldier who was stationed at Catterick can ever forget the experience, so too does Padgate seem to have carved its name on the memories of all RAF recruits called up there.

> We were met at the station by RAF lorries and went straight to Padgate, near Warrington, about 5 a.m. Breakfast was waiting and we were issued with a pint mug and a set of irons. The meal was porridge without salt, sausages and beans and a slice of toast. After a night travelling in a train it was not exactly what you would call a hearty meal.
> The next week was spent at Padgate getting kitted out and the various jabs etc. The issue of kit was exactly what you would expect in one of the 'Carry On' films. You paraded before a long counter and a NCO walked in front of you and shouted to an airman over the counter a size, and that was it. You got it and if it fitted you were lucky. The remainder of the week was taken up with getting your uniform altered, sending your own clothes home in a brown paper parcel and filling in endless forms.
> The best recollection of Padgate was the haircut. We all paraded in a large hangar and at the end in a small room were about six barbers going non-stop. I can distinctly remember an inscription outside the door of the shop, and it read: 'This is just a —ing farce, they shave you like a duck's arse.'
> (Corporal John Inglis, RAF Regiment)

Like most large and impersonal military camps where men were always in transit, Padgate offered little in the way of amenities. The food was consistently bad, the tea insipid – giving rise to the joke that it must be laced with bromide to reduce the men's sexual urges – the accommodation sparse and the NCOs

uncaring. Fortunately, the stay at kitting-out camp was only four
or five days before the recruits were broken up for posting to their
training camps. There the regime was dominated by bull and
drill, the severity of which depended on the posting: RAF
Bridgnorth was considered by most conscripts to have been as
bad as anything in the Army.

> At 5.30 a.m. I wake up shivering with cold [he wrote to his
> schoolfriend John Lee on 20 April 1950]. I don't know why, but it
> is quite the coldest place I have ever been in, in the mornings – like
> a fridge. Seeing everyone else asleep, and especially hearing
> everyone snoring, I always slump down again amongst the
> bedclothes. Golly, if you happen to wake up very early its the end
> as far as getting back to sleep is concerned for the snoring is
> incredible. You know how people give exaggerated impressions of
> snoring which make you laugh at their ridiculousness – well, it's
> just like that, only multiplied by 20.
>
> At 6.00 a.m. everyone tumbles shivering and weary out of bed;
> not all at the same time, for some people have to shave, whereas
> others can do that the night before and look fresh in the morning.
> It is a rule, by the way, that we shave daily.
>
> Corpl. Ingram: 'Is there any bastard here who's not got a razor,
> hasn't shaved before?'
>
> Timid AC/2: 'Me, corporal.'
>
> Corpl. Ingram: 'Well, now's the bloody time to learn. Buy a
> razor and scrape your —— face every day, see?'
>
> I dress as quickly as possible and dash out to the ablutions where
> there is a queue for the wash-hand basins (small, filthy, 20 for 120
> people, 1 plug between them, the rest stuffed with bog-paper and
> you wash quickly before the water runs away). The water is cold,
> hard and there are no lights in the place.
>
> Back to the billet. Make up beds – blankets folded in intricate
> way, mess tin and eating irons laid out just so on the bed. Then to
> breakfast. The meals here are quite good and I really enjoy them
> now. It's pig-swill of course compared with home cooking, but
> then it's a pig's life here compared with that at home. If there's one
> thing it teaches you it is the meaning of hard work. From 6.00 a.m.
> to 11 p.m. we are usually working all the time. After 5.30 p.m. we
> finish, but there are plenty of things to clean, polish and blanco.
>
> (SAC Graham Mottershaw, RAF)

Most Army conscripts would recognise Mottershaw's description of his basic training, but elsewhere at places like RAF
Wilmslow or RAF Compton Bassett the regime was less strict –
mainly because the numbers were smaller and the atmosphere in
consequence more placid.

I was in 'F' Flight where a Cpl. Perkins was in charge. Far from being the monster of fiction, he was not much older than the rest of us and was quite a pleasant and helpful person. His face was very pale and his voice hoarse, as if shouting was not natural to him. He got a severe dose of flu eventually but still turned out looking very grey (he never looked well at the best of times). His voice became a harsh croak and we had to strain our ears to hear his orders . . . skiving became a way of life. My father had told me, along with advice about swagger sticks and field sketching pads, never to volunteer (and to stay away from propellors), so when Cpl. Perkins came into the hut one evening and asked if there was an artist in the house, I chose to remain anonymous. Some fool blabbed and I was brought out from my hiding place among the others. I was told to report to the stores first thing and draw (yes, he actually cracked that golden oldie) a tin of white paint and a brush, using which I was to paint the hut numbers on their respective dustbins. Everything turned out for the best after all, and I spent a very pleasant sunny day of harmless amusement while everyone else sweated on the square within earshot but out of sight. I also gave my first pint of blood at Wilmslow along with a large number of others who shared the same base motive – avoiding an afternoon on the square.

(SAC David McNeill, RAF Coastal Command)

Other recruits remember being asked if anyone had short-hand, only to be ordered to the cookhouse 'because they are shorthanded'; and at John Inglis's intake at RAF Credenhall, near Hereford, the sergeant gave extra drill to all those who admitted watching John Wayne in *The Sands of Iwo Jima* at the camp cinema the previous evening. There were warrant officers whose humour could be less kind, especially on the firing range – 'Don't look down, feel for the trigger. If it had hair on it you'd find it!' – but for the most part the RAF adopted a more relaxed and good-humoured approach to recruits during basic training, especially to those who would be taught a trade such as wireless operation or aircraft control.

The final parade was a bit hit and miss as I wasn't considered good enough at drill to go on it and I was confined to hut-cleaning during the practices. However, due to some early postings they were short of numbers and so they risked using me.

The day before passing out parade we were allowed a late pass and we all piled off to Liverpool. After the third pub I was well away, lost my mates and didn't know where I was. By some miracle I found myself back at the railway station and some of my friends helped me back to camp. To sign in I had one standing either side of me to stop me from falling over. That

night was horrific – 24 blokes all moaning, groaning and being
sick.

(SAC John Dinning, RAF)

Getting drunk for the first time during National Service was an
initiation for many conscripts, and for some drink became a
means of forgetting the difficulties of service life, but it was not
that easy to obtain. The NAAFI served only beer and National
Service pay did not extend to any great over-indulgence. In the
Royal Navy, however, grog was served to all National Servicemen – a tradition not abolished until 1970, by when it was
something of an anachronism on board ships which carried
delicate electronic equipment. For all conscripts, though, the
daily ration of grog was a link with the navy of yesteryear.

> In our mess on board HMS *Dodinan Point* at Rosyth there was an
> old hand. He had been in the Navy for over twenty years, was in
> possession of three good conduct badges but had never progressed
> beyond being a 'killick'. We called him 'Stripey'. He was a father
> figure. If any misdemeanour occurred in the mess he would always
> accept the blame with impunity, because he knew we would be
> charged with an offence, but a respected old hand like him would
> not be – and, sure enough, he never was.
>
> He was PO's mess-man and as such was entitled to a daily tot of
> neat rum at 'Up spirits' time. The rest of us had a tot of grog – one
> part rum to two parts water. The benefit of getting neat rum was
> that it could be stored if not used. So old Stripey always had a
> supply from which he generously dosed us if any of us was ill with a
> cough or a cold. The cure was miraculous – I can still imagine the
> feel of over-proof spirit in my mouth. I cannot recall anyone taking
> advantage of his good nature.
>
> (Writer John G. McIlvean, Royal Navy)

Men like the senior leading hand softened the blow for many
naval conscripts away from home for the first time and feeling
homesick in a strange environment.

Along with many other National Servicemen, John McIlvean did
his basic training at HMS *Royal Arthur* at Corsham in Wiltshire,
the other major base being HMS *Victory* at Southsea. Entrance
to the Royal Navy was determined by the results gained at an
intelligence test during registration, and by the recruit's previous
naval experience in the RNVR or in the Sea Cadets. The navy
could afford to be choosy – at any given time National
Servicemen never provided more than 10% of its total man-

power. As a consequence naval conscripts had a good conceit of themselves, even if few found themselves being posted to responsible 'rate' positions – that is, being trained for gunnery, radar or communications. Most National Servicemen served their time in the Supply and Secretariat Branch working in administrative jobs: the only alternative was to sign on as a regular, an option which was frequently put forward with the lure that it attracted a higher rate of pay. On demob all National Servicemen had to serve with the Active Reserve, often as Petty Officers or commissioned officers.

Basic training differed in the Royal Navy in that only a fortnight was given over to drill and rifle practice to lick the young recruits into shape. (RNVR camp counted towards basic training.)

> On receiving my notice of 'call up' I was ordered to report to HMS *Victory*, Victoria Barracks, Southsea, on 7 September 1953 by 16.00. As an ex-Reservist I had to travel in uniform and take all my kit. We arrived in Portsmouth in the morning, and having large kit bags etc. decided to go to Victoria Barracks, dump them and then have a walk round until 4 p.m. The Petty Officer on the gate was most helpful and showed us into a room to leave our bags but when we tried to leave he became less helpful and refused to let us go. Lesson one.
>
> We were eventually 'classed up' and proceeded into basic training, starting with bull and dress. This held no fears for the ex-reservists but we encountered the famous 'Obadiah' on the parade ground. He was a CPO Gunnery Instructor, whose correct name I never knew, but he was known as 'Obadiah' throughout the navy. One of his quirks was, if a man made an incorrect drill movement, he had to march smartly to the middle of the parade ground, mount a dais and standing to attention shout to all points of the compass, 'My name is Obadiah, I pull the f— wire!' This caused great mirth to everyone else on the parade ground. Generally though, the Instructors there were a good lot who realised that their charges were nervous and in many cases homesick. The only times that I saw discipline strongly enforced was with the non-conformists who did everything to buck the system.
>
> (Writer William Nuttall, Royal Navy)

Sarcasm was not just the prerogative of Army and RAF NCOs. When Robert Greenshields complained that the sun was in his eyes during a parade at HMS *Royal Arthur*, the Chief Petty Officer ordered all six hundred recruits to turn around, much to his own humiliation. There was also a good deal of practical joking during basic training, engineered on the whole by the

Petty Officers who wanted to school their recruits in the
intricacies of naval lore and language. Knowing that a 'killick'
was a leading rating was almost as important as rifle drill and the
recruit soon learned that he never complained but 'dripped'.
Each day he washed out the 'heads' and not the ablutions and
Petty Officers vied for the chance to make a 'nig-nog' (raw
recruit) call the bows the sharp end.

The next step was a course in trade or seamanship training, and
for those bound for the Supply and Secretariat Branch that meant
a posting to HMS *Ceres* at Wetherby in Yorkshire. There, in
squads of twenty each, men were trained to become 'Writers', as
clerks in administration or in stores where they would be
responsible for accounting and stock-taking. Many had civilian
experience in banks or accountants' offices and the work came
naturally to them – indeed, the Royal Navy prided itself on taking
only qualified men – but in general it was a colossal waste of
manpower. Civilian labour could have been substituted for many
of the tasks given to National Service Writers, who in many bases
also had to contend with the hostility of the regulars who felt
inconvenienced by having to work with short-service colleagues.

For those posted to sea-going establishments little training was
given, and many men were consigned to inconsequential tasks.

> After leaving *Theseus* (where I worked on the telephone
> exchange) my principal duties were in the Reserve Fleet putting
> ships into 'mothballs'. Some of this work was quite dirty, chipping
> lead paint in the bilges wearing goggles and masks and having
> regular blood tests and de-ammunitioning ships with shells left
> over from the war. We had to make two trips to Scotland to fetch
> down ships to Portsmouth for the Reserve. There was a feeling of
> resentment, at least on my part, that we were being used as cheap
> labour.
>
> (AB James H. Austin, Royal Navy)

Given the Navy's reluctance to train men to responsible
positions unless they signed on as regulars, discipline could have
been a problem in dealing with the National Serviceman. On
ships such as the fleet carrier HMS *Ocean*, the centre of National
Service training operations in Scotland and a veteran of the
Korean War, good order was maintained by keeping the men
busy and making them understand that each job had a purpose.
At shore bases like HMS *Ceres* discipline tended to be stricter,
and there were examples of the same meaningless tasks which
disfigured military basic training – whitewashing coal, weeding
lawns with eating irons and so on; but on the whole, Petty

Officers preferred to maintain discipline with a mixture of toughness and good humour.

> At the end of our six weeks' seamanship training we had to 'pass out' and our intake was detailed to be Guard of Honour for the Second Sea Lord, Admiral Sir Guy Russell. Unfortunately we had one person who could not do rifle drill at all; despite being quite an intelligent young man, he was constantly falling foul of PO Lines because of this. We were all lined up to receive the VIP with Duffy (the awkward one) just behind me in the centre file, end man. PO Lines was adjacent to him on the flank. Just before the Admiral appeared I heard PO Lines muttering 'For f—'s sake Duffy . . . Faint!' Next thing he crashed to the floor alongside me and was removed. He was heartily congratulated by PO Lines later and this heralded a new and good relationship between them.
>
> (Writer William Nuttall, Royal Navy)

One of the privileges of joining the Royal Navy was that the uniform was generally a better fit, and recruits were encouraged to visit a tailor early in their training to acquire a 'tiddley suit', or best uniform. In 1950 the navy had revolutionised its standards of uniform for officers and men, and this move, too, benefited National Servicemen. The old working dress of baggy overalls gave way to light blue shirts and dark blue denim trousers; and for walking out, the traditional 'square rig' of collar, jumper and bell-bottomed trousers was modernised by the introduction of a coat-style, zip-fronted serge jumper. Conditions ashore and afloat were improved. Sheets were issued – this applied to all three services – and in the newer ships the hammock disappeared in favour of bunks. Despite continuing peacetime food rationing, which remained in force until 1954, meals were reasonably well-cooked, if limited in scope, although no one who served at HMS *Royal Arthur* in the early 1950s can ever forget the strange breakfast combination of kippers with prunes!

Because trade or seamanship training was more important to the Navy than basic training was to the Army and the RAF, men were given their postings at call-up. With the Army and the Air Force it was rather different. At the end of basic training each National Serviceman was interviewed by a Personnel Selection Officer (PSO) who made the final decision about his future employment. According to the Army rule-book this was the most decisive moment of the recruit's service, but in truth the interview often turned out to be something of a farce. Few PSOs were qualified in personnel selection – some were National Servicemen themselves – and most were inclined to be swayed by what had been written in the records by the MIO during registration. As a result the process was repeated, and men found themselves being posted to units which would make little use of their civilian skills.

'Do you play football or cricket? Do you swim?' the Orderly Officer at Dhekelia asked Peter Davies, a builder by trade.

'No,' he replied to both questions.

'What do you like then?'

'I like reading books.'

Davies was then posted as a Male Nurse III to the British Military Hospital at Nicosia in Cyprus. There he had to make a further choice between medical or surgical duties, chose the latter, and found himself doing all the jobs no one else wanted to do.

For all the men passing out at eight-weekly intervals, the options were trade or professional training at home; for some, a posting abroad; and, for a few, designation as Potential Officer Material (POM) and removal to the officer training wing. Most POs had been singled out or encouraged to apply for officer training half-way through basic training, and had been separated off from their original squad early on. For them a path had been marked out, although many would stray from it: for everyone else there was a passing-out parade, usually followed by a boozy party and then home for a week's leave, resplendent in a perfectly bulled uniform. The worst was over, they had all been told, and the best was yet to come.

Chapter Three

THIS SEAT OF MARS

One of the first differences noticed by just about every National Serviceman during that first leave was that uniform still bestowed some benefits. In the early days at least, with memories of the war still strong, they might be treated to drinks in pubs or given free passes to dance-halls or cinemas. Going home wearing the 'best blue' uniform of the Royal Air Force, the distinctive black beret of the Royal Armoured Corps or the kilt of a Highland regiment, could be a heady experience for an eighteen-year-old who might have been a schoolboy a few months earlier – even though there were old sweats at every turning, ready to deflate youthful egos.

> After square-bashing we had one week's leave, so I got a warrant and went home to Perth. I can remember going out in town and I went to my old barber for a haircut, feeling like Douglas Bader in my uniform. The barber said, 'Have you joined the ATC, then?' Boy was I deflated. My own pal had been called up a day after me and he was in the Royal Artillery. We were both home together strutting round the town in uniform when we saw an old postman we knew from work days. He took one look at the pair of us and shouted across the High Street, 'Thank God there's a navy!'
>
> (Corporal John Inglis, RAF Regiment)

Parents, too, took a positive attitude towards National Service. Fathers who had been called up in World War II looked on conscription as a fact of life, an experience which their sons had to face as part of the scheme of things. A few thought that if Britain was to retain a pre-eminent place in the world she needed strong armed forces; others thought that if they had done their duty, so should their sons; men of all political shades felt that National Service was good for national discipline; even a handful of the old left lent their support because they believed that all potential revolutionaries should have some military experience. (One distinguished Scottish trade union leader turned on opponents of National Service with the remark, 'How many of you street fighters can fire a rifle?') The majority were agreed that National Service could do little harm and that, on the whole, it was 'a good thing'. Most fathers had had words of advice to offer to their sons when they were called up – never to volunteer for anything, how to skive – and for the most part were pleased, as one father put it, to see their sons 'go away boys and come back men'. And mothers, who had worried about losing loved ones during World War II, could watch their sons going off to the armed forces fairly secure in the knowledge that they would not see active service.

This was not a view shared by the armed forces which, as we have seen, were continuously in action during the period of National Service. To keep their men fighting fit, trained and in a constant state of readiness meant that life in most active units could be tough. It was certainly the view of most Regular officers that it should be.

> I had a squad at Dunbar Castle with National Servicemen who'd just been called up and I did make life uncomfortable for them because the standards were appalling and one must remember that drill, bull and discipline are necessary to obtain efficiency. I gated the whole platoon myself, NCOs included, because the standard was so appalling . . . ultimately my platoon won the award for the best platoon in the Company and they welcomed this experience. They didn't think it was such a joke though when they got out to Germany and found that I was their Platoon Commander again! But at least I was the devil they knew. When one got out to a regular battalion you did not make life deliberately uncomfortable, there was too much to do, but it's all part of the growing up experience and might be called the induction of indoctrination into the armed forces.
>
> (Major W. R. R. Bruce, 4th/5th Bn. The Black Watch)

Bill Bruce joined The Scots Guards in 1946 as a volunteer to avoid being sent down the pits as a 'Bevin Boy' and was commissioned into the Black Watch as a short service officer. There he was responsible for training the first intake of National Servicemen, and found that 'if a man came into the Army with the idea of enjoying himself and making the best of it for his two years, he did well.'

Having given their men a basic training in how to act like a soldier, sailor or airman, the next step was to transform them into fighting men, to give them all something useful to do. This could mean battlefield training in Britain or Germany for infantry recruits, sea-going experience in the Royal Navy, or learning about strategic support in one of the Army corps or the RAF; but for the majority of National Servicemen, particularly in the Army, it meant an indoctrination in the art of administration. As many recruits were to discover, it was one thing to strut along the High Street in a uniform but quite another to sit behind a desk in a featureless office, dealing with the endless forms required for the movement of ordnance stores, or working out the entire battalion's pay, minus deductions for damages (9*d*. for the replacement of a china pint mug).

THE ARMY

Unknown to the National Serviceman, the interview with the PSO had placed him in one of the six Summed Selection Groups (SSG) which would help to determine the course of his future training. It had always been assumed by the Army that recruits allocated to SSG 1 to SSG 3+ would get high-grade jobs, while those on 3— to 5 would be assigned to run-of-the-mill work requiring little or no training. Although allocation to an SSG was the final responsibility of the PSO, other factors were taken into account, such as the educational standard achieved before call-up, general aptitude and performance during basic training.

According to a confidential memorandum of 1949, it had been calculated that to provide adequately for the requirements of the Army each intake of recruits would have to contain men with SSGs in the following proportions:

Above median	*Below median*
SSG 1 — 10%	SSG 3— —20%
SSG 2 — 20%	SSG 4 — 20%
SSG 3+ —20%	SSG 5 — 10%

By 1949, largely because of deferments and the disturbance to education during the war, the National Service intakes were unable to conform to the Army's prearranged ideal. The percentages were never achieved: in 1947 only 4% were allocated to SSG 1, and only 15% of the entire annual intake reached the upper three (of eight) educational standards, those of school leaving certificate standard or above. Two years later, 84.8% of the recruits had educational standards ranging from elementary

('full-time general education to the age of 14') to illiteracy
('unable to read or write'). This led the military planners to the
unpalatable conclusion that 'The quality of intake now reaching
the Army, whilst failing to provide its high grade requirements, is
producing an embarrassing number of men whose ability and
capacity for learning is so limited that they are capable of
performing only the most simple administrative and general
duties.'

Ideally, the Army would have preferred all its National Service
recruits at a later age, once they had completed further education
courses, apprenticeships and other trade training. This would
have provided better educated and more mature recruits, but by
subordinating the talents of trained men – engineers, graduates,
tradesmen – to the needs of the Army, it would also have had a
disastrous effect on the nation's economy. Although a pressure
group was formed within military circles to lobby for a later
joining up age, it was never a political starter. (Another school of
thought had it that recruits would be more malleable when they
were sixteen.)

Things did improve by the mid 1950s when the effects of the
1944 Education Act began to be felt, but even that act, thought
revolutionary in its time, heightened the dilemma faced by the
military planners in determining a recruit's SSG. An 11-plus, or
qualifying examination, determined at the age of eleven whether
a pupil went to a grammar school – generally the path to a
profession or tertiary education – or to a secondary modern
school which gave a broad technical education, ending at the age
of fifteen. Even by 1955 the number of grammar school pupils
had not risen above 10% of the school population (only in
Scotland, with its different system, was the number higher);
admittedly this was twice the number of pupils in pre-war years,
but, broadly speaking, it meant that higher education was still the
preserve of the middle classes.

In many cases recruits did have a frighteningly low standard of
general education – an abiding memory of many National
Servicemen is their shock at widespread illiteracy amongst their
new mates in the barrack-room, and the preference for reading
comics like the *Dandy* and the *Beano* – but the Army's rigidity in
imposing its educational guidelines was also to blame. The recruit
who told his corporal during basic training that an equal-sided
triangle was also an equilateral triangle would not be given much
credit for his knowledge; whereas a smartly turned-out soldier,
willing to obey orders, could be given plus marks towards his

allocation to an SSG for holding his Sten gun correctly. Whether or not he knew that his arms were forming an equilateral triangle was another matter.

> To bolster the dearth of experienced personnel we got another sergeant . . . still a young fellow, he was a soldier's soldier – immaculate kit, gleaming boots, half-inch hair, but overweight. All 'Yessirs' and flamboyant salutes. But he could hardly read or write. He was consigned to the wagon-checking function, which he 'oversaw'. His signing of all the stuff I typed for him was painfully slow, requiring pauses, lip movement and so on to complete the signature. He and I conflicted because I was scruffy and irreverent, but nevertheless we co-operated through mutual need. Every week he and his crew stole a ton or so of coal from the various yards and sidings they had access to, and we stole food from the various messes our room-mates had access to, and I typed his weekly report and weekend roster, both of which he presented with his quiet flourish. He wasn't a bad sort at all, but I cannot see how inability to function in a job should be rewarded as his was.
> (Corporal Iain Colquhoun, Corps of Royal Engineers)

From the military point of view, the fact that the NCO was a good soldier and carried out his appointed tasks efficiently was usually enough, but many National Servicemen found it a great trial to be ordered about by men they considered to be their intellectual inferiors. 'We only have to teach ridiculously simple stuff – the standard of the highest is about that of a boy of 14 or 15,' Ian Macleod, an RAEC sergeant in Germany, told J. M. Lee.* 'Not even up to School Cert standard.'

In the first years of National Service a sizeable proportion of graduates and well-qualified school-leavers made it to the Royal Army Educational Corps as Sergeant-Instructors, or 'schoolies'. It was their task to get soldiers through the Army's Certificate of Education: quite a few sergeants of war-substantive rank had been either threatened with demotion or reduced to corporals on account of their lack of formal education, and were anxious to regain their stripes, pay and privileges. For most conscript RAEC sergeants, National Service was a pleasant time bounded by classrooms, libraries and elementary teaching; if it was tainted at all, it was only by the knowledge that their rank had been gained

*J. M. Lee, Professor of Politics at the University of Bristol, was determined unfit for National Service but acted as 'link-man' in the correspondence of his fellow sixth-formers at Henry Mellish Grammar School in Nottingham. These letters provide an invaluable first-hand account of National Service in the years 1949–1951.

by virtue of their civilian qualifications and not by their military expertise. National Servicemen served as 'schoolies' throughout the period and were generally respected by the men who came under their wing. To the rank and file the 'schoolie' had the ultimate skive, but older officers could be chary of RAEC sergeants, thinking them 'bolshy' or 'unsoldierly'. And there was, too, the lingering memory of the slightly subversive role played by the education corps in World War II.

> The RAEC obviously worried about the 'politicising' charge: in his introductory address to the sergeant-instructors' course the School Commandant at RAEC Wilton Park told us they didn't want 'any dirty-pink LSE types' in the Corps. Our intake was generally so apolitical as to be mystified or amazed by his remarks.
> (Sergeant Richard Storey, Royal Army Educational Corps)

For those recruits in the upper echelons of SSG who were not officer material, the next stage in National Service was a posting to a training regiment if they belonged to one of the Army's corps – Royal Engineers, Royal Signals, Royal Army Service Corps, Royal Army Medical Corps, Royal Army Ordnance Corps, Royal Electrical and Mechanical Engineers, Royal Military Police, Royal Army Pay Corps, Royal Army Veterinary Corps, Military Provost Staff Corps, Royal Army Educational Corps, Royal Army Dental Corps, Royal Pioneer Corps, Intelligence Corps, Army Physical Training Corps or the Army Catering Corps (given in order of precedence). Men in the infantry or a regiment of the Royal Armoured Corps stayed with their unit to complete their training. Those considered to be unskilled or unreceptive to teaching were posted immediately to units in this country and abroad, where they were generally given the most menial tasks to perform.

Men posted to infantry regiments which were not stationed abroad spent most of their National Service at home depots, where they were trained as clerks and then employed on the weighty matter of the Army's records. Some were lucky, like Lance-Sergeant Alan Rattray who served with the 2nd Battalion, Scots Guards, at Chelsea Barracks in London, where a considerable time was spent parading for Royal duties and other ceremonial occasions. Today he still admits to feeling 'a touch of pride' whenever he hears his old regiment mentioned, an emotion infantrymen are perhaps more prone to share than any other servicemen. One of the first duties of all infantry training sergeants was to instil into their recruits a knowledge of, and a pride in, the regiments' traditions, so that National Servicemen would remember that it was the Argylls which had held the thin red line at Balaclava, that the Devonshire Regiment had started life as the Duke of Beaufort's Musketeers, that the badge of the Duke of Edinburgh's Royal Regiment contained a China dragon, that the North Lancashires were also known as 'The Loyal Regiment': it was emphasised again and again that the recruits had not so much joined the army – they had joined a regiment.

> Before going in I was determined to avoid service if at all possible. Having lost that particular battle I was somewhat surprised to find that after basic training I had been sufficiently brainwashed that I was totally defensive towards the Wiltshire Regiment, proud to be in the WR and would hear no criticism of it!
> (Private R. H. Bulford, 1st Bn. The Duke of Edinburgh's Royal Regiment)

This *esprit de corps* extended not just to those who spent most of their time in rifle companies, but also to those – the majority – who worked as clerks. One of the by-products of National Service was an increase in paperwork in a battalion's Orderly Room and in the Quartermaster's department, due largely to the constant turnover of men. Equipment had to be handed out and accounted for, pay had to be calculated and demob arrangements made: most National Service clerks had an understudy waiting to take over, and this doubling up added to the sense of confusion which frequently reigned in the Orderly Room. Not surprisingly, perhaps, the surface lack of order was resented by the Regular NCOs who often looked on their National Service colleagues as nine-day-wonders and treated them accordingly. But whether employed in an administrative capacity or as riflemen, each recruit had to be schooled in the use of weapons and given basic battlecraft experience, which usually entailed a course with an infantry training battalion. Thus, in the early 1950s, a Cameronian, say, who had joined up and completed his basic training at the regimental depot at Winston Barracks in Hamilton, would then proceed to Dreghorn Barracks in Edinburgh for a ten-week posting to the 1st Bn. Royal Scots, at that time the Lowland Brigade's training battalion. Thereafter, like Bill Kerr, he would return to the bourne of his own regiment for further training and employment.

> At Dreghorn I did not feel a part of the regiment, although I was made to feel at home by the other Orderly Room clerks. In the Royal Scots Fusiliers I felt part of the regiment. By example as

well as by instruction the senior NCOs and Warrant Officers instilled a pride in oneself and the regiment and I felt that the battalion was well trained, although the Fusiliers and junior NCOs, particularly in the rifle companies, were nearly all National Servicemen with a constant turnover.

(Corporal W. L. Kerr, 1st Bn. Royal Scots Fusiliers)

The system allowed infantry regiments to strengthen their links with the traditional recruiting areas, and in so doing build up a feeling of mutual obligation. Most Cameronian recruits came from Lanarkshire (Bill Kerr's Royal Scots Fusiliers recruited from Ayrshire and the south-west of Scotland) and the regiment was quick to build up a close relationship between the Depot and the local County Council. Similar links were created by the English county regiments, and the return from Korea of the Gloucestershire Regiment – the 'Glorious Glosters' – was a signal for tremendous public excitement when they marched through Bristol to receive the freedom of the city. In turn, passing out parades at the end of basic training became family affairs and most National Servicemen were left with the feeling that they belonged to an organisation which really did take a close interest in their care and well-being. Occasionally, infantry recruits would be posted to specialist arms like the Intelligence Corps or the Joint Service School of Languages; they could also be cross-posted to another regiment in the same brigade, but the general rule was that, once enlisted in a regiment, a man served on its strength until the end of his National Service.

For the specialist back-up corps, the post-war years brought with them problems of a different nature. All had expanded during World War II (the REME had been formed as a separate corps in 1942); all had unprecedented numbers of men in their ranks; and all had made giant strides in the type of equipment they handled. Much of it was highly complicated in operation and maintenance and demanded a reasonable standard of skill and application, yet demobilisation in 1945 and 1946 meant that all the corps suffered wastage of valuable trained personnel. As a consequence, each revamped its structure to allow the minimum amount of time in basic and trade training so that recruits could be prepared quickly and efficiently for service in a field unit.

To meet the needs of the peacetime army, the Corps of Royal Signals, which accepted a high percentage of National Servicemen, evolved a much enlarged Signals Training Centre consisting of six training regiments and a depot regiment. After being called up in the Royal Signals the recruit would be assigned to 7 TRRS at Catterick. Following basic training the most suitable recruits were then trained in wireless operation, cipher work, telephony or telegraphy: thereafter, the most competent became instructors themselves. The Royal Signals had a reputation – not altogether undeserved – for providing a particularly severe code of discipline during basic training; most recruits discovered, to their surprise, that trade training was a more civilised and practical affair.

> How different the world seemed a few months later when the square-bashing ended and the sub-zero Yorkshire winter was replaced by the warm and welcoming atmosphere of Bohemian Brighton, where I found myself at a Royal Signals cipher school which kept a low profile in buildings just off the main Lewes Road.
>
> Life at 4 (Ind.) Signals Squadron, where the total complement numbered fewer than one hundred, contrasted dramatically with the khaki expanse that was Catterick Camp. There was a marked contrast, too, in the all too serious activities at the cipher school and the goings-on just a threepenny bus ride away, where, on Brighton's saucy sea front, the Permissive Society was being nursed through its infancy by Beatniks and other outrageous people who populated the beaches and the bars of Britain's most liberal town in the first few months of the Swinging Sixties.
>
> 'Don't go to such-and-such a street,' warned the rather naive CO. 'It is a dangerous and pernicious place.' Needless to say, the self-same street was duly explored and found to be neither dangerous nor, when we had looked up the dictionary, pernicious, but for all that, Brighton after Catterick was like leaving a crematorium and entering a disco.
>
> (Corporal Denis Gane, Royal Corps of Signals)

To the joy of all recruits, morse code was gradually discontinued after 1945. However, there was still a need for cipher clerks, men trained in the complexities of coding and decoding; and along with telecommunication training, it provided skilled work for the high calibre National Serviceman. Men like Signalman Findlay, who had completed an apprenticeship in Post Office telephones prior to call-up, came to regard their Signals' training as forming part of their continuing education: 'By this time I had been assigned to a 22-week course as a Line Technician. I didn't know it at the time but it was a very good course technically and attracted a substantial technical allowance on completion.' With the Corps being called upon to provide a complete system of communications from the War Office downwards, a strategic wireless network was developed, and equipment such as teleprinters and VHF wireless sets became more refined as a result.

In other specialist corps, especially in the Royal Engineers and the REME, it soon became apparent that the National Servicemen who had completed trade apprenticeships were of a higher standard than many of the Regular recruits, and so corners could be cut during trade training. Although many skilled men had slipped through the MIO's net during registration, a reasonable proportion did find their way into responsible and challenging tasks in the army's engineering branches.

> I was sent first to Lydd, Kent, to the AA Command School for training in electrical instruments. It was my own line of work and I was grateful for the good grounding in electrical theory and practice I was given. From the officers down, there was an acceptance of us recruits as lads being trained in engineering. Looking back, there was a kind of public school atmosphere at the training school. There was little 'military' intrusion. One was always encouraged to do well in studies and practical work.
> (Craftsman Frank Thompson, REME)

Graduates or apprentices holding their HNC could go far in the REME, even as National Servicemen. Because there was a shortage of armament artificers in the technical branches such as radar servicing, groups of National Servicemen were trained in high technology skills and promoted to the financially rewarding rank of Leading Artisan Sergeant. The courses took place at Arborfield, near Reading (Nos. 3 and 5 TRREME) for telecommunications and radar, and at Bordon, an ex-Cavalry barracks of Crimean War vintage (Nos. 4 and 6 TRREME) for armaments and vehicles. Less skilled personnel were trained as mechanics or taught to drive – one of the practical skills for civilian life to which all National Servicemen, of whatever arm, aspired. Most men in the RASC were given the opportunity of putting themselves forward for drivers' courses, but in other arms it was a privilege only given to the lucky few and instruction could be haphazard.

> I was whisked away (from WOSB) to Kinmel Park near Rhyl where I was more or less taught to drive. It was basic infantry training all over again but with an hour a week for driving instruction on a variety of vehicles with a variety of instructors. One I recall had a thin stick with which he rapped knuckles at every mistake; just the thing to inspire confidence while piloting a big three-tonner along country lanes or on the north Wales coast road. In spite of this I managed to scrape through my test – the

only one I have had, and which laid some sort of foundations for over thirty years of accident-free motoring.

(Gunner Martyn Thomas, Royal Regiment of Artillery)

Soldiers learning other trades could be treated with equal tardiness. NCOs unused to taking recruits through crash courses would either throw up their hands in horror at any display of ineptitude and then impose even stricter standards of discipline, or they would ease up, telling themselves that the men were, after all, only temporary soldiers passing through. Clerks, for example, were supposed to learn how to type reasonably efficiently – and many did – but for every man given a decent term of instruction, there was another whose training was careless and rudimentary.

I can now laboriously bash out a few words on the typewriter without looking at the keyboard [he wrote to J. M. Lee]. This is known as touch-typing. Looking at the keyboard is known variously as 'skiving' and 'an offence'. However, when it comes to typing to music in order to gain rhythm (or something like that) I mess up the keyboard and jam the machine. We are always asked if we are having any difficulty, and on replying yes, are told, 'Continue with the next exercise.'

(Private A. J. Bayley, Royal Army Service Corps)

The art of skiving – malingering to one's own advantage – will be examined later, but Alan Bayley's remarks hit on one of National Service's greatest anomalies. It had been introduced to swell the army's manpower and make it a more efficient fighting force, yet one of the first lessons passed on by the Regulars, the 'old sweats', was to keep out of trouble by appearing busy or by playing the chameleon. During trade training and thereafter, army camps would be full of men busy doing nothing or merging into the scenery whenever an officer hoved into view. During PT a mixture of shouts and exaggerated movements could deceive the onlooker into believing that every effort was being put into the exercises; men marching at the double going nowhere in particular at least *looked* efficient; mechanics standing around a 3-ton truck with its bonnet open might be examining the engine – or just busy discussing last Saturday's football results. The problem was that although the Army needed trained men – and in most cases was prepared to go to considerable lengths to get them – instructors were thin on the ground in the early years, and then they got bored. There was also the problem of dilution: an Army Order issued at Command level, for instance, aimed at increasing efficiency in the training of Cooks, Class II, could become just another piece of unwelcome bumph in the Orderly Room. Unless there was a real desire to improve the training of apprentice cooks, there was always the danger that a repugnant order would not be acted upon; or if it were, only in a half-hearted way. Judging by the avalanche of complaints about Army food, many were left with the impression that little training had ever been given to the men of the Army Catering Corps.

When the training was good, however, most recruits were agreed that it was very, very good.

> The quality of the training at Arborfield was absolutely first class. It was so good in fact that I could now walk into either a 3 Mk. VII radar set or a 4 Mk. VI radar set, switch it on, operate it, calibrate it and I could also do all the servicing on it. With the exception of one or two fire picquets or the odd guard, there were no regimental duties at all – I think there was a muster parade in the morning which was a bit of a shambles, then we all marched off to our classes. The training started at half-past eight and went on until five, with three-quarters of an hour for lunch. We weren't messed about at all, everything there was done to make sure that the quality of the training we received took precedence over everything else.
>
> (2nd Lieutenant R. J. Wyatt, REME)

Trade training in the infantry lasted ten weeks; in the specialist units it could be anything from twenty to thirty-six weeks, depending on the level of skills involved. Men in the RASC were trained at the Corps' Central Training Centre based at Aldershot (Nos. 1, 2 and 5 TR), Farnborough (No. 3 TR) or Yeovil (No. 6 TR), and were taught how to drive, how to service their vehicles and how to load them tactically – that is, on the principle of 'last in, first out' in order of necessity.

The Royal Engineers and the Royal Regiment of Artillery provided perhaps the widest range of crafts: everything from plumbing to bridge-building, from gunlaying to radar operation. In 1947 and 1948, at the time of the reorganisation of the Army, the Royal Artillery had escaped the worst upheavals of amalgamation and disbandment, and in 1950 it still had 69 regiments, fourteen of which were grouped with TA units in Anti-Aircraft Command. Of the remaining regiments, about half were field artillery units, a quarter medium or heavy units and the rest were assigned to field force anti-aircraft duties. Their equipment, too, was beginning to change, and by the late 1950s missiles like the Corporal and the Honest John were beginning to be deployed with RA units of BAOR, along with new and more sophisticated battle-field weapons such as the 105 mm Abbot self-propelled gun and the 155 mm towed howitzer. Very few National Servicemen were allowed to have much to do with the gunnery side of the Royal Artillery and most were designated to back-up duties, servicing vehicles or in administration. (To be fair to the Army, those National Servicemen instructed in gunnery usually found that the technical skills were too difficult to master in the short time allotted to them.) Nevertheless, Sappers and Gunners tended to have a good conceit of themselves and their Corps or Regiment – in the Army's Order of Precedence, the Royal Regiment of Artillery stands fourth and the Corps of Royal Engineers fifth, after the Life Guards and Blues and Royals, the Royal Horse Artillery and the regiments of the Royal Armoured Corps – and their battalions maintained the same standards of discipline and regimental spirit as were found in the infantry. In fact, perennial shortages of infantry for active service meant that Sappers and Gunners were often called upon to act as footsloggers, and all recruits in both arms were given extensive weapons training.

Although attention to bull was never to be so strict as it had been during basic training, it remained a fundamental of Army discipline. A man caught with filthy webbing could be put on Company Orders and confined to barracks (CB) for seven days. More serious charges – falling asleep on guard duty, mishandling weapons on the firing range, being drunk and disorderly, arriving back late from leave – could entail punishment under Section 40 of the Army Act, 'conduct prejudicial to good order and military discipline'. Those punished under Commanding Officer's Orders could expect 28 days CB, stoppage of pay, and additional guard duties or allocation to such menial tasks as spud-bashing, washing latrines, gardening or painting. More serious offences could lead to a District Court Martial which was permitted to imprison men for up to two years, or to a General Court Martial which had lengthier prison terms and even the death penalty at its disposal. Mostly, though, punishment was meted out for quite trivial offences and at the whim of an inspecting officer or NCO.

> I had the dirtiest rifle in the Army. I tried to change it early on, but was told to 'go away', Army style. In vain I poured Brasso down the muzzle and pulled it through time after time. No use. It looked fine from the muzzle end, but from the breech it was as rusty as old iron. Must have been a trick of reflected light. General Inspection: a thousand men on parade with rifles. Me tucked away in the middle rank to avoid detection. Officer chooses to

inspect middle rank! He took one look through my rifle and screamed across the parade ground: 'I look at this man's rifle and what do I see? Bloody spiders!' Visions of the glasshouse loomed large. Thankfully, the platoon corporal gave him some explanation which let me off the hook. Phew.

(Corporal Derek Stoddard, Royal Army Service Corps)

To be marched at the double, minus belt and cap, into the CO's office, flanked by two NCOs, was supposed to be a humiliating experience, one which every soldier wanted to avoid. It became a skilled operation for the soldier to know how far he could go in defending his point of view to his superiors.

The Army never fails to surprise you. On the last day of my three weeks on CB I was parading behind the guard in Full Field Marching Order (which contained 72 separate sets of brass, all gleaming) when the Orderly Officer said to the Guard Corporal, 'Charge him, dirty brasses.' I could not believe my ears, my brasses were immaculate. After the parade I spoke to the Corporal and he agreed that they were clean. The following day I was on orders and the Commanding Officer asked the Corporal whether the brasses were dirty and to my horror he said, 'Yes, Sir.' The CO then asked me if I had anything to say before he passed sentence and I thought to myself, 'in for a penny, in for a pound.' I said, 'If you give me any more CB I will not be responsible for what happens.' Then I held my breath. The CO never batted an eyelid. 'Admonished; march him out, Sergeant-Major.' Admonished meant a slapped wrist but no punishment. This was one of the black moments, but as in most cases, it had a silver lining. Young men are born optimists!

(Private Terence Davenport, Royal Army Medical Corps)

In fact, very few National Servicemen suffered extreme penalties, the exact number being hidden by the government's Thirty Year rule regarding access to public papers; confinement to barracks and extra guard duties were the sum of most military punishments. If an NCO could not pin anything on a soldier he disliked or whom he suspected of skiving, there were other insidious ways of inflicting misery. Men could be picked on to do guard duty several nights in succession in addition to a normal day's work, and then called out in the early hours of the morning and inspected. Another hated task was the fire picquet or night-time fire watch, but it was the monotony of guard duty – plus its general uselessness – which pulled at the heartstrings of most National Servicemen.

It was eery doing guard duty in winter (at Shoeburyness). Every five days we did a twelve-hour stint; two hours on, four off, protecting the workshops from I don't know what – they were near the beach and about half a mile from the guardroom. We had no weapons of any kind and there was no phone. On a pitch black night with the wind howling through the trees, or on a foggy night with becalmed ships in the river blowing their foghorns, you need strong nerves.

(Gunner Martyn Thomas, Royal Regiment of Artillery)

During the 1950s guard duty in the United Kingdom temporarily took on a front-line aspect after the IRA successfully raided military bases in search of arms and the Army tightened up its security. For a few months guards became more vigilant and circumspect, but the birds had flown, leaving locked gates and jittery nerves. Even at the best of times guard duty was regarded as a chore, at worst a punishment. Unfortunately the Army leaned towards that view, too, and those soldiers who disliked their period of National Service could see it only in a ludicrous light – the reluctant guard standing watch over his equally unwilling fellow men.

About this time the IRA robbed the REME depot at Arborfield of guns and ammo. A new picquet was created – the armoury picquet. One man on the roof all night, two locked inside, four patrolling outside. So naturally the two inside fell asleep, putting out the lights. At 1 a.m. the orderly sergeant kicked on the door, wakening those inside. One of them, startled in the dark, pulled the very loud alarm, wakening the camp, causing embarrassment to the orderly sergeant, because the errant soldier had a good excuse. 'He thought they were breaking in.' Twenty minutes of uproar later, the sergeant went up a ladder to find the 'missing' roofman, who was still, poor soul, fast asleep. These lads, supposed to guard all night, got no relief at all from their daytime commitments of classes, parades, evening duties and so on. Several fell asleep in their classes, to further possibilities of charges and CB. 36 hours of constant alertness/activity would not be expected or tolerated anywhere in the civilised world, except in extreme circumstances such as war.

(Corporal Iain Colquhoun, Corps of Royal Engineers)

At the end of the trade training, all recruits were posted to regular units in the United Kingdom or overseas. Those who wanted to travel could express a preference for service in the major commands, BAOR, MELF, Far.ELF and, during the Korean War, for attachment to one of the battalions fighting in the Commonwealth Division. Postings were made according to

necessity and to a man's training. The endemic shortage of
infantrymen meant that depleted battalions in overseas postings
required a constant transfusion of men, so that the National
Serviceman serving in an infantry regiment had an odds-on
chance of going abroad. For the others, especially for those not
involved in extensive trade training, postings seemed to be as
arbitrarily, even as casually, arranged as any other facet of service
life, and inevitably there were periods of longueur.

> Following the completion of trade training we found ourselves in a
> void. At this time the war in Korea was in progress and, if I recall
> it correctly, for some reason or other we all applied for postings
> there. As they were not too sure how postings were being sorted
> some of us were put into a new kind of torture called 'holding
> troop'. If the first six weeks had been difficult, my three or so
> weeks in holding troop were horrific. The lance-corporal in charge
> was a sadist and picked on me from the start, in particular because
> I spoke nicely. I could do nothing right and he hounded me from
> pillar to post for about nineteen hours a day. I think that is the
> nearest I have ever been to becoming a murderer.
> (Signalman R. G. Jones, Royal Corps of Signals)

The holding troop or the transit camp were limbos of a
particularly pernicious kind, emphasising all that was dreary and
dehumanising about life as a National Serviceman, and they are
worth mentioning as a counter-balance to the frenetic activity of
basic and trade training. Inevitably, with the Army growing into
an amorphous mass, constantly breaking in and then releasing
short-service soldiers, the system would sometimes break down
and men be condemned to lengthy periods of time-wasting in
anonymous transit camps or the idleness of holding troops.

It was as trained soldiers that the Army got the best out of its
National Servicemen and the National Servicemen got the best
out of the Army. Pay went up, the uniform could be improved by
tailoring, Regulars became less chary, some men were promoted
to corporal or even to sergeant, and leave was granted more
generously. After trade training it could be fairly said that the
Army began to regard its young conscripts as soldiers and not as
unwelcome visitors to its ranks.

THE ROYAL AIR FORCE

The first surprise awaiting many National Servicemen in the RAF
was that they could progress through their service without ever

seeing a plane, let alone flying in one, although some bases were prepared to send up non-flying airmen on short joy-rides in elderly Ansons or Dakotas. The general feeling was that unless aircraft came within a man's ground responsibilities, he had no need to go near one. Thus a wireless operator from ground control could be given the opportunity of the occasional flight but the same privilege might not be extended to a clerk.

Normally, aircrew had been selected at the time of registration – they had to sit a separate board – and during basic training they had been earmarked as officer cadets and kept a caste apart. Towards the end of basic training, as in the Army, there was a chance to be chosen for officer selection (the only sure course to aircrew training) but only the best recruits were taken. Anyone wanting to train as a pilot had to become an officer and consequently the RAF put a good deal of pressure on its POs to sign on as regulars on short-service commissions. At the time, the inducements seemed to be an attractive alternative to the rigours of square-bashing.

> Within a few days of arriving at Padgate, we were marched to the camp cinema where we saw, for the first time, an officer. He was recruiting for aircrew, the available categories being pilot, navigator, signaller and air gunner. We were warned that the aircrew medical was rigorous, the required educational standard was equal to school leaving certificate, but the benefit was the replacement of normal square-bashing by 'light foot drill'. The first two items were no problem to me and the third had a distinct appeal. I remembered the promise a month later when a typical day's activity consisted of 'circuits and bumps' in a Tiger Moth all morning, running from one lecture to another – navigation, aviation medicine, engines, airmanship etc – all the afternoon, followed by marching and rifle drill until 9 o'clock at night. About 10% of us came forward to volunteer for aircrew selection.
> (Sergeant Peter Kilmister, Flying Training Command, RAF)

The cost to the nation of reorganising Flying Training Command pushed up the Air Estimates from £498 million in 1953 to £621 million in 1955. As a result, every penny had to pay and the aircrew training course at RAF Hornchurch was deliberately severe, demanding high standards of intelligence and technical skills: those who could not make the grade as pilots were assigned to navigator or air gunner categories, but those who failed completely were condemned to the oblivion of menial work for the rest of their National Service. Rather than terrorising its recruits during trade and professional training, the RAF seems to have preferred treating its men rather like tightrope walkers. Those who got through their courses by virtue of skill and application could expect a fair deal; those who fell from grace for whatever reason rarely got a second chance.

Because the RAF only took recruits with a higher standard of education, it expected more of its National Servicemen and in return treated them better during the next phase of their instruction. Discipline, which had been uniformly strict during basic training, became more relaxed, bull became a thing of the past, and the NCOs let down their guard to display a more friendly face. There were exceptions, usually amongst officers who had wartime aircrew experience and thereafter been given ground duties. Along with certain NCOs they took a dim view of National Servicemen, and those selected for officer training could generally expect a hot time. For the most part, though, as in the Army's specialist corps, recruits being trained for trades like wireless operation or air traffic control found that the courses were relaxed and enjoyable experiences.

> RAF Compton Bassett lay on the north side of the A4 just before Cherhill, and was overlooked by an immense white horse carved in the hillside. When I arrived, the horse had a tricolour effect due to the Boy Entrants, who occupied part of the camp, tipping cans of red and blue paint down it. The atmosphere was completely different from Wilmslow – so long as you turned up for classes and dressed reasonably smartly, no one seemed to bother where you went at other times. You had to apply for a 24- or 48-hour pass to stay away overnight, but this was mainly because the appropriate ration entitlement had to be issued for whoever you were staying with since certain things like tea were still rationed, and also to have a note of your address in case a war started in your absence. Civilian clothes were mostly worn off-duty and security was non-existent, with people wandering in and out at all hours.
>
> (SAC David McNeill, RAF Coastal Command)

David McNeill had been posted to RAF Compton Bassett as a 'Tele. Asst. (U/T W/OP)' and it had taken him some time to work out what his posting meant. Translated, it read 'Telegraphy Assistant, (Wireless Operator, under training)': like the other armed forces, the RAF also had its bewildering system of initials and abbreviations. The course was 18 weeks long and included morse, message procedure and radio theory; as the minimum passing-out speed for sending and receiving morse was eighteen words, barely anyone failed and the classes at Compton

Bassett settled down to a pleasing routine of instruction in standard procedures and elementary radio electronics.

> There seemed little point in attending the early morse classes beyond a periodic visit to keep from getting rusty, and so I was excused them along with Gerry Turner who had attended a similar radio school in Liverpool, and who appeared to have made as much of radio theory as I had. We wandered about the camp during the spare hour and, depending on the weather, sat on the grass or went down to the cafe, a wooden shack at the main gate where the 'Blue Tango' and 'Delicado' played constantly on the jukebox, just chatting and happily idling our time away. Apart from the freedom to come and go and the civilian clothes, the officers and NCOs were virtually invisible. Some instructors were NCOs but the only other one we regularly came into contact with was a very jolly little Flight Sergeant who woke us up in the morning by shouting and banging on lockers and who made sure that the lights were out at night and that we were safely tucked up in bed. He was seldom seen at any other time. The Orderly Officer, with Orderly NCO in attendance, wandered through the mess at mealtimes, murmuring in time-honoured style, 'Any complaints?' But what they all did in between times was a mystery.
> (SAC David McNeill, RAF Coastal Command)

Men being trained in a specialised electronic trade were highly valued by the RAF, another reason for the more generous attitude of the authorities. Much of the equipment dated back to wartime development and by today's standards had a Heath Robinson-ish look. Before the invention of transistors and printed circuits, radio and radar equipment relied on wiring, valves and cathodes which were constantly failing and having to be located and then replaced; wireless-telegraphy communication between ground control and aircraft relied on morse in the early 1950s, forcing operators to strain through the crackles and fizzes in their earphones to give and receive messages; even fighter plotting still used the old wartime tables and magnetic pieces denoting aircraft. All the equipment had to be serviced or calibrated by the men themselves, and although most of the work was fairly elementary, the RAF took the view that there was little point in aggravating men by imposing unnecessary bull and drill. During trade training men were excused boots, and even on courses for clerks and cooks the atmosphere was less hurried than it would have been in the Army. One unlooked-for consequence was that men became bored more easily and time could hang heavy on their hands; most jobs had to be spun out, and finding enough to do during the day could be a difficult task for men involved in basic duties. The secret was never to look conspicuous and always to appear busy: during trade training many National Servicemen remarked that their camps had the relaxed, understated calm they associated with wartime films about service life, almost as if they were all decent chaps about to whizz off to do battle with 'Jerry'.

Discipline was more strictly imposed on operational bases where a feature of everyday life for all National Servicemen was the fire picquet. Every three weeks each recruit had to be on fire-watch between 5 p.m. and 7 a.m. with only four hours allowed for sleep. It was a hated duty, and although less frequently imposed than in the Army it always came as a shock to recruits used to the relaxed atmosphere of their huts. Once basic training had been completed there was no longer any need to keep spotless the floors of the living accommodation, and the cry 'Pads!' was no longer heard in the land. A curiosity of RAF life was that floors, once cleaned and polished, could then not be walked upon with boots, necessitating the use of 'pads' or huge wads of blanket tied over footwear to prevent them scratching the high polish. A ritual at the end of basic training was for each Flight to slide up and down the huts' floors wearing tackety boots, destroying eight weeks' worth of spit and polish and leaving a dreadful mess for the next intake to bull up again.

The one arm to impose military standards of bull and discipline during trade training was the RAF Regiment.

> Bull was terrible. Whilst I was in the services we had a Bull Night one night every week and everything had to be spotless. If when the Old Man came round next day all was not right, you had another Bull Night and another inspection the following day. At one camp I was at, the coal bucket had to be emptied and bulled up with steel wool. The shafts of the billet's sweeping brushes were scraped each Bull Night with a razor blade. On kit inspections our PT shoes were under the bed and we put varnish on them to make them sparkle. I wore belt and gaiters for two years and every night you had to blanco them and do your brasses.
>
> (Corporal John Inglis, RAF Regiment)

Formed by Royal Warrant on 1 February 1942, the RAF Regiment's principal duties were of a para-military nature – the defence of RAF airfields against low level air attack, the training of its personnel in defence skills and the direction of crash rescue services. During the war its complement had mushroomed to 85,000 officers and men in 240 operational squadrons, and although many units had been subsequently disbanded it was still a force to be reckoned with. It reached a peacetime high in 1952 when it consisted of 18 Wing headquarters and 47 squadrons made up of 720 officers and 7,196 men. Because of its specialist role it attracted not only the best recruits but also those physically fit enough to stand up to its rigorous schedule of training.

> After a few weeks' training doing constant rifle drill you suddenly found one day that the rifle was no problem and the drill was a piece of cake. After that you really began to enjoy life and I enjoyed the challenge rifle drill produced.
> We did endless training with all sorts of weapons, rifle, Bren, Sten, pistol, piat, grenades etc. This sort of training was done in a disused camp a few miles from our main camp (RAF Watchett). Initially as we marched to the training camp the NCOs would shout 'Sing or double?' As we were carrying Brens, rifles etc, we would sing like hell. The Hit Parade that I can remember was Jimmy Young singing 'Too Young', Kay Starr in 'Wheel of Fortune' and Johnny Ray in 'Cry'. Not exactly marching songs, but it seemed a lot better than doubling. Then after a few weeks, as we got fit, the NCOs would shout 'Sing or double?' and we would reply 'Arseholes!' and double without much trouble.
>
> (Corporal John Inglis, RAF Regiment)

Prestige in the RAF Regiment was particularly high, and although other airmen scoffed at the bull their fellow recruits had to suffer, there were decided advantages in opting for this arm. Basic regimental training was given at RAF Watchett, in Somerset, where men stayed under canvas during the summer and living conditions were generally good; thereafter there was a choice of specialisations – AA gunner, signaller, armourer, air defence – most of which demanded a course in driving at RAF Weeton, near Blackpool. Service with the RAF Regiment, especially during the early 1950s when it was being expanded, also carried with it the chance of service with the 2nd TAF in Germany, whose men were housed in comfortable and relatively modern ex-Luftwaffe bases.

The RAF also managed to get the best from its men by appealing to their corporate pride, because even in peacetime it still carried some of its wartime mystique, memories of the Battle of Britain, the Thousand Bomber Raids, the Dambusters. Officers and men who had survived the war felt that as the RAF had been in the vanguard of the war against Hitler, they had a right to look upon themselves as the nation's premier striking force. By the mid-1950s even the government was encouraging that belief. The post-war Labour government might have cut back the RAF's wartime status, but under the post-war administrations the Conservative government was intent on strengthening the air force's cutting edge. A nuclear-armed V-force had been evolved, the 'stand-off' bomb was being evaluated, the Lightning supersonic fighter made its first flight in 1957, and various ballistic missiles were in different stages of development. Although there was still a good deal of muddled thinking over the country's air defence policy (the abandonment of the TSR 2 tactical combat aircraft, the costly decision to drop the American Skybolt missile, the closure of the Blue Streak project, for example), the RAF spent a good deal of time and effort during the 1950s rejigging its methods to meet the ever-changing needs of modern warfare. This meant that men trained in specialised trades generally led interesting service lives and, even though their number was being reduced in the second half of the decade, very few National Service recruits in the RAF felt that they were not performing a useful task. Obviously there were those who found themselves doing boring clerical duties or carrying out pointless tasks in non-operational bases, but for the most part the training was not only good: it was seen to have some purpose. As David McNeill, a W/T operator put it: 'I can joke about the whole thing now, but RAF Coastal Command did perform a useful defence function and being a wireless operator made you feel a vital link.' Even those who thought their duties mundane or repetitive were agreed that in time of war they would be essential to the nation's security.

THE ROYAL NAVY

Although the Royal Navy had set its face against any overall reliance on conscription, it continued to need regular intakes of National Servicemen to solve its manpower problems of the 1950s. By 1954 the first of the post-war 'seven years' short service men were leaving the navy in large numbers, and they were not being replaced in any quantity. So severe were the difficulties facing naval planners that in March that year the battleship HMS *Vanguard* and the carriers HMS *Implacable* and HMS *Indefatigable* – although all less than ten years old – were placed in reserve, for lack of crews to man them. Other smaller vessels were placed in mothballs, and shortages of fuel meant that sea exercises had to be curtailed or even cancelled: four years earlier, the Home Fleet's Training Squadron had spent most of its time moored at Portland Harbour and few improvements had been made in the intervening period. The strain on personnel caused a rash of discontent to sweep through the fleet, and 1954 saw reports of malicious damage on leading capital ships like the carrier HMS *Eagle*. To offset those problems the Admiralty stepped up the social improvements begun in 1950, one much-needed innovation being the reduction of a ship's commission to eighteen months, thus lessening the sailor's period of separation from his family.

Nevertheless, it would be fair to say that throughout the decade the Royal Navy was regarded as something of a Cinderella by service chiefs and that their attitude had a deleterious effect on both the recruiting and the employment of National Servicemen. In no area was this more clearly seen than in the attitude taken towards the employment of aircraft carriers, an argument which limped on well into the 1960s. When the carrier HMS *Ark Royal* was commissioned in 1955, some sections of the press, led most notably by the *Sunday Express*, attacked the ship as a white elephant, incapable of meeting the needs of modern aerial warfare, prone to attack by land-based bombers, and useful only in limited support of amphibious operations. The failure of the Admiralty to argue the case for continuing naval airpower was symbolic of a lack of direction and of an inability to define clearly the navy's role in Britain's defence system. Public scepticism with Britain's defence policies in the 1950s added its toll to the navy's recruitment problems, and as a result the average National Serviceman in the Royal Navy found himself in an anomalous position. Regarded as a stop-gap measure and therefore not suitable for long-term training, he was nevertheless a vital cog in ensuring that naval manpower was kept up to strength, on paper at least. To help make good its deficiencies in 1954 the navy was allowed to take on 6,500 National Servicemen as opposed to 2,000 in the previous year: without them, it was tacitly agreed that even more ships would have to be laid up. It was not until 1959 that the intake was reduced to its lowest ever figure of 500.

The majority of National Servicemen trained as Writers and spent their service at shore establishments where they were involved in basic administrative duties; those sent to sea as Captain's Writers were transferred frequently, largely because it was considered safer not to tamper with the postings of regular seamen. During his twelve months' service as a Stores Assistant,

Robert Greenshields served on four separate vessels – the destroyer HMS *Nonsuch*, the sloop HMS *Redpole* and the aircraft carriers HMS *Formidable* and HMS *Warrior*. His experience was not untypical, as the employment of National Servicemen in the Supply and Secretariat branches released regulars for seagoing 'rate' positions. At some shore bases the tedium was frequently relieved, as in the Army and the RAF, by assignment to general tidying up duties.

> Periodically we had a break from classes for a week in which we had to perform routine tasks about the camp. I had a marvellous number in charge of a whitewashing group. We got rained off frequently and retired to the Buffers Store to drink tea. During the Second Sea Lord's visit, I and my party were happily whitewashing a bridge in the camp when along he came with the Captain and the Commander and all his retinue. I called my party to attention and stood at the roadside, when to my horror he stopped and came across to speak to me. I saluted with a spray of whitewash and was asked what I was doing. 'Whitewashing stumps, sir.' I felt like saying something else but didn't dare. After some questioning he asked what branch I was in and was informed, 'Writer, sir.' He seemed horrified and asked the Captain why a Writer was doing such a menial task. This was passed down the line and eventually the reply came back, 'Period of workshop, sir.' He informed the Captain that he felt that some more fitting task could be found. Of course, I was not consulted and would have preferred to have been left in peace. Later I was summoned to the Guard Room, given a rollicking for causing trouble and detailed as sentry on the Main Gate, in full dress with rifle . . . I did not thank the Admiral for his intervention.

(Writer William Nuttall, Royal Navy)

The Admiral's concern may have been heightened by the growing sense of despondency which had crept into the Senior Service. Shortly before his visit a number of marker grenades had been found in the engine-room of the submarine HMS *Artemis*, and only swift action had prevented a serious fire. Other acts of vandalism reported at the time included cutting electrical leads on capital ships and putting sand in the steering gear. Much of the discontent was caused by the navy's continued reliance on its manpower to carry out mundane tasks like chipping paint or cleaning bilges, and it was not until later in the 1950s that this work was carried out by automatic devices.

The Royal Marines also accepted a limited number of National Servicemen and by 1949 the service had expanded to 13,000 officers and men. They were trained at Eastney Barracks,

Portsmouth, for gunnery and sea training, at Chatham for pre-embarkation training, and at Stonehouse Barracks for infantry and amphibious warfare training. Service as a National Service-man was also possible in the Royal Marine Commando forces, which maintained units at home, in the Mediterranean and in the Far East. Some National Service naval officers were encouraged to fly with the Fleet Air Arm as pilots or navigators, but this option was discontinued when obsolete carrier aircraft like the Attacker, the Sea Fury and the Wyvern were replaced by the Sea Hawk jet fighter and the Sea Venom all-weather fighter. The introduction of angled decks, steam catapults and the mirror deck landing device had greatly increased the safety of naval aviation; at the same time, it had made it decidedly more complicated.

As the period of National Service ran its course, there was something of a sea-change amongst service chiefs with regard to the training of short service recruits. Between 1949 and 1957, in the Army and the RAF at least, it was generally thought worthwhile to allocate time, finance, material and personnel to the training of skilled craftsmen, engineers, pilots, radar oper-ators and the like, because there was a tremendous shortage of Regulars capable of fulfilling many of those roles. There was also the not-inconsiderable benefit that skilled men would continue their training for up to four years in the reserves, thus giving the Army especially a respectable strategic back-up. Men returning to TA camps as trained mechanics or wireless operators were more likely to be of some use to the Army than men trained in clerical duties, for whom annual TA camp was a boring waste of time. By the same token, the Army usually found that it had little idea of what to do with its Reservists who had spent their National Service pushing a pen in the Orderly Room or the Pay Office. By and large, it would be fair to say that when the armed services gave a man a competent and interesting technical training the dividend would be worthwhile and the National Serviceman tolerably happy.

> The W/T part of the Signals section was located in two rooms in the control tower (at RAF St Mawgan). There were five receivers complete with headphones and keys linked to the transmitter about a mile away on the top of a hill. Theoretically, we worked a 3-watch system, but in practice often there was no night flying so that there was quite a bit of time-off. The messages consisted mainly of routine weather and position reports from the Lancasters,

and if there were a dozen of them in the air at once on training exercises it was quite hectic if more than one tried to communicate at the same time on the one frequency. It is like someone interrupting a conversation, but it didn't take long to learn virtually to speak to two people at once in morse, using codes both official and unofficial. All unofficial procedures were of course frowned on, as was the development of a 'fist'. This meant a particular style – some operators tended to slur the symbols together, others clipped them with exaggerated spacing. I found myself developing a drawl, with the first dash of a symbol drawn out and the rest clipped. Most operators did something like it and you could often tell who was at the other end by the style alone. The habit was discouraged for that very reason, since it was common during the war to trace enemy troop movements in this way . . . Other operators had various talents. Some could carry on a coherent conversation with several aircraft at once, sorting them out into an orderly queue, and the rare ones like Ivor Yelland who came from nearby Redruth could make sense of things which others could barely hear (and this was a job where acute hearing was a basic qualification).

(SAC David McNeill, RAF Coastal Command)

Tasks like that gave the intellectually inclined the reassurance that their skills were being used, and helped, too, to allay the fear that two years away from books and disciplined learning would stem their intellectual growth before going on to college or university. Where the training was indifferent or the job boring, neither side gained.

Towards the end of National Service all three services took less trouble training their conscript rankers, although officer training continued until 1960 when a total of 35,000 National Servicemen had been given commissions. By then it was no longer worthwhile to train men as specialists when they might only have one further year to spend in uniform. Regular recruiting had begun to improve, and not unnaturally the forces wanted to concentrate on men who would be with them for a long period. The large training establishments needed for the constant flux of recruits were also wasteful, as was the employment of large numbers of officers and NCOs to staff them. The Royal Navy and the RAF were the first to stop specialist training, but the Army continued to offer technical training to a minority of its best recruits until the end of National Service. This was largely due to their need for trained National Servicemen to act as instructors, and the Army's point of view was well captured by *The Covenanter*, the regimental magazine of the Cameronians, when the battalion said farewell to its last National Servicemen in December 1962.

Now National Service is coming to an end and we are turning over to an all-Regular battalion. This will create many problems, not the least of which will be the difficulty of finding Regular specialists who can fill the many vital gaps which have been appearing with increasing regularity in recent months. No doubt these difficulties will be overcome, but even so, we shall miss the willing and cheerful presence of our many friends who joined us temporarily from all walks of civilian life.

Chapter Four

OFFICERS AND GENTLEMEN

One of the most far-reaching decisions taken during basic training was the separation from the squad of those recruits considered to be potential officers. At the end of the period, or in some cases halfway through it, army POs were placed in a separate officer training wing to prepare for the hurdles which would determine whether or not they were worthy of holding their sovereign's commission. During their interview with the PSO, recruits could put themselves forward for officer selection; and provided they had attained a high SSG, had a good school record and had performed well in basic training, their requests would usually be smiled upon. For the most part, though, the Army was looking for its officers, first and foremost, amongst ex-public or grammar school boys who had completed CCF training to Cert. A standard, and who would be considered socially acceptable to most Officers' Messes.

Although the Army contained fewer polo-playing officers of independent means than it did prior to 1939, its officer corps were still dominated by those it held to be 'gentlemen', most of whom had been educated at the country's leading public schools. Some infantry and most cavalry regiments still only took their officers from the scions of the aristocracy and landed gentry, or from wealthy families with socially acceptable backgrounds. The post-war Labour Government had tried to democratise the officer caste by removing the necessity to pay fees at the Royal Military Academy, Sandhurst, and by making it easier for rankers to apply for commissions, but these were largely cosmetic exercises. The reforms hardly touched the potential National Service officer who had to possess a good education, social confidence, some previous military training and a certain conceit: most of those qualities, the Army generally agreed, were to be found in the products of a public or grammar school education. Not without reason, National Servicemen came to believe that it was pointless putting themselves forward unless they had those qualifications; although it has to be said, too, that many public schoolboys and university graduates refused to be considered as potential officers on a point of principle, because they disagreed with the whole system.

Once selected as a PO, the recruits remained behind at the basic training camp while their fellow squaddies proceeded to trade or professional training. This was usually the first formal indication of the divide which separates the officer from the rank and file.

> And then the day came when I moved up the hierarchy from simple trooper (Royal Armoured Corps) to PO (Potential Officer), and as this was the cavalry where it was unthinkable that POs – who were also presumably PGs (Potential Gentlemen) – should mix with the brutal and licentious soldiery, I was moved to the more luxurious PO wing. And that was that. My friends went to the specialist Gunnery, Driving and Signals wings and I saw them before I departed for Eaton Hall. But already the barriers were up and the friendliness was mixed with wariness. I was about to become an officer and, in the cavalry, officers belonged to a different species and lived in a different world. How were my friends to know that it was a world I had no desire to inhabit? I simply wanted to get out of the hell of Catterick and I did. I wish I could have taken them with me.
>
> (2nd Lieutenant R. M. Morgan, 1st Bn. Gordon Highlanders)

There followed a further fortnight or so of fatigues and training – carried out under reasonably harsh conditions to see how POs reacted to them – culminating in the first hurdle, the Unit Selection Board (USB). Here, the potential officers were interviewed by a senior officer. Those who passed progressed to a War Office Selection Board (WOSB), known to one and all as a 'Wasbee'. At Catterick, in interregnum before the two boards, the men moved into the Somme Lines where the accommodation was better but the regime more severe. During the early half of the 1950s, POs moving into the officer training wing were subjected to an uncharitable practical joke known as the 'grip':

> Sometime before 6 p.m. a sergeant appeared and ordered all present to their feet. An officer (a captain, as I remember) followed him in together with a medical officer – not the one we had seen earlier. The officer explained that 4 Squadron was not a holiday camp and much more was expected from officers and

> potential officers than from ordinary soldiers. Accordingly, the squad could not have the benefit of the usual weekend rest. He stated that we and our kit were in a disgusting state and that it was his intention that by the time our normal commander returned from leave on Monday we and our kit would be immaculate. Therefore an immediate start would be made on cleaning and bulling up kit, boots and uniform for inspection at 8 p.m. that night.
>
> (2nd Lieutenant A. A. Faucheux, Royal Army Pay Corps)

That morning, Anthony Faucheux and the other members of his squad had been given smallpox inoculations which usually called for a period of rest until the effects had worn off. But for them there was to be no break, in spite of their increasing grogginess. Several times that evening the officers and NCOs returned to harass them, but worse was to come the following day.

> Saturday morning after breakfast there was a full kit inspection during which the MO complained of the state of the barrack-room ablutions and latrines and stated that they were not hygienic. As a result the squad was ordered to clean out and paint the barrack-room, clean and bull up the latrines for an inspection on Sunday.
>
> Whitewash was provided and those of us who were physically able (three had become ill as a result of the vaccination and the previous day's exertions) split into three groups. I was in the barrack-room group because my height was useful for painting the ceiling.
>
> It took until lights out at 11 p.m. to do the work – after which we again fell into bed.
>
> (2nd Lieutenant A. A. Faucheux, Royal Army Pay Corps)

After 36 hours of being bullied and pushed around, Faucheux's squad walked into the canteen on Sunday morning to be greeted by a round of applause: their 'NCOs' and 'officers' were none other than the recruits from the senior intake who had borrowed the uniforms to trick their new colleagues. Far from causing any offence, their practical joke – a tradition at Catterick – was considered to be good for discipline and morale and therefore tolerated by the senior officers.

The period in the officer training wing provided the final preparation for the next and perhaps the most vital step – the two or three-day examination at the WOSB, usually held in a discreet military building with outlying grounds.

> The Board consisted of a number of senior officers and we were put through a series of interviews and practical tests. These

involved working as a team under a leader and trying to get, say, an oil drum over an obstacle with the minimum of equipment and facilities. This was to discover if one had the qualities of leadership.

(2nd Lieutenant Ian Duncan, Corps of Royal Engineers)

The testing of potential officers at a WOSB fell into six main parts. At the top of the list was the assignment known as 'situations', whereby a group of five would be confronted by five challenges with each man taking his turn as leader. Then there were written tests followed by interviews with the inspecting officers; the theoretical side was crowned by each PO having to give a lecture on any subject (frivolities were discouraged); and after that came the final interview, during which questions were fired at the candidate by a senior officer while other board members noted the reaction. The last part of the examination was purely social: officers from the examining board were present at all meals to inspect table manners and to listen in to conversation. It was widely assumed by most candidates that the officers were there, too, to see if their charges could hold their drink.

No more than 70% of those tested at any WOSB passed the board. It was a tightly compressed examination requiring a broad range of practical and theoretical skills, and it was meant to be so. A potential officer who could talk wittily and intelligently on Clausewitz and war, but who could not get five men across a twenty-foot chasm with ten feet of rope, was unlikely to pass. The reverse, too, was true: what the army wanted was good all-rounders. WOSB also inculcated the need to succeed at all costs. Having escaped the mindless routine of basic training and its indifferent food and accommodation, few POs were anxious to return to it. From WOSB onwards, the fear of failure was a powerful spur.

At the end of the course you'd all line up and a captain or a major would walk round with little pieces of paper on which it said passed, failed or deferred, which meant that you could come back in six months' time and try again because they thought you were a pretty good chap but not quite good enough yet. They walked along with these pieces of paper, saying, 'Hard luck, number 36,' 'Good luck, number 42.' They got to me and said, 'Hard luck.' I was extremely depressed.

(2nd Lieutenant R. J. Wyatt, REME)

Bob Wyatt was deferred, but despite his initial disappointment tried again six months later. On that occasion he was successful and was eventually commissioned into the REME.

Those who failed WOSB were RTU'd – returned to their original
unit – the ultimate disgrace.

Men wanted to become officers for many different reasons –
social or personal, to escape the humdrum life of the ranker,
because it seemed the right thing to do, or simply because they
were curious. But one over-riding factor was that selection as an
officer seemed to be a logical progression from military experience gained at school. Boys who had done well in the CCF found
it easy to master the intricacies of drill and weapon training, and
were not disturbed by bull or by officious NCOs. They were more
likely to be confident and positive in their attitudes to their
superiors, able to appear decisive yet circumspect in their
dealings with their fellow men, and to possess an air of authority.
    There were many National Servicemen who would have
applied for officer selection but for their fear (not altogether
groundless) that they did not have the right accent or social
background, or that they would be unable to afford the higher
expenses of the Officers' Mess. In fact, money – or the lack of it –
could be a problem. In 1948 a National Service lieutenant was
paid 11s. a day (55p): twelve years later, in 1960, this had only
risen to 13s. (65p). There were allowances for purchasing the
uniform and accessories but in a smart infantry regiment which
insisted that its officers dress correctly in the Mess, expenses
could be higher than the uniform grant. Some regiments only
asked their National Service officers to wear service dress but
Anthony Faucheux converted his £12 uniform allowance into a
dinner jacket which his CO permitted him to wear in Mess, and
which served him later on his return to civilian life. Unlike their
Regular counterparts, though, few National Service officers ran
up large Mess bills.

After a short period in the limbo of a holding unit, the majority of
successful candidates passed on to Eaton Hall, near Chester, the
army's school for training and examining officers for service in the
infantry (including the Brigade of Guards), REME, the Corps of
Royal Military Police, the Intelligence Corps and, occasionally,
the Royal Marines. Eaton Hall also provided basic officer
training for the RAOC and RAEC. Men bound for the Royal
Artillery, the Royal Engineers and other corps were trained at
Mons Officer Cadet School at Aldershot. Regular officers

continued to receive their instruction at the Royal Military Academy, Sandhurst.

For boys who had been at boarding school, Eaton Hall proved to be a home from home. Built in its present form towards the end of the nineteenth century as the seat of the Duke of Westminster, it was a gaunt, overbuilt, yet not unattractive pile set in extensive parklands. Attached to the main building was a private chapel, its clock tower a miniature replica of Big Ben, but Eaton Hall's most distinguishing feature was its famous 'Golden Gates'. These vast ironwork pieces were heavily ornate and painted in black with the ornamental flourishes picked out in gold. With the long avenue of trees behind them, they framed perfectly the distant building, giving the whole prospect the aura of Evelyn Waugh's Brideshead with its 'new and secret landscape'. The illusion was punctured only by the brick huts and other austerity buildings which littered the grounds, a legacy of the war years when Eaton Hall housed the Royal Naval College, Dartmouth.

The accommodation inside Eaton Hall, however, left little to be desired. Cadets – as they had now become, complete with white collar tabs and a white disc behind their cap badges – were quartered four to a room in the elegant staterooms, all suitably furnished and with ample 'bed space'. After the squalid ablutions of basic training the bathrooms at Eaton Hall were positively luxurious, and no cadet who trained there has ever forgotten the outsize baths and capacious washbasins, all set in marble and resplendent with ornate brass taps and fittings. From the very outset of their course it was the intention of the army to accustom its cadets to the dignity of being an officer and of living in the self-contained world of the Officers' Mess. To Bob Wyatt it was just like being at an exclusive 'military boarding school. The people there were almost entirely from public schools and all the feelings you have at a public school were there in exactly the same way.'

There were other changes, all equally agreeable. Civilian clothes, usually a lounge suit, were worn off duty, allowing the more worldly cadets to sport suitably distinguished old school ties. In the early days of National Service the Platoon Instructors dined with their cadets in the Mess and encouraged an interest in military and regimental customs as well as the social niceties of a regimental Mess. It was the rule, too, that all NCOs should address the cadets as 'sir'. Presumably this innovation was to condition the young men to their future rank and help them react to it, but the NCOs at Eaton Hall and Mons had developed the use of the word 'sir' to make it sound more like an insult than an act of deference:

'Mr Jones, *sir*. Am I hurting your horrible lanky hair, *sir*? Well, I should be, *sir*. It's long enough for me to stand on, *sir*. Just like a girl's or a nancy boy's, *sir*. You're an idle, dirty, little officer cadet, *sir*. Get it cut. Understand, *sir*?'

Intakes, 60-strong, arrived every fortnight; each intake was divided into two platoons, and the Platoon Instructor (normally a captain) remained with his cadets throughout the sixteen-week course. The School was organised into a headquarters with a Commandant (Lieutenant Colonel), a Headquarters Company and three Training Companies, each of which was commanded by a Major. Other Company staff included 8 Platoon Instructors, a Company Sergeant Major, a Company Quartermaster Sergeant, clerks and storemen. A small detachment was based at Oke-hampton in Devon to oversee the Battle Camp, one of the highlights of the course during which cadets spent three days in mock battle conditions.

The course was divided into two parts, the Primary Phase (six weeks) which provided elementary training in basic military subjects common to all arms, and the Advanced Phase (ten weeks) which concentrated on tactics, weapon training, drill, administration, PT, morale, signals, transport, fieldcraft, hygiene, military organisation, military law and education. In all the training the emphasis was on the platoon, the intention being to turn out a 2nd Lieutenant who, after further practical experience, could exercise effective command as a platoon leader.

From the very outset of the course a strong element of competition was introduced amongst the cadets; points were awarded for all exercises, and at the conclusion the cadet with the top marks would be presented with the coveted Belt of Honour. Quite apart from the threat of being RTU'd – few ever were – there was the more tangible fear that poor marks could mean a posting not to a regiment of one's choice but to a relatively lowly corps. To this end, the Platoon Instructors encouraged their cadets to compete against one another and much of the course was designed to allow cadets to pit their wits against their fellows'. In one of the exercises, a Tactical Exercise Without Troops (TEWT), cadets were presented with a tactical problem and asked to provide a solution, each cadet taking it in turn to be commander of the force attacking or defending a position.

TEWTs normally took place in the War Room which contained a large relief map, and the instructors at Eaton Hall went to some lengths to achieve realism.

> Now and again I was called into the war games room to play a most vital role. Together with a few handpicked men we were issued with three cigarettes and took up position beneath a large table upon which was a relief map of a battlefield.
> Lighted cigarette at the ready I kept a keen eye on the officer in charge of the lower room party, and at a given command I would inhale deeply and blow smoke through a hole in the base of the relief map. Up above, as the battle progressed, billows of smoke would appear at strategic points on the map as 'explosions' occurred. I never really got to know the significance of the 'explosions' I was responsible for, but there were many of them in a Woodbine and when the battle was over it was not cordite but a haze of burned mellow Virginia which hung over the battlefield.
> (Private David Rees, 1st Bn. Royal Welch Fusiliers)

Dai Rees – known as Rees 40 to his friends in the Royal Welch Fusiliers – was posted to Eaton Hall in 1949 as part of a general duties squad. (It is the custom in Welsh regiments to distinguish between all the Williamses, Reeses, Joneses etc by adding the last two Army numbers to their names. Thus 2200640 Private Dai Rees was known simply as 'Rees 40'.) In addition to smoking cigarettes in the War Room he took part in Battle Camps by letting off thunderflashes and firing blank rounds of ammunition from a rifle to provide authentic sound effects during the mock battles. 'I wasn't even the enemy,' he recalls. 'All I was doing was firing a rifle into the air to create an atmosphere.'

The Army put a good deal of faith in the Battle Camp as it was the only sure means of seeing how its future officers would react in a near approximation of battlefield conditions. In his study, *On War*, Claus von Clausewitz reasoned that manoeuvres and training should be as realistic as possible to prepare the officer for the noise, danger and mayhem of real warfare, and that military leaders should be 'inoculated' in advance of the experience. His philosophy was taken to extremes during World War II when both the allies and the Germans used live ammunition at battle camps in an attempt to simulate the conditions which officers would face in combat. In peacetime, risks of that kind were rightly considered to be impossible. Nevertheless, the British Army continued to believe that battlefield inoculation at an early stage in an officer's career did prepare him for the sound and fury of actual combat, and although Rees 40's efforts with his cigarettes and his blanks might appear absurd, they did fulfil a necessary training function at Eaton Hall.

Another part of the course designed to test self-confidence and military initiative was the 'playlet'. Groups of cadets would be asked to dramatise an incident to illustrate a basic military point such as the importance of maintaining vigilance whilst on guard duty. For example, a sentry would be seen to fall asleep, thereby endangering his comrades, the point being rammed home by the representation of a terrorist attack on a platoon while the guards slept. Other playlets might be more theoretical, or designed to make a moral point such as the need for officers to retain their authority over their men. A favoured theme was that of the officer who courts popularity – the playlet might dramatise an incident in which the men refused to obey an order because they had become used to the officer calling them by their Christian names. Cadets would also be asked to give 'lecturettes', both to demonstrate their grasp of a subject like hygiene and to show that they could get a basic point over to their men.

At Mons Officer Cadet School, cadets bound for the Artillery or the Engineers quickly discovered that their course lived up its reputation of being tougher than that offered at Eaton Hall.

> The ten weeks were taken up with basic 'infanteering bull', i.e., map-reading exercises and mock battles. Perhaps we had polished things as Sappers but as Officer Cadets we bulled the bull. Quite incredible how one can make the studs on boots shine. Knife-edge creases and boots one could see one's face in were the order of the day.
>
> (2nd Lieutenant Ian Duncan, Corps of Royal Engineers)

One of the reasons for the rigorous training at Mons was that it provided such an intensive course, cramming into six or ten weeks the basic elements of the Primary and Advanced phases of the Eaton Hall course. Thereafter, cadets proceeded to their respective corps' headquarters for further training, the Sappers going to the School of Military Engineering at Chatham and the Gunners to various training regiments. Mons also trained officers of the Royal Army Pay Corps and they finished their courses at Devizes where the training presented few problems to those cadets who had completed civilian accounting or actuarial courses.

Another reason was that Mons stood in Aldershot, known to generations of soldiers as 'The Camp' or 'The Home of the British Army'. Designated in the mid-nineteenth century as the main training garrison in the south of England, Aldershot had slowly spawned an impressive conglomeration of barracks, camps and training grounds; so firmly had the army placed its imprint on the town that it was well-nigh impossible to escape the military presence. Mons had been established as an Officer Cadet School in 1948 and was housed in Mons Barracks, built in 1926, and until 1940 the headquarters in Aldershot of the Royal Corps of Signals. It stood north of the Basingstoke Canal, off Princes Avenue, near the Military Stadium and the recreation grounds.

The standard of drill at Mons was predictably high and no cadet who marched onto the square could ever forget the awesome figure of RSM Brittain of the Coldstream Guards, who was in charge of drill and reputed to have the loudest voice of command of any Warrant Officer or NCO in the British Army. Intakes to the school arrived every fortnight and passed out at the same intervals, the passing-out parades being particularly impressive and following the form carried out at Sandhurst. While the band played 'Auld Lang Syne' the men passed out slow march off the parade ground and up the steps of the school, followed by the Adjutant mounted on a charger. With so much tradition surrounding them and with the interested eyes of the rest of the Regular Army on them, the cadets at Mons were kept up to the mark by their NCOs and training officers: most felt that the standard of instruction and the subsequent emphasis on drill and bull were extremely high.

> Mons Officer Cadet School was extremely tough – mainly the pressure of the timetable and the threat of being RTU'd if you failed either the technical tests or the physical pace or were generally not up to it. Again, the support of friends was a key factor.
> (2nd Lieutenant Patrick Tolfree, Royal Regiment of Artillery)

That sense of co-operation and comradeship described by Patrick Tolfree was a constant factor, too, of Royal Air Force officer training. Perhaps because discipline tended to be more relaxed in the RAF, and perhaps too because the relationship between officers and men tended to be less distant, team work and team spirit were greatly encouraged during all steps of officer training.

> The first weekend there was my twenty-first birthday and I was granted privilege leave by the Squadron Leader. The others were confined to camp and during my absence my fellow cadets cleaned my bedspace to sparkle like a mirror . . . After six weeks we

transferred to RAF Spitalgate for six weeks OCTU. Here we were under observation all the time. We had to work very hard but our Warrant Officer was most helpful as our instructor.

(Pilot Officer C. H. Berthelot, RAF)

Nor was this an isolated incident, born of a special occasion in a young man's life: RAF cadets and their instructors tended to be helpful to the members of their intake, mainly because the majority of the cadets had been pre-selected for officer training. This did not mean that their courses were less rigorous than those conducted by the Army; both services applied exacting standards to their officer cadets, but it was generally agreed that, once it had earmarked its potential officers, the RAF was less inclined to ditch them – unless, of course, they failed to come up to the mark in a wide range of subjects.

> Officer training was rather different because it was competitive. There were wild rumours about a high 'chop-rate', but in fact after a three-month course 89 out of 91 passed. This led to a good deal of tension and a desire to 'do the right thing'. As an example there was a boxing match; I loathe boxing and preferred to listen to Bellini's *Norma* on the radio. My friends all thought I was foolish – one ought to be seen at the ringside by the instructors. But I didn't go – and I still passed.
>
> (Pilot Officer D. L. Bird, RAF)

In fact, Dennis Bird's preference for opera did not harm his future prospects: at the end of his National Service he became a Regular officer and retired in 1968 with the rank of Squadron Leader.

The RAF selection process was similar to a WOSB. The emphasis was on intelligence and initiative, the intention being to turn out a Pilot Officer capable of taking a responsible administrative post or, in the case of the RAF Regiment, of fulfilling the function of a platoon leader. National Servicemen – all had to be officers – who wanted to fly had to apply separately before registration to the four-day aircrew selection course at RAF Hornchurch, where the standard of medical and aptitude tests was deliberately high. Once called up, the successful candidates had to appear for basic training, but from the very outset it was understood that they were to be treated as a caste apart.

> When I received my call up papers and reported, it took a considerable amount of time to convince the sergeant in charge

that I had actually been to Hornchurch and had been selected – even though I showed him the relevant letter – because he assured me that it was not possible to apply privately. One had a tremendous sense of superiority when reporting to Cardington on the first day of service because the vast majority were treated rather poorly, whereas I and one or two others who had been pre-selected for aircrew were treated as gentlemen.

(Flying Officer Peter S. Jones, RAF)

Graduates, too, were generally encouraged to apply for a commission prior to basic training: the RAF was particularly keen to encourage graduate and aircrew officers to apply for short service commissions, an option which had obvious attractions – regular officers enjoyed superior conditions and a higher rate of pay.

Although the RAF placed great importance on catching its potential officers before they registered, the opportunity for selection did exist during basic training. As with the army, considerable significance was placed on the candidates' education, public and grammar schoolboys being given precedence, and on their social backgrounds. Most officers commissioned in this category were posted to ground duties, usually in administration, and were trained at RAF Spitalgate, near Grantham in Lincolnshire. It was also possible to volunteer for aircrew selection at this stage, but it was a precarious process involving so many hoops that only the most committed – those who had escaped the pre-selection process – ever got through.

Potential aircrew officers who had passed the Air Ministry's selection boards were sent on *ab initio* pilot and navigation courses with the rank of Acting/Pilot Officer. There, in the early 1950s, pilots were trained on Chipmunks and Prentices, and after 60 hours flying proceeded to Advanced Flying Schools. These specialised in operational conversion to jet aircraft like the Meteor T Mk. 7 for fighter training, or twin-prop aircraft like the Mosquito T Mk. 3, FB Mk. 6 or PR Mk. 34 or Varsity, for bomber or transport training. Operational training continued during the first six months of a pilot's attachment to his first squadron, and it generally took a year to eighteen months before he was proficient in all-weather flying. It was for those reasons – the length of the training and its complexity – that National Service pilots were encouraged to apply for regular commissions. It was a condition of their service that all National Service and Short Service aircrew had to enlist with the Royal Air Force Volunteer Reserve (RAFVR) after demob, and to continue weekend flying for four years. When the government disbanded the RAFVR in May 1957, on account of the cost and complexity of modern jet aircraft and in the mistaken belief that the days of the manned fighter were numbered, the decision sounded the death-knell for the training of National Service aircrew.

It was that ordnance, too, that presented Flying Officer Peter Jones with one of the least expected, more enjoyable and perhaps most unique experience of any group of National Servicemen. After kitting-out at Cardington he proceeded to RAF Kirkton-in-Lindsey for a 3-month officer training course, which culminated in his being accepted for jet-fighter training with other NATO pilots in Canada.

> On the 4th September 1956, the few who had been selected sailed on the French liner *Flandre*, first class from Southampton to New York, and had a superb time. After half a day in New York we went by train to London, Ontario, where we stayed for two days being briefed on Canadian ways and being kitted out, etc. It took two days by train to go to Moose Jaw, where we stayed from the 16th September 1956 to the 31st May 1957. We were taught on a Harvard Mark II single-engined propellor aircraft with dual control, and logged up a total of 194 hours flying. This included solo, formation, night instrument and low level flying.
>
> During a holiday between the 8th and 23rd February 1957, four of us managed to cover 5,500 miles in 16 days using three cars, travelling from Moose Jaw, where the temperature was 30 degrees below freezing, to the Mexican border where the temperature was high enough to swim in the sea. We needed three cars because unfortunately two of them 'died' on us during the journey. We visited places like Las Vegas, Los Angeles, Hollywood and San Francisco.
>
> We were transferred to Portage La Prairie near Winnipeg on the 23rd June and stayed there until the 12th October 1957. There we were taught on the Lockheed Silver Star single jet engine twin-seater and a further 84 hours flying was logged. On completion of that course, wings were gained.
>
> (Flying Officer Peter S. Jones, RAF)

Although a fully fledged pilot, Peter Jones' adventures were not yet at an end. Later that month, October 1957, he returned to Britain on the liner *Empress of England*, only to be told that his services would no longer be required. He had been caught up in the government's decision to abolish the RAFVR: it was inappropriate to convert him to the new British jets such as the Hunter and the Javelin, and with no other suitable work at their disposal the RAF offered immediate demobilisation to their

Silver Star pilots and seemed 'quite pleased' when they accepted. Peter Jones' National Service had only lasted seventeen months, and after demob he was promoted to the rank of Flying Officer.

The pilot training courses were of necessity extremely tough, and became increasingly so as the weeks progressed. It was one thing to make a slight error of judgement in a slow and friendly trainer like the Chipmunk, quite another in a military jet which dealt severely with any slip of concentration. Potential pilots who make too many mistakes – of any kind – soon find themselves on a slippery slope.

> The successful cadets on the *ab initio* pilot and navigator courses automatically became Acting/Pilot Officers; those who failed on both academic and 'officer material' grounds spent the remainder of their two years doing the most menial tasks – an incentive to succeed. Those who failed the academic subjects but who showed officer potential were transferred to the RAF Regiment. Those who were bright but who were not 'officer material', e.g., had rural accents, were reselected for signaller or air gunner categories. My transition from cadet pilot to cadet gunner was occasioned by a misunderstanding – I mistook the Station Adjutant, who was scruffy and driving a lorry, for a lorry driver.
> (Sergeant Peter Kilmister, Flying Training Command, RAF)

Peter Kilmister spent the rest of his National Service with the rank of sergeant as an air gunner instructor, a trade which was fast becoming obsolete with the introduction of jet bombers. His experience was somewhat unusual, in that of all the services the gulf between officers and men in the RAF was not considered to be too great an obstacle; hence the presence, one suspects, of a scruffy and unshaven Station Adjutant. On most active bases the relationship was reasonably relaxed, especially between the officers and men of aircrew and their ground staff.

> If you were on the flying wing it was very free and easy – this was everybody who was actually out on the airfield. You didn't wear a hat, you didn't salute officers, you didn't wear shiny boots – you were all fairly free and easy. When you saw an officer, you said, 'Good morning, sir', or something like that – this was because you weren't wearing a hat and couldn't salute him. And you didn't wear a hat because it could get blown off or sucked in when aircraft engines were running. It was a most enjoyable time.
> (SAC Donald Turner, RAF)

After his trade training, Donald Turner had been posted to RAF Marham to service the radio equipment on the 'V' force bombers which had been formed as Britain's principal nuclear strike force. Marham housed the Valiants of 148, 207 and 214 squadrons, and the introduction of these high speed jet bombers was to change the face of the RAF's frontline strike capacity. The runways at the V-bomber stations had to be extended and strengthened along with the taxiways and hard standings; new lighting and landing aids had to be introduced together with enhanced air traffic control systems, and the entire back-up technical services had to be re-equipped. Consequently, there was a powerful feeling of togetherness amongst the aircrew and the ground staff, a feeling that they belonged not merely to a team, but to a team responsible for manning the nation's nuclear strike force.

Commissioned National Servicemen in both the RAF and the Army were generally welcomed into their respective Messes by their fellow officers for the simple reason that they were fulfilling the essential task of the junior subaltern or pilot officer. Simon Coke, who was commissioned as a National Serviceman in the 3rd Bn. Coldstream Guards, was treated with 'friendly indulgence' by his new comrades in arms when he joined the battalion: 'It was only five years since the end of the war, so the regiment was used to young short-service commissioned officers.' In the Queen's Own Cameron Highlanders at the same time, Lieutenant Alexander Dunbar thought that 'the Regulars put up with the conscripts good-heartedly. They weren't a threat, nor a great nuisance. Among the subalterns there was not much difference between conscripts and regulars.' Later, after serving in Palestine, he realised that as a 'totally green officer' he had been something of a liability, and that the Regulars had gone to some lengths to keep him out of trouble. There were, of course, exceptions to the hand of friendship. Sandhurst and Cranwell-trained officers of the same generation as the National Servicemen tended to regard themselves as a superior breed, and there were dyed-in-the-wool traditionalists of the old school who looked upon National Servicemen as birds of passage and therefore not really an integral part of the armed forces.

Curiously, the widest gulf between the Regular and the National Serviceman seems to have come at NCO level. The National Serviceman who held his sergeant's stripes by virtue of his superior training or technical ability was often given a hostile reception in a Sergeants' Mess which contained a majority of men who had fought their way up the ranks to gain their coveted three stripes. This was particularly true of National Service sergeants in the RAEC and REME.

> After the course was finished we were promoted sergeants and sent off to the most awful part of my training in the Army. You were a man with three stripes but you were nothing more than that. You had got your three stripes because of your technical expertise and the large length of training you'd had. You did not have any skill in regimental duties and it was thought that if you wore three stripes you couldn't simply be a technician: you had to be something a little more than that and you certainly had to learn something about drill because in the units to which you were going you were probably going to have to conduct parades so you needed to learn a little about that. So we all were sent off to a course which was specially arranged for Leading Artisan Sergeants at 4 Bn. at Bordon in Hampshire. That was absolutely terrible, the worst part of the training that I had been through. It was ten times worse than going through officer cadet training. The junior NCOs were nasty, awful little people. Although they were only lance-corporals or corporals, they had the power over us as sergeants during this training and to lead us whatever sort of life they wanted. They were Regulars, and they resented very much National Servicemen coming in and after a year having the rank of sergeant. They couldn't appreciate this and they certainly didn't enjoy it, and they made us aware of the fact that they didn't like it. They gave us the hardest possible time they could. There was one particularly awful little lance-corporal there and I always said to myself, 'I will come back, you little bastard, when I'm really at a correct rank, and I'll lead you a hell of a life.' I did come back when I was commissioned but I'd forgotten all about it by then, and although I saw him again I didn't take it out on him even though at the time he was taking us through training I certainly felt like it.
>
> (2nd Lieutenant R. J. Wyatt, REME)

In fact, had it not been for the fully trained National Service Leading Artisan Sergeants of the REME, the corps would have been hard put to fulfil its increasingly intricate technical function during the 1950s. But all too often, as Bob Wyatt testifies, the presence of a National Serviceman with three stripes on his arm was a red rag to the hard-bitten Regular. And in the RAF, too, National Service sergeants were treated to equal amounts of condescension.

> My main reason for not signing on was the hostile attitude of the Regulars towards National Servicemen. I encountered this frequently as I was the only National Service staff instructor, and the

all-too-often repeated 'present company excepted, of course' did
nothing to dispel my resentment. I spent a month at the Medical
Rehabilitation Unit where aircrew NCOs and officers, Regular
and National Servicemen, mixed freely. An expression which
some thought particularly amusing was 'bloody National Service
(spit), RAF Regiment (spit), Acting Pilot Officer (spit).'
(Sergeant Peter Kilmister, Flying Training Command, RAF)

Regulars have always dominated the NCO (or equivalent)
command structure of the British armed forces; indeed, there is a
school of thought common amongst many groups of servicemen
that it is the corps of sergeants who really make the British Army
work. The RSM of an infantry battalion was (and still is) a very
important figure, in some respects as vital a component as the
commanding officer. He is the link between the officers and the
men, and as he will have served longer in the regiment than most
of the officers, his experience and knowledge of procedure,
customs and precedence are never undervalued. The same can be
said of the other NCOs in key positions, men with the rank of
CSM or CQMS. For the most part, they owed their rank not only
to their educational attainments but also to length of service and
experience, and could see no reason why young and well-
educated National Servicemen should be given positions of
authority as sergeants or officers.

You do not ask about the National Service officer but I will give
you my opinion of this character anyway. He tried desperately to
be an officer, but all told, he was despised by his soldiers, barely
tolerated by the senior ranks and treated as the lowest form of
animal life by the RSM. Under NO circumstances was he allowed
to 'lead' the platoon, the Platoon Sergeant was the be-all and end-
all of that body of men, the National Service officer was head in
name only. Don't misunderstand me, there were some very good
National Service officers, but their lack of experience and, in some
cases, their complete lack of common sense was like a red rag to a
bull as far as the Regular servicemen were concerned and they
were made to feel that they had a very long way to go before they
could be accepted as soldiers, let alone officers. In most cases, the
National Service officer was thrown into a situation for which he
was totally unprepared, a situation which can be compared to a
trainee lion tamer in a cage with 30 odd wild killers, hell-bent upon
destroying him.
(Staff Sergeant D. F. Phillips-Turner, RAOC)

That comment, voiced by a Regular soldier who served for 22
years, many of them as a senior NCO, could be applied to any
young tenderfoot officer, conscript or Regular, but in the case of

the National Serviceman it has a more oblique application. Whereas a freshly commissioned subaltern or Pilot Officer would progress fairly steadily up the middle ranks and become more experienced as he did so, the National Service officer usually had only a bare year's service and left the armed forces at about the time he was beginning to be most useful to them. It was that brevity of service which disgruntled the Regular NCOs, and they could see no reason why a superior education or family background had been preferred to experience in gauging military effectiveness. Amongst National Service NCOs, the hostility shown by their fellows was often a deciding factor when they refused to sign on as regulars.

Nevertheless, in spite of the criticisms of the professionals, the National Service officer did perform a useful function in the Regular Army and in the RAF (the Royal Navy ran 'upper yardsmen' courses for potential officers and a small number of National Servicemen received commissions). Their civilian talents were usually put to good use – the RAMC was well supplied with trained doctors and officers – and, in infantry regiments, all subalterns, Regular and conscript, tended to be treated alike. In Malaya, during the Emergency, National Service 2nd Lieutenants led patrols into the jungle in the relentless war against communist terrorists, and served there with commendable bravery and tenacity. Often only the young and the fit could survive the arduous conditions; in much the same way, RAF instructors of Flying Training Command discovered that young National Servicemen, with their ability to pick up flying techniques and their quick reactions, made excellent pilots, so that the ending of National Service pilot training with the closure of RAFVR in 1957 was much regretted.

The National Service officers also brought a fresh approach to the demands of their job. Because they were temporary guests of the forces they could be more critical of some of the obvious shortcomings. A Regular officer might accustom himself to those quirks – such as regimental custom where age-old usage had led to abuse – but a National Service officer could see through them and, if he so chose, decide not to conform.

> I had not asked for the cavalry, I wanted to be a Gordon Highlander like my father and brother before me, but the cavalry it was to be until I escaped from the nightmare of Catterick to Eaton Hall Officer Cadet School and subsequently to a commission in the Gordon Highlanders. Because I became an officer myself I was able to draw comparisons between the contemptuous aloofness of the cavalry officers at Catterick, who seemed to pass most of their time

at the races, and the active interest of the Highland officers, whose knowledge of their men and of their families was my first introduction to a style of leadership which I have tried to imitate as a Headmaster. Perhaps I was just unfortunate in the type of officer I encountered at Catterick, but they seemed to me to be shallow and frivolous men, content to leave their soldiers and their troops and squadrons to the mercy of the uncertain tempers of the NCOs.
(2nd Lieutenant R. M. Morgan, 1st Bn. Gordon Highlanders)

The Gordons drew most of its men from the north-east of Scotland and had its depot in Aberdeen; consequently, like most line infantry regiments, it was akin to a close-knit family. The type of leadership qualities which Robin Morgan picked up from the regiment included the lesson that he should put his own needs behind those of his men: in Malaya he would not eat or take a shower after a jungle patrol until his men had been attended to. It also meant looking after his platoon's welfare – giving advice to the man with girl friend problems, or to the married man who had run into financial difficulties. For a twenty-year-old officer these were questions of experience whose answers could not be found in any textbook, and most National Service officers had to learn on their feet as they progressed through their military service. A combination of authority, common sense and good nature pulled most of them through the awkward moments when they encountered emotional crises beyond their immediate experience. There was, too, the arrogance of youth. As one ex-National Service officer put it: 'When you're twenty you think you can do anything. At that age you think you'll live for ever.'

With good reason, the possession of a commission was considered to be a bonus when applying for a civilian job once National Service was over. Employers were thought to smile more kindly on a candidate for a management position if he had been awarded a commission during his military service, believing that he would be more mature, more capable and more able to manage men than someone who had not been put in a position of authority at an early age. During the 1960s, when the Army was promoting the advantages of a short service commission, its advertisements included that belief as a fact, and the majority of National Servicemen who were commissioned incline to the view that their promotion was a positive advantage.

It was a useful experience, broadened my outlook on life, and enabled me to meet a lot of people I would not otherwise have done and visit a lot of places I would not have gone to.

(Pilot Officer C. H. Berthelot, RAF)

I certainly matured greatly during that period, made friends who have turned out to be lifelong and believe that – because of both those facts – I enjoyed Oxford much more than might otherwise have been the case. It was a fantastic opportunity for an eighteen-year-old to command a platoon.

(2nd Lieutenant Simon Coke, 3rd Bn. Coldstream Guards)

I was two years older when I went to university – almost everyone else except medicos were. I had travelled. I had matured. I had been in danger. I had been in command of men. I was tougher, more confident, more hungry for learning. I had learned to drink.

(Lieutenant Alexander Dunbar, 1st Bn. Queen's Own Cameron Highlanders)

It was beneficial. It was useful when I joined the Colonial Agricultural Service in Uganda, particularly with regard to office administration, care of stores and so on.

(2nd Lieutenant Archibald Dunbar, 1st Bn. Queen's Own Cameron Highlanders, attached 1st Bn. The Gordon Highlanders)

I was glad to have done it and to have met the people I did. It gave me an outlook and confidence in 'man management' for my profession.

(2nd Lieutenant A. D. S. MacMillan, 1st Bn. The Royal Scots, attached 1st Bn. King's Own Scottish Borderers)

Another reason for their sense of satisfaction was the pleasurable social life led by the officer caste of Britain's armed forces. Junior officers were generally encouraged to behave boisterously on Mess nights, during which heavy drinking would be followed by rough games of high cockalorum and British Bulldog. Most officers had passed straight from their public schools through Sandhurst or Eaton Hall into the army, and consequently there were those who looked upon the Mess as an extension of their schooldays. New subalterns were 'dined in' on their first guest night, when all drinks were charged to the accounts of their brother officers and the evening usually ended with a variety of initiation rites designed to test the new officer's ability to enjoy himself, hold his drink, remain on his feet, and still retain a sense of humour. It was all light-years away from the life of the rank and file and, although it could be an overwhelming experience at times, there were few National Service officers who did not enjoy the pleasures – and the rigours – of the Officers' Mess.

Life as a National Service officer was good. I think we had about £6 or £7 a week, which just about paid the Mess bill and left you with a few shillings. In fact I remember that at the end of my National Service I could even afford to run a car, so we must have been pretty well off. The food in the Mess was very very good and all the various functions and activities which went on there were pleasant, so I don't think that anyone who was an officer during National Service would have any complaints on the sort of life they led.

(2nd Lieutenant R. J. Wyatt, REME)

On demob, many National Service officers went on to complete university degrees. For many it was a liberating experience and they claim that two years' military service had given them an added maturity which made undergraduate life more agreeable. Others found the transition difficult. In some Oxford and Cambridge colleges especially, ex-National Servicemen were frequently alarmed to discover that their fellow students regarded college life as a civilian equivalent of the Officers' Mess. A frequent comment of National Servicemen who went on to obtain degrees was, 'Few bores were more shunned at university than those who could not stop talking about their National Service experiences. The officers were generally the worst, too.'

The critics were the men who wanted to put National Service behind them as quickly as possible and to start life afresh, freed from what they now saw as the shackles of a commission. There were those, too, who embraced the politics of the Left, and who remembered their incarnation as officers with embarrassment. 1956, the year of the Suez crisis, saw thousands of young people take to the streets of London to voice their disapproval of Britain's action; by the end of the decade, the Campaign for Nuclear Disarmament had attracted large numbers to its membership and their protest marches to Aldermaston, centre of Britain's nuclear research, had become an annual pilgrimage. Indeed, protest movements generally had become fashionable amongst the young, especially amongst the country's undergraduate population, many of whom were ex-National Servicemen. In that ambience there were obviously those who preferred to keep a discreet silence about their commissions.

The mood was caught in the literature of the period, particularly in the work of writers like John Osborne, John Braine, Kingsley Amis, Alan Sillitoe and David Storey, who provided an interesting sidelight on the social scene and introduced characters alienated from post-war society. Because they cocked a snook at literary convention the press labelled them 'Angry Young Men'. Also published at that time – and vaguely associated with the movement – was Andrew Sinclair's novel *The Breaking of Bumbo* (1959), which follows the sad career of Bumbo Bailey, Old Etonian and National Service officer in a famous Guards' regiment, who destroys himself by speaking out against British involvement in the Suez crisis.

> OK. Suppose we beat Egypt. We lost anyway. We've got to sell ourselves to live, and who'll buy Johnny Bull, with a Boer War musket in his hand? We don't want our Empire, say we (minus Beaverbrook). Give it away, as long as you still buy British. We only want to trade. We don't want to fight. Cyprus – a police action. Kenya – restoring order. Got to protect British lives. Oh, we think we're so damn wonderful still. And all we are is a lousy punch-drunk ex-champ, between a couple of real big men, jockeying around for the k.o., not caring two damn hoots about us. One swift back-hander from either of them, and we're on the canvas. But, by Christ, we can make such a big bang when we fall. We can make the biggest bloody bang they've ever seen. And then the big men will make big bangs too, and we'll all sit round pulling crackers, bang, bang, bang, bang, till we're all dead, but great, wonderful, heroic, unbeaten Britain, didn't she go out with a bang!

Later, Bumbo commits an act of mutiny when he attempts to subvert the members of the battalion's rugby team by persuading them that they should refuse any order to go to war against the Egyptians over Suez. As a result he is cut down to size by the regiment's officers and forced to resign to save the good name of the Brigade of Guards. Sinclair himself served as a National Service Ensign in the Coldstream Guards, and his novel remains a classic statement of alienation from the military world; the path taken by Bumbo Bailey from basic training at Caterham, through officer school at Eaton Hall, to a commission in the 'Redstone Guards' is as instantly recognisable as is his ultimate self-abasement and delusion with the soldier he has allowed himself to become. In its subject matter and in Sinclair's choice of language *The Breaking of Bumbo* is very much a product of its times, retaining a period charm which the years have not dispelled.

Being a National Service officer, as Bumbo Bailey discovered, was a temporary affair with military life; while commissioned, he had to obey his orders as 'merely the umpteenth Young Ensign, whose job was to make the perfect perfection by the application of the rules'. It was on this level that their Regular officer colleagues trusted them and, when the time came for demob, it was in these terms that most National Servicemen regarded their commissions. The majority view was that it had been an interesting interlude which, despite its restrictions, had provided the opportunity to assume responsibility at an early age. In 1959, years after his time as a short service officer in The Border Regiment, Edmund Ions was surprised by his sense of regret when he noticed that his old regiment had been amalgamated with the King's Own Royal Regiment to form the King's Own Border Regiment. Ten years later, in 1969, when further amalgamations were taking place in the British Army, he came to terms with his military experiences as a commissioned officer, first in the army of King George VI and then of Queen Elizabeth II.

> Rationalisation was the cry. This is not to say that today's smaller army is not intensely professional and fully adequate to its tasks. It manifestly is, and man for man it is probably a more efficient fighting machine, equipped with much better weapons and with greater firing power. But I wondered if the rationalisers really grasped that the fundamental problem today may be the sense of belonging. One cannot *belong* to a logistical matrix. Glancing at the Army List, I found few of the names I knew at Sandhurst. Most had wanted to join their county regiment: they were not ashamed to say so. Many would have retired early, denied the promotion they had good reason to expect when they entered the profession with high hopes. Some I knew were dead. Those that remained were largely taken for granted during long years of peace. Yet peace is a fragile commodity, and democracies take their armies for granted more than dictatorships are inclined to do. That is their weakness and their strength.
>
> For myself, I recognised a private debt, chiefly to men older than myself, who tried to make a soldier out of me. If they did not quite succeed, nevertheless there was a debt, difficult to convey precisely.[10]

Other National Service officers, too, will recognise the very personal nature of that private debt.

Chapter Five

EVEN THE BAD TIMES WERE GOOD

With the exception of the public schoolboys who had spent up to ten years of their childhood at boarding schools, or the deferred men who had completed apprenticeships or university courses, National Service in the 1950s represented the first period away from the steadying influence of home. Instead of having to conform to the demands of the family, men found themselves detached from the network of domestic relationships and the constraints of their teenage years. Although for many that rupture was only temporary, it did bring with it a new sense of freedom. Life in the services might have been bound by a web of regulations and traditions, but there were periods of free time and leave during which young men could flex their muscles, released from the shibboleths which had governed their behaviour at home, school or work. Despite the introduction of the modern social services in the immediate post-war years and the changes they had wrought on British society, the role of the family had not lessened and most young people still learned from their parents their social and political outlook and their attitudes towards behaviour and morality. While at home they continued to be subject to those standards: National Service offered a period of dislocation from many of the social and moral assumptions which had guided their earlier years.

Other facts of life remained much the same. Public transport had a pre-war look to it and could be a dirty and tedious experience. Relatively few families had cars – just over two million in 1950 – and trunk roads had not yet spawned motorways; air travel was still the province of the wealthy. Currency restrictions prevented much travel abroad and most people still took their holidays in Britain. Until the consumer boom of the latter part of the decade, incomes remained relatively static; the average weekly wage for a male worker of £3 10s. 11d. (£3.55) in 1938 had only risen to £8 8s. 6d. (£8.42) in 1951. During the greater part of the period of National Service few families had additional sums of disposable income to spend on consumer durables, holidays or other luxuries – even had they been available in any quantity. Alcoholic drinks were still fairly expensive, and drink-related problems did not become a substantial problem until the relative affluence of the late 1950s and early 1960s. Most surveys indicated that the majority of young people thought that sex before marriage was wrong* and, in any case, contraception was not always widely available and certainly not a subject for discussion. The most widely used forms of entertainment were the cinema, still a cheap leisure time activity, and football matches, then enjoying attendance figures unheard of two decades later.

National Service helped to break the mould in which most young men had been cast in the 1950s. Travel became the norm, with recruits and servicemen regularly going from home to camp and then from one camp to another. REME Craftsman Frank Thompson, for example, had to travel to Blandford in Dorset from his native Stornoway on the island of Lewis – 'a hell of a long way from the barren Hebrides!' – and after basic training, was subsequently stationed at Lydd in Kent and Tonfanau in North Wales. In the two years of his service he only went back to Lewis once and 'tended to go to London to savour its cultural delights rather than make the long trek home.' Horizons could be broadened by seeing other parts of Britain just as much as they could be by travel abroad; but it was not just the exposure to the sights and sounds of other cities and regions that appealed to most National Servicemen – it was also the chance meetings with other young men in the same boat that mattered greatly. Friendships were usually a soothing balm during the inevitable periods of boredom and staleness which made up their service lives.

*'Despite the importance that the majority of English people give to sexual love in marriage, the majority think that both sexes should approach marriage with no prior sexual experience. Slightly more than half the population in the case of men, and nearly two-thirds in the case of women, disapprove of any sexual experience before marriage. Roughly an eighth say that they do not know. A third of the population in the case of men, and just under a quarter in the case of women, are in favour of some sexual experience before marriage.' Geoffrey Gorer, *Exploring English Character* (1955). Gorer based his results on surveys he carried out in the *People* newspaper in January 1951.

National Service afforded a unique opportunity to experience communal living and to meet youths from all walks of life. For instance, I had a coalminer next to me in the barrack-room on one side and an Oxford undergraduate on the other side of me. There were approximately forty of us in one barrack-room, so one had to learn how to live with people. Everyone developed a remarkable frankness and honesty. People used to often leave their money on the bed after pay parade, knowing it would be there when they came back from tea. We also had wonderful discussions in bed at night on the 'usual subjects' and also our future plans after demob. Alas, I have lost touch with most of my platoon now but I have never regretted having had to do National Service as I had always led a very sheltered life at home with my parents, so you can imagine the shock of Army life and language on me during the first few weeks.

(Lance-Corporal M. Jones, REME)

One of the recurring regrets of all National Servicemen is that they did not always take the trouble to keep alive the important friendships made during their periods of service. As the years rolled by after demob it was all too easy to forget to reply to letters or to lose forwarding addresses as men married, had children and bent their minds to domestic matters. Also, men changed quickly on their return to civilian life, and incidents which had seemed all consuming or just plain humorous in the services soon began to pale.

Yet some friendships lasted a lifetime, and there were National Servicemen who found adapting to civilian life a difficult experience simply because 'mates in civvy street' never seemed to be the equal of those they had met in the services. Partly, the reason lay in the intensity of the experience. Having to share cramped and Spartan living accommodation twenty-four hours a day meant that every recruit had to learn to give and take: men might be warned to keep out of their mates' bed space, but the last Woodbine would be shared and if a man were lucky at cards the whole platoon would be treated to an evening out at the camp cinema. Similarly, the system of helping mates who could not cope, which had blossomed during basic training, continued throughout a man's National Service. Beds would be made up by all members of the barrack-room, brasses would be polished and boots bulled, uniforms and kit pressed to exact specifications: it was almost a case of 'them and us'. If men felt that they had managed to pull the wool over the eyes of a superior, then it was one up for the ordinary squaddie.

Like all compact societies, the system had its checks and

balances and maintained its own moral code. As long as a man kept within the general unwritten rules of the barrack-room – by helping out, sharing his belongings, lending money or cigarettes, keeping himself to himself – then harmony reigned. If he stepped out of line, retribution could be swift and pitiless. Most National Servicemen are agreed that, although the stealing of military property was endemic and a soldier's kit was fair game, personal property was sacrosanct. A man caught stealing a mate's money or his cigarettes could expect little mercy.

> In the winter of 1950 the camp was being run down, so there were only six of us left in the billet at Gosford. (3 Anti-Aircraft Group Workshops, REME.) We were all pals but there was a Welshman put into the same hut and then cigarettes started to go missing. One of the lads put a pen mark under the tip of his cigarettes and left them lying in his locker. They disappeared and the Welshman was found to háve them – it was a cold frosty night, so we took all his clothes off, carried him about three hundred yards and threw him into a burn that ran through the centre of the camp.
>
> (Craftsman A. Yule, REME)

NCOs usually turned a blind eye to barrack-room justice, and those who suffered at its hands were not encouraged to press complaints. For one thing, it could lead to a charge, and for another it could bring further private retribution – one of the inexorable rules of Army logic was that a man who allowed an item of equipment to be stolen could be put on a charge, too, for failing to look after his public or his private property. Besides, it has long been a convention in British schools to frown upon tale-tellers and sneaks, and, as many National Servicemen had quickly discovered, the Army in many ways resembled a well run, if over-strict, boarding school.

By the same token, a man who burnt his boots beyond repair during the obligatory burning and bulling sessions could be put on a charge for damaging government property, and there were even examples of men being put on jankers for injuring themselves during PT sessions or accidentally getting themselves sun-burnt. (The charge, again, was 'damage to government property'.) Few men bothered to report sick unless they were completely incapacitated, for the good reason that it was such a palaver. In order to report for sick parade men had to appear in full kit with their uniforms bulled to the peak of perfection, and woe betide the man who did not pass the sergeant's gaze.

> I knew one lad, a driver, Sapper Stewart, who had ulcers before induction and who was lying whimpering with pain rather than

report sick. He drank Milk of Magnesia or some such. He had
gone in once to sick parade at Chester, and wound up charged,
three days jankers for failing to bring his irons with his mess tin,
and a threat of a further charge of malingering if he ever did it
again.

(Corporal Iain Colquhoun, Corps of Royal Engineers)

Not unnaturally, a system based on rigid rules, many of which
were palpably absurd, attracted a good deal of combined
opposition; hence the united front frequently presented by the
barrack-room, and the strength of individual friendships. It also
encouraged the art of 'skiving'.

A feature of just about every military camp – at home or
abroad – was that in some corner there could be found groups of
men idling away their time, sweetly doing nothing and making
sure they were not caught. Raw recruits may have voiced initial
astonishment when they found men hiding in the latrines having a
sly smoke, 'just like at school', but they quickly accustomed
themselves to the notion that the 'skive' was an accepted and
acceptable part of military life. On one level, a skive could be
mere time-wasting and was therefore not always discouraged by
the authorities. A man sent to sweep out the Sergeants' Mess, for
example, knew that it would take half an hour at the most, but
because two hours had been allotted to the task he either had to
spin out his labour or do it quickly and then make himself scarce.
The important thing was not to be caught; or if you were, to have
a watertight reason for being where you were found. Elsewhere
in the day's routine, tasks could be made to appear more
important than they really were.

> The Higher Authorities here love to jump upon small soldiers with
> dirty brasses or undone buttons, but the main occupation is
> wasting time.
> 　E.g. 2 hours queuing for inoculations
> 　　　1¾ hours for casual pay parade
> This, of course, is during the time allotted to various types of army
> instruction and is cheered by the ranks as 'a big skive'.
> 　　　　　(Private A. J. Bayley, Royal Army Service Corps)

Other skives could be quite elaborate, involving the complicity
of the rest of the barrack-room and aimed at breaching military
authority. LAC James Tod remembers that because kit went
missing at such an alarming rate, the men at RAF Hednesford
developed a game of 'kit leapfrog' during stock-taking. After No.
1 Billet had been inspected and its contents checked, gear and kit
would be hurriedly transferred to No. 3 Billet while the inspecting

officer was doing his rounds in No. 2 Billet. Nothing was ever found to be missing, even though in many cases the same kit had been counted twice.

Occasionally, too, men could be misplaced and forgotten about: that was considered to be the biggest skive of all. AC1 David Price and three fellow airmen spent an idyllic six months during the summer of 1947 stationed at RAF Ferryside, an abandoned air-sea rescue base near Carmarthen. Ostensibly their job was to prevent squatters taking over the camp – one of the many ways by which the homeless highlighted their plight and the general housing shortage in post-war Britain; but, in the way of things, their existence was forgotten. Each week their rations would arrive from RAF Pembrey and be shared with the local people in return for home-cooked pies and cakes. One of the men was married and his wife came to stay with him in the nearby village. It was all too good to last, and retribution came in the shape of an officer making a casual and unexpected visit while the little group was sitting down to its evening meal. An ex-aircrew flight sergeant, slightly unhinged, was let loose on the unit, and evenings in the pub and home-cooking quickly became a thing of the past. Later, while attached to a maintenance unit, Price saw an aircraft fuselage slip off a 'Queen Mary' transporter, its back broken. Undeterred, the men hid it at the back of a remote hangar and despatched another fuselage with fresh paperwork. They were never caught.

Most of the best skives could be worked in camp, where the routine was settled. It was easy to find places to hide away, or to bend the ear of friendly clerks in the Orderly Room to misplace or alter displeasing orders.

> Occasionally I also contrived to assist other airmen to extend their weekends slightly by signing 36-hour passes for them, forging the Warrant Officer's signature so well that I doubt whether he could tell. I was considered quite an expert at this and although it was a despicable practice, all I was actually doing was enabling the holder of the pass to return to camp later on the Sunday night than he would need to have done otherwise. He was entitled to leave camp anyway but without a pass it was necessary to return by midnight and this was somewhat early for someone travelling quite a distance by train.
>
> (LAC B. J. Tipping, RAF)

Another good camp skive was to be 'excused boots', a much-sought privilege awarded on medical grounds, which allowed its holder to wear civilian shoes. There were also elaborate schemes

1. 730 days to go. A squad of recruits on Day One at The Barracks, Berwick-on-Tweed. Sergeant Laidlaw, DCM, sitting centre.

2. The Quartermaster's Stores. RAOC platoons collect kit and kitbags, Aldershot, March 1948.

3. You're in the Army now. Recruits of the King's Own Scottish Borderers try on their Glengarry bonnets.

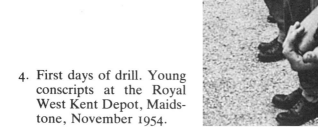

4. First days of drill. Young conscripts at the Royal West Kent Depot, Maidstone, November 1954.

5. Now clean the uppers! A critical inspection in the Welsh Guards' barracks, Caterham, 1948.

6. This is how it's done. Lance-Corporal Dowden's model kit lay-out, The Barracks, Berwick-on-Tweed, March 1947.

7. Get those arms straight! PT at the Guards' Depot, Caterham, May 1948.

8. A soldier's best friend. Young Guardsmen learn to strip and assemble a Bren gun, Caterham, May 1948.

9. The End Result: Army. The Lady Mayor of Berwick-on-Tweed inspects a King's Own Scottish Borderers' passing out parade, The Barracks, Berwick-on-Tweed, May 1952.

10. The End Result: RAF. Passing out parade, RAF Wilmslow, May 1952. David McNeill fifth from right wearing glasses.

11. The End Result: Royal Navy. John G. McIlvean's 1223 Class. HMS *Royal Arthur*, June 1949.

12. Was it all worth it? F4 Squad, RAMC Crookham after 3 months' training, 18 May 1958. Peter Davies standing middle row left.

13. Spit and polish. Men of 1st Bn Royal Ulster Rifles scrubbing equipment, Queen's Hill Camp, Fanling, Hong Kong, May 1953. George Savage kneeling on left of group.

14. A fairly regular job. Sweeping up at RAF Jever, Germany. 1952. John Inglis second from right.

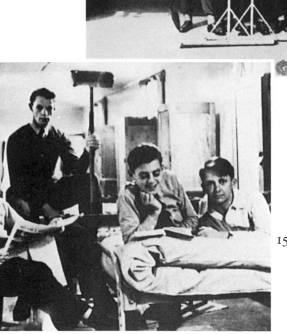

15. There'll always be a bull night. RAF Pucklechurch, 2 July 1956. Mike Burdge standing right.

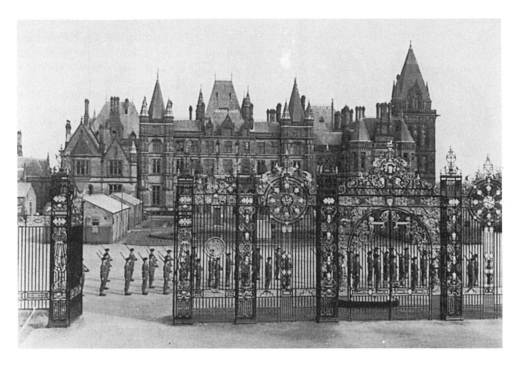

16. Officers and Gentlemen. The Golden Gates of Eaton Hall officer cadet school, April 1954.

17. Field Marshal Slim takes the salute at the passing out parade at Mons officer cadet school, September 1952.

18. The spirit of 'the mob'. National Service sailors on the focsle of HMS *Sirius*, Portsmouth, 26 February 1950. James Austin standing third from left.

19. First issue of pyjamas, RAF Weeton, September 1951. John Inglis with sickle.

20. Just having some fun. Derek Pilkington after training as a Regimental Policeman, Royal Army Pay Corps, Waller Barracks, Devizes.

21. Cookhouse fortnight. Men of A Squadron, 3rd Training Regiment, Royal Engineers, make music at Morval Barracks, Farnborough, July 1953. Ian Duncan standing centre with 'sword and shield'.

22. Off duty and nowhere to go. RAMC recruits at Crookham, 1958.

23. Transports of delight I. The troopship *Empire Fowey*, formerly the Nord Deutscher Lloyd passenger liner, *Potsdam*.

24. Transports of delight II. An Avro York troop transporter, derivative of the wartime Lancaster bomber.

25. NAAFI Club, Chatham, 1957. Members drinking in the cocktail lounge.

26. Celebrating the Coronation with a cuppa. NAAFI mobile canteen in Germany, June 1953.

27. Army Cup Final, 1957. 1st Bn Royal Welch Regiment versus 1st Training Regiment, Royal Engineers.

28. Cyprus 1958. 'So we camped in a river bed "because they don't get much rain in Cyprus."'

29. Suez Canal Zone. Naval petty officers and ratings enjoying an afternoon at the Old Victoria Lido, Fayid during the visit of HMS *Newcastle*, March 1948.

30. 'Snatch Squad' drawn from 1st Bn Duke of Wellington's Regiment for a raid over the Chinese lines, January 1953.

31. Scenes at the dockside in Pusan, Korea when the 1st Bn Duke of Wellington's Regiment embarked aboard the troopship *Asturias* for service in Gibraltar.

32. The Emergency in Malaya. Men of the King's Own Scottish Borderers move through the jungle on patrol.

33. No more soldiering for me. Lt. Col. A.B.M. Kavanagh says farewell to the last National Service 'Dukes' at the last demob parade of the 1st Bn Duke of Wellington's Regiment, 2 October 1962.

34. Happy days are here again. Demob day, RAF Pucklechurch, July 1957.

to steal coal or coke for the barrack-room stoves; these were usually executed by men on guard duty, and as with every profitable skive the over-riding principle was to avoid being caught.

Equally fertile ground for a good skive lay in confusing the military mind, especially when it had to cope with an unusual problem. If a difficulty could not be solved by strict adhesion to the rules, then the incident could be strung out for several hours and involve a growing number of men, each willing to offer his own words of advice, often with unlooked-for results.

> One shit-pit incident happened when someone put a live cat down the hatch and it rested on a piece of cardboard meowing piteously. The Orderly Sergeant asked for volunteers to be lowered in a rescue attempt . . . no one volunteered! So the Pioneer Section set about digging a tunnel. The Orderly Officer said the cat had to be put out of its misery . . . so a six-foot iron rod was aimed and dropped . . . missed and disappeared into the muck. The Orderly Officer then sent for gun-cotton to blow the cat up . . . which would have been interesting, but finally the Orderly Sergeant had the great idea of shooting the cat, which they did.
>
> (Rifleman George Savage, 1st Bn. Royal Ulster Rifles)

Incidents of that kind could, of course, happen in civilian life, and skiving had become something of a tradition in British industry by the 1950s, but in the Army a waste of time involving a good many people (and in this case a cat) was an event to be savoured. Tying up the services of an Orderly Officer, an Orderly Sergeant and a platoon of men for an hour or so was no mean feat; obviously, had it been a real emergency, the incident would have been swiftly resolved, but its bizarre nature, allied to the traditional British regard for animals, caused heads to be scratched and time to be wasted. In other words, it was a good skive, something to be relished and laughed at again in the NAAFI that night.

To some extent, officers and NCOs condoned a degree of skiving because they knew that in the administration of such a large organisation as the Army it was virtually impossible to account for each man's movements during every hour of his service. Knowing, too, that when large groups of men are assembled together in an environment not entirely to their liking they would find ways and means of avoiding unwelcome tasks, the Army took a reasonably benevolent view towards mild skiving, provided that it did not interfere with discipline. Therefore, men discovered hiding and smoking in the camp's latrines would probably be let off with a warning, but a platoon on a 'night scheme' found hiding in a wood and avoiding their part in the exercises would face a charge. Besides, the Army had several unofficial yet well-known disciplinary measures of its own to counter-balance the liberties gained by skiving.

> By this time (1955) the snow had started and was to remain until the end of March. It was very cold but our instructors kept us too busy to notice. We were not subjected to the sort of thing one now associates with the paras, but the exercise and constant activity made us extremely fit. As we approached passing-out parade, the 'bull' became intensive. An early indication of how the military mind works was seeing lorry loads of 'clean' snow being deposited on top of the dirty snow which had been cleared from the drill square.
>
> (Signalman W. Findlay, Royal Corps of Signals)

It is perhaps not surprising that the word 'skive' has military origins and that it came into general usage in 1916, the year in which conscription was first introduced in Britain. Forty years later, it was one of the most common terms in service use.

If new words had to be mastered along with the forces' network of abbreviations, then another language, too, had to be learned.

> After two weeks, our flight was to be allowed out of camp for the first time on Saturday afternoon and we were gathered together in one of the huts on Saturday morning to be lectured by Corporal Wanless on the proprieties of being out in uniform for the first time. It went some thing like this.
>
> 'Right, you f—ing lot. I suppose you'll be f—ing off to Liverpool this afternoon as quick as your f—ing legs will carry you. I can't understand why it's got to be f—ing Liverpool. The place is crawling with f—ing SPs who'll delight in booking you for dirty buttons or boots. Why don't you go to Chester instead? There's a f—ing lovely cathedral in Chester.'
>
> Of all the inappropriate adjectives to describe a cathedral this takes the biscuit and has remained in my memory. Whenever the name of Chester crops up in conversation, on the radio, or I read it in a newspaper, my wife (who shares my memory) and I look at each other and smile, because we both know that 'There's a f—ing lovely cathedral in Chester!'
>
> (LAC Byron T. Denning, RAF)

The widespread and monotonous use of foul language in the services was a simple fact of life, one to which even the most fastidious recruit had to accustom himself. For many it was their first introduction to four-letter words, included in almost every conversation in a dull, repetitive and brutish way, devoid of any sexual connotation. On the one hand, NCOs adopted hectoring insults spiced with crude words and phrases – many of these admittedly inventive – as a means of abusing their men; on the other, bad language was endemic, a reflection of the monotony and repetitiveness of much of service life. A platoon wakened every morning to the violence of an NCO banging metal lockers and shouting, 'Hands off your cocks and on with your socks!' was hardly likely to begin the day in a pure frame of mind.

> The first drawback is that we have to get up at 6.15 in the morning [he wrote to J. M. Lee]. Lights out is at 10.30; it's of no earthly use to try to get to sleep before that since everyone else sits around talking. The talk consists of filth and blasphemy which surprises even a vulgar person like me; more sensitive and sheltered natures must suffer hell . . . Generally speaking, the crowd in this billet are crude in the extreme, but quite manageable and likeable beneath the surface.
>
> (SAC Graham Mottershaw, RAF)

Initial surprise at the prevalence of swear words in just about every sentence soon gave way to a blasé acceptance. Most men were surprised to find that the same litany of bad language entered their own vocabularies, and just as surprised to discover that it left when they returned to civilian life. Some refused to tolerate it and regarded the paucity of language as demeaning or insulting to their intelligence. One National Service officer who made a point of discouraging swearing in his company found that it was impossible to ban bad language completely. He was travelling in a vehicle which broke down in the wilds of Salisbury Plain: after a lengthy delay and much humming and hawing under the bonnet, the driver turned to the officer and gave his reason for the breakdown. 'Eee, sir,' he said, 'the fooking fookers fooked!'

Short and direct words originally used to describe a sexual function, such as 'fuck', became all-embracing adjectives; a stupid fellow was invariably referred to as a silly 'bugger' or a silly 'cunt', without any reference being made to either word's original meaning; God's name was frequently taken in vain. In that respect, the words were used so indiscriminately that they lost any real meaning and became boring insults; but on another level they revealed the callous insensibilities of the men who served in the nation's armed forces. George Orwell may have argued that because the British working classes use four-letter words to describe natural functions, their usage is obscene but not immoral; but there is a world of difference between using the word 'fuck' to describe sexual intercourse and applying it indiscriminately to anything from a rifle to a cathedral in Chester.

Nevertheless, it would be wrong to suppose that many National Servicemen worried over-much about the linguistic bankruptcy they discovered in the armed forces; for there were those, too, who were astonished or delighted in varying degrees by the idiomatic inventiveness they discovered in the barrack-room. Being able to 'swear like a trooper' was an important part of the bonding process with young men from different classes and backgrounds and from different parts of the country.

> I particularly remember the comradeship in the barrack-room in my first fortnight, along with a very mixed bunch from the northern towns. The next bed to me was occupied by an Indian from Liverpool. The first night after lights out, he said, 'If anyone comes near me, I've got a knife here and I'll knife him.'
> Fortunately, after two days he was taken off to hospital with what the troop bombardier told us was 'galloping syphilis', and we never saw him again. There were other Liverpudlians in the barrack-room and their language was appalling. In every sentence a very basic four-letter word was used – usually very humorously.
> (2nd Lieutenant Patrick Tolfree, Royal Regiment of Artillery)

As well as having to put up with constant swearing, the matter of sex itself had to be confronted. Since the beginnings of warfare and the creation of organised armies there has been a strong connection between a young man's first sexual experience and his first experience of battle. In primitive societies both were considered to be part of the initiation of a young boy into manhood, and that notion was carried over into the armies of the world by successive generations of soldiers. Virility, sexuality and bellicosity became confused, and in time of war the army became a haven of jumbled erotic thoughts. 'To some people, carrying a gun was like having a permanent hard-on,' remembered a young American veteran of the war in Vietnam. 'It was a pure sexual trip every time you got to pull the trigger.'

Although few National Servicemen were to fight in their country's service, the tradition of the 'rapacious and licentious soldiery' died hard, and accounts perhaps for many of the preening and boasting attitudes adopted by British soldiers. In their book, the very action of putting on a uniform was enough to increase their erotic appeal. (It also accounts, perhaps, for the preponderance of sexually-based swear-words which could be used to question a soldier's parentage or accuse him of effeminacy, the ultimate soldier's crime.)

In any barrack-room, sex formed the major topic of conversation, led usually by those who were sexually experienced – or pretended to be. Stories of sexual prowess during the last leave could make the virgins in the company feel inadequate or jealous, and the neighing of the barrack-room stallion could be thoroughly unsettling. If their evidence alone were taken, National Service could be regarded as a time of complete sexual licence, but as Arthur Marwick notes in his recent social history of post-war Britain, 'Expressed attitudes towards sex are notoriously hard to disentangle from actual sexual behaviour. Loudmouths may be the shortest in actual performance; the discreet may be quietly living it up.'

As in any other peer group there was an immense variety of sexual attitudes amongst National Servicemen, and age-old double standards continued to be upheld. The over-riding opinion in Britain during the 1950s, held by both men and women, was that sex before marriage was wrong, yet it was also felt that a man should have some sexual experience before he married. (23% of the women in Gorer's survey thought so, and 34% of the men.) While many National Servicemen conformed to the profile drawn by such surveys in their attitudes to sex, a high proportion admitted that they gained their first sexual experience while stationed abroad where sex was cheap or available and where it was considered 'manly' to make at least one visit to a brothel. At home, sex outside marriage was not only frowned upon morally, it was also relatively difficult to achieve; furthermore, contraceptive devices were perhaps not as conveniently available as they were a decade later. Around 5% of the births registered each year during the 1950s were illegitimate.

Faced with a large number of young men who were naturally inquisitive about sex, the services adopted a pragmatic solution to the problem. Their chief fear was that men would contract a venereal disease and thereby render themselves unfit for further military service: this was particularly true of overseas postings where prostitutes had a ready-made clientele. To counteract this threat, recruits were shown medical films – usually hideously graphic – emphasising the consequences of advanced venereal disease, and these were backed up by awful warnings from the medical officer. More profitably, all three services provided their men with free contraceptive sheaths before they went on leave – in the navy these were playfully known as 'sports gear'. With good reason they were issued at all bases, whether at home or abroad.

> The small town of Wetherby was invaded every weekend by hordes of girls from Leeds, known as 'The Leeds Commandos', because they were 'in action in all weathers'. Some even operated through the wire fence of the camp. Taff Bish and I often had the duty of patrol and used to hide until some poor trainee and his lady friend achieved a near climax. Then we would leap out and beat the fence with our sticks, making the whole structure rattle and spoiling the final ecstasy.
>
> (Writer William Nuttall, Royal Navy)

The forces' interest in sex was not just confined to things mechanical. Realising that a sizeable number of National Servicemen were surprisingly ignorant about it, the Army produced several informative booklets on sexual matters, such as Major-General Frank Richardson's down-to-earth *Advice on Sex* which he wrote for 1st Corps, BAOR. For many it was a revelation, as sex education in schools during the 1950s tended to be so sketchily described and couched in such prim language as to be almost confusing. According to General Richardson's thesis, it was quite commonplace for young National Servicemen to feel 'unnatural' or to complain of being 'undersexed' after listening to the latest round of boasting in the barrack-room[11]; therefore it was the Army's duty to lend some ethics to sexual relations. Usually this concern began and ended with an embarrassed talk by the padre, although there were some officers who realised that their men's sexual problems could not be swept under the carpet. In the best cases this extended to sympathy and support when marriages or long-lasting relationships broke down, but most National Servicemen found the provision of such advice scarce. All too often, the general view was that sex was a matter which could be handled like any other item of military equipment, and that it was all a question of supply and demand.

> The Regimental Christmas dance held in a base in the middle of nowhere was an experience not to be forgotten. The plan was to book the NAAFI Hall at the polo ground in Fayed – the nearest town – convey the troops in a convoy of trucks to the venue, then send the trucks around the Canal Zone to bases where there were some women, e.g., hospitals and signals units, pick them up and take them to the dance. This took a couple of hours during which time the troops got drunk and had started fighting with each other or were too drunk to dance – those who were neither made a dive for the girls, and in the resulting chaos the female officers in charge

of the girls decided not to take any chances and to return to their units. I recall getting one dance with a pretty dark-haired Irish girl. After the girls were delivered, the trucks returned to pick up the troops, many of whom by this time were unconscious and had to be manhandled into the trucks. I remember one such character awaking on the trip back to camp and gleefully shouting that it was raining – only to find that someone at the front of the truck was busily relieving himself into the wind. The dance was a great reliever of tension but not, I feel, in quite the way that the CO had hoped.

(Lance-Corporal Bob Downie, Royal Army Ordnance Corps)

It was a familiar scenario. Servicemen deprived of female company would turn to drink and then start fighting when dances were arranged, leaving senior officers with the opinion that any attempt at organising 'socials' for the men was best left alone. On the whole, the services preferred not only to discourage any contact between their male and female branches, but also to deny the presence of a female unit on a military base. One RAF airman put on Guard Duty at a remote part of his station allowed curiosity to get the better of him and peered into a seemingly deserted room only to find a woman in a state of complete undress. Unfortunately for him, his Lady Godiva turned out to be a nonplussed WAAF officer; the camp police were called, and he was lucky to escape with a severe reprimand. The problem was not confined to the men's services: in 1957 two WAAFs were charged with soliciting American airmen in Bedford and dismissed the service.

Although talk in the barrack-room usually turned on fairly explicit sexual behaviour – penis size and masturbation being common topics – for many men the immediate problem was the girl they had left behind and what she might be doing in the boyfriend's absence. For those with wives the position was even worse: quite a few of the deferred men were married, and as no quarters were available to them they had to put up with two years' separation. Tearful farewells at mainline railway stations were a common sight throughout Britain on Sunday evenings as 36- or 48-hour passes came to an end, sundering a brief period of togetherness. The intense and artificial weekends spent together often did more harm than good, with the result that many relationships broke up: the arrival of a 'Dear John' letter was a signal for doom and despair which in extreme cases could lead to the recipient going AWOL. It was common for National Servicemen with domestic or emotional problems not to return to

camp after a weekend leave, and in such cases it was rare for the
service authorities to be sympathetic. Absentees were hounded
down by the services' police from whom they could expect little
mercy once caught. In spite of the attention they paid to sex
education and counselling, the services took a severe view of men
going AWOL in order to solve an emotional problem.

Another potential cause of sexual problems was homosexuality. Throughout the period of National Service it was still a crime
to indulge in homosexual acts: it was not until 1967 that the
Sexual Offences Act (England and Wales) decreed that a
homosexual act between consenting adults in private would no
longer be a criminal offence. This legislation, occasioned by the
efforts of Leo Abse MP and the work of the Wolfenden
Committee, excluded the armed forces from its conditions and it
remained a military offence for servicemen to be practising
homosexuals. A homosexual could state his sexual preferences at
registration and thereby seek exclusion from military service, but
doctors took a dim view of any such admission. Medical and
psychiatric opinion in the 1950s still largely regarded homosexuality as a perversion or deviation which could be cured; as a
result, the 'short sharp shock' of service training was widely
considered to be the correct therapy for any young man who
admitted that his sexual preferences were homosexual in character. It was – and remains – a military or naval offence to be caught
practising any homosexual act, and each year during National
Service and beyond a handful of men have been 'administratively
discharged' for that reason. (In 1984 the number was 87.)

Nevertheless, by virtue of one of the many double standards
upheld in the services to maintain good order, long-standing
homosexual relationships could be tolerated provided they were
not prejudicial to service discipline.

> Part of my growing up was to become aware of the more 'earthy'
> aspects of life such as homosexuality, which receives more
> publicity today, the result of which is that eight-year-olds talk
> about 'queers' and 'benders'. I did not find out about these things
> until aboard *Theseus* at almost nineteen years when listening to a
> discussion on the electricians' mess deck between two or three
> electricians. When the gist of their conversation finally sank in I
> was so outraged that I almost called them liars, but was then
> invited to see some of the people in question, mainly Officers'
> Stewards and Stewards making up in the electricians' bathroom
> which they shared. It took a long time for the truth to sink in and I
> was indignant about the whole thing. I even had a go (verbally) at

one or two of them; it was a thing I could not begin to understand. Looking back, I realise how naive I was.

(AB James H. Austin, Royal Navy)

Naval practice, in general, was to limit the number of known homosexuals in sea-going ships, and in many units tacit approval was given by senior officers to long-standing homosexual 'marriages'. Elsewhere – and this was the most common reaction – homosexuality was something to be feared and reviled and any man suspected of being 'queer' would be subjected to taunts and insults and, in the worst cases, to being beaten up. At the very least, and especially in the armed forces, exposure to homosexuality usually came as a shock, and something to be given a very wide berth.

> I remember at Weeton one of the Corporal Instructors was a bit AC/DC and he was known as Mary to all the occupants of our hut. The ablutions that we used were outside the back door of the Nissen hut and they too were a bit basic. The one thing that was always missing in the ablutions was the sink stopper and you had to soak a load of toilet paper and jam it in the hole or next time you went into Blackpool, buy a stopper which you then carried around with you. Back to Mary. I always gave him a wide berth but one day I ended up in the ablutions at the same time as him. He was nearly finished and I was busy mashing up toilet paper to make a plug. I can remember him smiling and saying, 'Do you want to borrow my stopper?' Christ, I was out of the toilets like a shot and never ever went for a wash if he was about.
>
> (Corporal John Inglis, RAF Regiment)

At the other end of the scale, some National Servicemen who later 'came out of the closet' admitted that during their time in the services they adopted super-tough and over-aggressive attitudes to mask any suspicion that they might be homosexual. After all, they had reasoned, homosexuals are sissies and pansies; far better to go out at the weekend, get drunk, get into a fight and bash up queers than to be thought one oneself. For the most part, homosexuality only entered the conversation in the barrack-room in the form of aggressive banter and crude jokes.

Next to sex, drink was the most commonplace topic of conversation in the barrack-room. In the early days of a man's National Service the odd bottle of pale ale or half-pint of cider was the greatest alcoholic indulgence – the weekly rate of 28s. (£1.40) in 1948 had only risen to 38s. (£1.90) in 1960 for a National

Service private. For that reason, the amount of spending money
the National Serviceman had in his pocket was exceedingly small
and even the much-vaunted 4s. (20p) a day was reduced by
stoppages for breakages, National Health Insurance and a 10d.
(4½p) clothing allowance. Most men were lucky if they held on to
£1 2s. 6d. (£1.25) a week – some men had to send some of this
home to help their families – and this came as a bitter blow to
men who had been used to drawing around £10 a week in well-
paid and skilled civilian jobs. Later, pay did improve and during
the last six months of a man's service he was liable to a Regular's
pay, which was £4 11s. (£4.55) in 1960 for a private and £5 19s.
(£5.95) a week for a corporal. Additional sums were also paid for
specialist skills such as marksmanship, ability at a trade, or for
training as a parachutist.

Between the wars there had been a marked decline in heavy
drinking in Britain, and this trend continued into the late 1950s
when the increase in public affluence gave people more disposable money to spend on drink. Cash for heavy boozing, then, was
always going to be in short supply for the average National
Serviceman: that said, National Service did give several generations of young men their first experience of going to pubs and of
getting drunk. Because the availability of alcohol was necessarily
restricted at the NAAFI, most drinking was done off-camp, and
for those National Servicemen who trained at camps in the West
Country or passed through the transit camp at Newton Abbot,
that meant cider – the drink whose first sip, according to Laurie
Lee, tasted of 'golden fire . . . wine of wild orchards, of russet
summer, of plump red apples'.

> Watchett is in Somerset where the cider do come from. We were
> warned about the strength of the brew but took it with a large
> pinch of salt. Needless to say, we went in to town to sample the
> product. It was called scrumpy and it didn't taste all that strong,
> but when we left the pub we were legless. The camp was a few
> miles from Watchett and I remember sleeping the night on the
> town cricket pitch. Thankfully it was a really warm summer and we
> suffered no ill effects and staggered back to camp about 5 a.m.
> (Corporal John Inglis, RAF Regiment)

John Inglis was lucky. The services cracked down on drunken-
ness, and punishments for returning to camp drunk could run
from additional guard duty to stoppage of leave. Any serviceman
who assaulted a superior while drunk could expect to receive at
least 28 days' 'jankers' after being put on Commanding Officer's
Orders. National Servicemen stationed at Catterick have vivid

memories of the riotous scenes at Darlington Station on Sunday nights as trains disgorged their soldier passengers, many of them much the worst for wear. Amongst them would be returning Scottish soldiers, who had had longer to get fighting drunk and made no secret of their dislike at finding MPs armed with paddy-sticks waiting to greet them. Running fights at both Darlington and Richmond stations were fairly common and often inevitable events.

At other times men got drunk to celebrate special occasions such as demob, when an entire billet would turn out to salute its departing mates, or Christmas, when the work of every camp would grind to a halt.

> On Christmas Eve some well-meaning friend bought me three beers which I didn't like, [he wrote to J. M. Lee] but drank because of the 'extra-specialness' of the day. When I got back to my billet everyone gathered together and we mixed up huge cocktails of Port, Dubonnet and Rum, singing 'Moonlight Cocktails'. Within half an hour I was swaying about, though I could see clearly. I denounced someone as a spy because they were drinking water in their mug. Sometime after 11 p.m. an officer appeared and we dispersed to our rooms. My bed wouldn't stay still and kept rocking like a ship. I was sea-sick and after that the next thing I knew was that it was 6 a.m. on Xmas morning when I woke up. Quite an interesting experience for a future novelist.
>
> (Private A. J. Bayley, RASC)

For those who lived within striking distance of a camp, weekend leaves were always possible; but for those who either lived in remote areas or were posted to them, entertainment had to be found locally. It was not worth David McNeill's while to make the long journey back to Glasgow to spend a few rushed hours with his family and friends while he was stationed at RAF St Mawgan.

> I went to a demob party in the Torpoint Inn in Plymouth in April 1953 (I know that because it was my birthday that weekend). We stayed both the Friday and the Saturday nights in the transit billets of RAF Mountbatten in Plymouth, the HQ of Coastal Command, 19 Group. Although in civilian clothes, we went in and out without let or hindrance, eating in the mess and visiting some of Nick's friends in the signals cabin. It would be unthinkable today, especially since for most of the Saturday we were all noticeably merry. That weekend was memorable in that it was the first time I was really properly drunk. We went to a theatre on the Saturday and the turns came on and went off with what seemed to me

bewildering rapidity. I kept leaning forward to the group of WAAFs who had accompanied us from the Torpoint, shouting my considered appreciation of each turn, but far from being embarrassed they spent their time screeching and giggling since they were all drunk too. It's a wonder we weren't all thrown out.

(SAC David McNeill, RAF Coastal Command)

The general rule was that each National Serviceman got fourteen days leave a year after eight months' service, with weekend leave at the discretion of the Commanding Officer and dependent on manpower requirements. Travelling time could be added to the longer periods of leave and a careful perusal of railway timetables could provide another day or so away. That, too, was regarded as a good skive.

On my first ship (HMS *Nonsuch*) I was told that all Scots people had requested to go on leave earlier so they could take the night train from London – I went to the Officers' Mess and asked to speak to the Captain. He told me it was OK so I left. The people who had told me were all hiding as it was supposed to be a joke on me but I had the last laugh: I was the only one who got away early and ended up with an extra day's leave.

(Stores Assistant Robert V. Greenshields, Royal Navy)

To cater for servicemen on leave in London, or for those passing through the city, there was the homely Union Jack Club in Waterloo Road which offered reasonably priced board and lodgings; other organisations, mainly voluntary, which looked after servicemen's interests included the YMCA, the Church Army, WRVS and Toc H. The principal provider of leisure and recreation, however, was the NAAFI* (Navy, Army and Air Force Institutes). There was a NAAFI in every camp, offering bar and cafeteria services, and on larger bases a well-stocked shop selling everything from shaving sticks to cigarettes. It also sold such necessary requisites as blanco and Brasso. Very often the NAAFI was a useful means of supplementing a soldier's diet, especially in camps where the catering was poor, and it also retained a hold on all servicemen's hearts as being the one place where they could escape from the regimentation of service life. By the post-war period the NAAFI had become a big business

*NAAFI was founded in 1921 in succession to the Canteen and Mess Co-operative Society, which had been in existence since 1894. During World War II its turnover was £200 million, it employed 120,000 members of staff and it maintained 10,000 establishments in over 40 countries. Even in the immediate post-war years it was able to keep its prices down to 1*d.* for a cup of tea and 3*d.* for a cup of coffee. An average meal (sausage, egg and chips) cost only 1*s.* 9*d.* (8p).

enterprise with a global network, and therefore an integral part of service life. On that level it did sterling work, but it is perhaps indicative of the services' indifference to their men's well-being that the voluntary services were such an important adjunct to National Service life. Men were constantly on the move, trains travelled without restaurant or buffet cars and frequently left their passengers stranded at late-night stations: for all those weary travellers, cups of tea and beds were provided by cheerful volunteers, doing their best to oil the wheels of the military machine.

One feature of NAAFI life was that the more enterprising committees would organise dances or jazz concerts on camp, at which a live group would play; bands with exotic names like Mike Daniel's Delta Jazzmen, Denny Coffey and His Red Hot Beans and Mick Mulligan's Magnolia Jazz Band. In his volume of memoirs, *Owning-Up*, George Melly paints a vivid picture of being a member of a jazz band on the road during the 1950s, and in one instance describes playing at an RAF base 'remarkable for the terrifying appearance of the two coachloads of girls imported by the authorities to dance with the trainee airmen'; but it was not jazz on the base which interested most National Servicemen. It was the opportunity to hear it in provincial cafés, in Soho jazz cellars during all-night raves, or in sedate town halls up and down the country. Jazz had gained an early foothold in Britain in the 1930s; strengthened by the influx of American servicemen during World War II, it had become by the 1950s the province of a younger generation who argued passionately the various merits of trad, mainstream, Dixieland and bebop. Their followers were fiercely loyal and evolved their own distinctive uniforms of duffle coats, battledress and open-toed sandels – almost anything would do provided it were extreme – and their heroes were Ken Colyer, Chris Barber, Humph Lyttleton, Alex Walsh and Monty Sunshine. Their bible was the *Melody Maker*, and their heaven, from 1956, the annual Beaulieu Jazz Festival organised by Lord Montagu.

> At Compton Bassett I got friendly with two people early – Mike Lowery and Adrian Stuart. Mike was from Sidcup and was slightly older than the rest of us, having had deferment as an art student at Woolwich Polytechnic. He was a great jazz and blues fan, a friend of Mick Mulligan (of the traditional jazz band of the time) and of George Melly and was a regular visitor to Humphrey Lyttleton's club in Oxford Street. We used to go to the jazz club at the camp where the band was so pure that they scorned drum kit and

double-bass and had a washboard and tuba in the real Dixieland marching tradition. It was run by a Senior Technician who had an enormous 78 rpm record collection rescued from London junk shops and street markets, which included originals by Big Bill Broonzy and Muddy Waters, and classics like 'Black Diamond Train'. Adrian, who was from Aberdeen, preferred classical music. There was even a thriving record club for that, which we went to often.

(SAC David McNeill, RAF Coastal Command)

Jazz, with its hint of rebellion and its mannered art school anarchy, had an obvious appeal to young people; but by the mid-1950s new sounds were being heard in the land. Skiffle and rock and roll had equally ardent admirers, and soon film producers were beginning to realise that there were other kinds of youth in Britain – those who frequented espresso coffee bars, formed skiffle groups, or stormed cinemas brave enough to exhibit the American film *Rock Around the Clock* with Bill Haley and the Comets. Young people outside the services had enough money to demand their own forms of entertainment, and film and television producers fell over themselves trying to provide it. Television's *6.5 Special* came to the small screen in 1958 featuring stars like Lonnie Donegan and Don Lang and His Frantic Five, while Tommy Steele found himself the subject of a film biography in *The Tommy Steele Story* before he was even twenty-one. Other popular films dealing with the music revolution were *It's Trad Dad* and Tony Richardson's *Momma Don't Allow*; Frankie Vaughan, another singer in the hit-parade, starred in *These Dangerous Years*, while from America came *The Girl Can't Help It*, featuring the pneumatic Jayne Mansfield and a host of top entertainers.

Comedy films also attracted large audiences with the 'Doctor' and 'St Trinian's' series winning deserved acclaim; the 'Carry On' films provided a peculiarly British sense of humour (*Carry On Sergeant* guyed the Army and National Service and was therefore not to be missed), and *The Goon Show* and *Two Way Family Favourites* attracted the largest radio audiences in the forces during the 1950s. Newspapers, too, offered their own form of entertainment, and the *Daily Mirror* earned a special place in most servicemen's hearts by campaigning for better conditions in the country's armed forces. In fact, never before had British newspapers had it so good, with combined sales above 16 million throughout the decade.

At most large camps National Servicemen were encouraged to

organise their own types of leisure and recreation, and for those men fortunate enough to be good at sport their service careers could be one long skive. Sportsmen who had represented their country or gained county or district honours were more or less assured of the chance to represent their service or unit, and were treated accordingly. Most were excused military duties altogether or found their way into 'cushy' billets so that they could devote more time to training; and during the period of National Service, inter-service matches or tournaments could be exciting affairs featuring several international sportsmen. The Scottish full-back Ken Scotland represented the Royal Signals in the Army Rugby XV and England's fly-half, Richard Sharp, played for the Royal Navy. Other notable National Service sportsmen who played for their country and for their service included the England footballers Bobby Charlton (RASC) and Duncan Edwards (RAOC), and the England cricketers John Edrich (RASC) and Doug Padgett (Royal Signals). A large number of professional footballers and men who had signed forms with senior clubs were scattered throughout the forces, and to be good at football was a passport to a relatively easy life.

> When I arrived at Port Said the camp PTI called out for all soccer players to fall out. I had learnt from experience that if you wanted a game of soccer you had to say you had signed for a league side. I chose Wrexham.
> When I arrived at Amman my soccer prowess had arrived ahead of me so I had to keep up the pretence. Anyway, I got away with it and fitted well into the camp team. My sporting needs were fully catered for with swimming and boxing and I also played a bit of rugby.
> (Lance-Corporal Griffith Roberts, Royal Corps of Signals)

Because of the preponderance of Scottish professional footballers in English league clubs it was generally – and usually wrongly – assumed that all Scots were good soccer players. As a result not a few Scottish National Servicemen had the same experience as Griff Roberts and managed to get away with the deception.

At home in Britain, the 1st Training Regiment, Royal Signals, was synonymous with excellence at rugby football and cross-country running and, naturally, good sportsmen tended to gravitate towards it or were pulled in that direction by the regiment's 'talent scouts'. One of the anomalies of service sport was that rugby players from the Union and the League codes were allowed to play together in the same teams, a situation which would not have been tolerated by the civilian sporting authorities: this, too, was one of the reasons for the success of the 1st Signals at rugby football. Even those who did not represent their unit at any senior level were encouraged to take up some kind of team sport; games away from home could be a welcome break in routine and in that way many men found they increased their circle of friends. Whether or not they played any team games, though, most conscripts admitted that they reached the peak of their physical fitness during National Service. From the services' point of view, sport was considered a good thing: it kept men fit and team games had the useful military function of maintaining motivation to succeed, and of developing leadership qualities.

Pleasures could take other, less obvious forms, and it came as a surprise to many National Servicemen that these could be provided by their own attitudes to the unit or regiment in which they served. Wearing a distinctive uniform gave many a man an agreeable sense of pride, especially when he felt that the right to wear it had been won the hard way. The Royal Marine Commandos and the Parachute Regiment only took very limited numbers of National Servicemen, and so severe was their training that selection was confined to the best recruits. Men permitted to wear the green beret of the Commando forces or the paratrooper's red beret regarded themselves as a race apart, and even after training continued to nurture a fierce sense of competition amongst themselves.

A National Serviceman did not have to belong to an élite or highly motivated fighting unit to develop that same sense of pride. A Guardsman in ceremonial dress could experience it while engaged on duties with the Royal Household, or it could come to him wearing a kilt and Balmoral, marching in perfect step behind the pipes and drums of a Highland regiment. Sailors have remarked on similar sensations, part pleasure, part sentimentality, while standing to attention on board the deck of a warship as it slipped into Plymouth roads. Few airmen, too, failed to be stirred by the sight and sound of one of the surviving piston-engined aircraft of World War II, whether it was a Spitfire banking lazily in the clear winter sky above Malta or a four-engined Lancaster bomber returning home from patrol at first light of day.

> I have always felt sorry for anyone whose first flight was in a metal tube bound for the Costa Brava. Apart from the privilege (and that may sound pompous, but it's true) of being occasionally and unofficially part of the crew of a flying legend, this was a real aircraft, built, flown and maintained by real people. It was no computer-controlled mystery of high technology wrapped and

sealed in bland streamlining. It could be understood by ordinary human beings, like a huge old-fashioned car, and the frailty of the straining components which kept it from plunging headlong into the sea could be seen only too clearly. It was oil-stained and patched. The paintwork was scuffed by clambering mechanics and the patterned surface of the wing spar was scratched and shiny. The paint was worn from the controls and the stuffing was coming out of the seats. There were pipes, wires and switches and huge scorch-marks fanning out over the wings from the exhaust ports. It was a noble, beautiful, majestic, tatty old wreck and we shall never see anything like the Avro Lancaster again.

(SAC David McNeill, RAF Coastal Command)

The hero of the Thousand Bomber Raids over Germany during the war, even in peacetime semi-retirement the Lancaster had lost none of its aura of power and elegance. By the early 1950s the survivors had been relegated to maritime patrol duties with Coastal Command and were gradually being superseded by Shackletons and American-built Neptunes. On being retired, the remaining Lancasters were sent to the breakers, a sad and undignified fate for such an historic aircraft. David McNeill enjoyed several flights on Lancasters flying out of RAF St Mawgan, even enduring an air test – trials in which a recondi-tioned aircraft was 'flown to the limits of destruction by one of a carefully selected number of the hopelessly insane, who was usually Polish.' Being thrown about the sky in a creaking aircraft flown by a merciless crew turned out to be a stomach-churning experience, made worse by the landing when the pilot made a wrong approach over a river valley. The sudden cold air caused the Lancaster to drop, and disaster beckoned before the Merlin engines surged back into life putting the plane on a correct descent. Not all 'joy-rides' were as eventful as that and on most RAF operational bases non-aircrew personnel could get in at least one free flight, provided they were prepared to push themselves forward.

At ATDU Gosport I remember going on detachment to RNAS Culdrose from where we would fly out to the Isles of Scilly and test drop torpedoes which would later be recovered by MTBs and brought back to Penzance and Newlyn. I flew on one such test in October 1949 in a Barracuda with Flight Lieutenant Salter as pilot and recall seeing the SS *Fantee* aground on the Seven Stones between Land's End and the Scillies. In succeeding days we watched as she broke up and sank with her cargo of bales of cotton and mahogany. We also watched the small boats trying to salvage what they could. I now regularly holiday in the Scillies and two

years ago (1982) found two huge mahogany tree trunks on the
beach – brought up by divers from the *Fantee* which I had seen sink
twenty-three years previously.

(LAC Byron T. Denning, RAF)

At bases like RAF Limassol on Cyprus where service life was
relatively relaxed, all it required was a quick word with flight
control and the National Service radar or W/T operator could find
himself the passenger in a Meteor trainer doing circuits and
bumps or, more adventurously, in an Anson on a communications run to Alexandria.

Ceremonial, the bane of basic training with its insistence on bull,
could provide pleasures of a different kind once the intricacies of
uniform and drill had been properly mastered. However much
men usually disliked guard duty, there were times, too, when it
rose to the memorable and could be seen as a necessary and
relevant military task.

> Feeling like a mannequin as your mates put the finishing touches
> to your dress prior to Guard Mounting Parade – followed by the
> blackness and the coldness of the night's vigil as one paraded
> round the camp perimeter doing your stag, armed with a pick
> handle – better than the poor sod on the Main Gate Guard having
> to stand still and on the alert for the Duty Officer swooping or any
> other passing big-wig. Yes, also a feeling of pride in the squad and
> of having mastered the drill – the esprit de corps – the feeling that
> you were never left out on a limb as there was always someone to
> help with, or share in, your troubles.
>
> (Lance-Corporal Bob Downie, Royal Army Ordnance Corps)

Other National Servicemen have memories of the solemn
dignity of taking part in a firing party and coming face to face with
death for the first time in their young lives.

> One tends to remember the brighter and pleasanter and amusing
> side, but inevitably there were the others as well. Like acting as
> part of the Guard of Honour at the funeral of the entire ten-man
> crew of an aircraft which crashed in the Moray Firth. They were
> part of my course, were friends – one in particular, Roger, was the
> first friend I made within hours of arriving at Padgate on my first
> day in the service.
>
> (Sergeant R. Darbyshire, RAF Coastal Command)

For them the volley of rifle fire and the poignant strains of the
'Last Post' have left indelible memories. There were other equally
powerful rituals which have left lasting impressions, none more

momentous than the rare sight of a serviceman being ceremonially drummed out of the services. While stationed at HMS *Ceres*, training to become a naval Writer, William Nuttall was a member of the drum and bugle band which played drum rolls while the Master of Arms cut off all the buttons and badges of a Steward discovered stealing from the Officers' Quarters. The ceremony took place in the Drill Shed in front of the entire company and was designed to instil a sense of awe into the men who witnessed it. After reading out the charge the sentence was then carried out, the final indignity being the slashing of the prisoner's shoe-laces before he was led to the Main Gate and ejected. It might have been simpler to have slipped the man out of the back gate, but his public humiliation was a cogent reminder that every serviceman had a responsibility to his fellow men.

Music was not just for solemn occasions. A fundamental part of military ceremonial was the regimental band, and National Servicemen of a musical frame of mind fortunate enough to be selected for instrument training were usually on to a good thing. Not only were bandsmen paid more for their skills, but their duties could be lighter, especially during the summer months when military bands were much in demand at shows and fêtes. In Scottish regiments pipers were very special soldiers indeed and in some cases their rewards could be substantial.

> Soon after completing my square-bashing I joined the pipe band. I had played the pipes at school and on requiring to do National Service I decided before signing that I would make as much of it as possible. One way of doing that was joining a pipe band and the Scots Guards' pipe band was deservedly famous. Prior to my demob we went on a tour of the USA and Canada – we spent 12 weeks there, we travelled 24,000 miles, we did 65 shows in 56 cities . . . Audrey Hepburn's guardian had been a Scots Guards officer and when she heard we were in town in LA she invited us out to the MGM film studios where she was making a film called *Green Mansions* with Lee J. Cobb and Anthony Perkins. We joined them on the set and watched part of the film being made.
>
> (Piper Drew Bennett, 2nd Bn. Scots Guards)

With the band of the Scots Guards, Drew Bennett also took part in the Royal Tournament at Earl's Court, the Trooping of the Colour at Horse Guards and the Edinburgh Military Tattoo; his skills as a Highland dancer took him to perform at the Royal Caledonian Ball and at 'countless other memorable engagements'. Nor were those all the benefits: the extra money gained from his piping and dancing helped to finance his studies at art college once he had completed his National Service. (On the sporting side he also skied in the BAOR team.) As in most cases in the forces, opportunities of that kind only came about when the serviceman could prove that he had ability and was also prepared to push himself forward for selection.

National Servicemen with good 'A' or 'Higher' level passes in languages could be selected for training at the Joint Service School of Languages, which was based at Bodmin in Cornwall before being transferred to its last home at Crail, near St Andrews in Fife. Its principal task was to train National Servicemen to 'A' level standard in Russian, a task which took nine months; thereafter, the top recruits would be posted to further intensive training courses at the School of Slavonic and East European Studies of the University of London, or to the Department of Russian at Cambridge. The rest would be posted to the Intelligence Corps or to the intelligence departments of the RAF or Royal Navy where they were engaged on basic translating duties relevant to British intelligence. Learning Russian in such a short time, and in some cases perfecting it to degree standard, was a prodigious feat and one which never failed to draw the admiration of the servicemen's teachers. 'They had to work hard at their Russian and it must sometimes have seemed a real grind,' recalls Professor G. H. Bolsover, who had charge of the course at London. 'But they were always conscious of the progress they were making. They knew that they were doing something which was worthwhile. Very few of them failed to pull their weight or had to be sent off the course and this in itself was a good indication that the great majority considered the exercise to be worth the effort they were required to put into it.'

The intensive study of Russian for services' use had been developed in the aftermath of the Korean War when the USSR had emerged as a potential enemy and the rush was on to pick up detailed intelligence about the country and its armed forces. The results of the exercise are still classified but the energy and commitment of those National Servicemen who took part must have yielded results, even if it was only in the translation of Russian printed material. It also gave birth to a teaching phenomenon of the 1960s: after years of being considered a specialist, even unwieldy language, Russian emerged as one of the growth areas in British education. As a result of their linguistic training many ex-National Servicemen returned to schools and universities as teachers of Russian, and helped revolutionise educational attitudes to the language and to the methods of teaching it.

At other times, postings offering an unusual training could be a matter of luck. To this day some ex-National Servicemen cannot understand why they were fortunate enough to end up doing interesting work, but one thing remains certain: once he had experienced it, each man was loathe to give it up.

> Some three months or so later (after arriving in the Suez Canal Zone) there was a notice requesting applications to go on a course as 'Observer Report Writers'. One of my colleagues, knowing that I worked for a newspaper, suggested that I should put in for it. In any case, as he said, it was an opportunity for a month at a new camp. A few weeks later I was told to go to Moascar, near Ismailia, to Army Public Relations. Ostensibly it was for a month, then to return to battalion to write appropriate stories; in actual fact I stayed with PR for the rest of my service . . . We met quite a few visiting foreign correspondents, mainly British, but several Americans as well. As you might expect, the PR detachment was quite small, about twenty in total and mostly from different regiments and corps. For instance, the colonel was a Sherwood Forester, but others were from the Royal Fusiliers, Cheshires, Royal Scots, HLI, Borders, RASC, RE, Life Guards and Royal Military Police. It was much more interesting work than being with the battalion and several PR photographers went on to press work in civilian life, including Bill Walker, with whom I now work on the *Cumberland News* and Peter Balton, now with *TV Times* and formerly with *Picture Post*.
>
> (Private Alan Byers, 1st Bn. The Border Regiment)

As most National Servicemen had discovered early in their service lives, the organisation of the armed forces seemed to depend less on logic than on the swings and roundabouts of their own fortune. When the fates were kind, National Service turned out to be a profitable and enjoyable time, fully justifying the Army's claim, made in its *Guide for the National Serviceman in the Army*, that National Service was 'in truth, an education in itself'.

Chapter Six

IS YOUR JOURNEY
REALLY NECESSARY?

At the end of World War II Britain's armed forces were strung across the globe from Germany to Japan, from the Adriatic to the Caribbean, and most strategically important places in between. In Europe the British army of occupation was settled in north-west Germany; meanwhile the victorious Eighth Army had swept up through Italy to enter Austria, where the southern provinces had been earmarked as the British zone. On the way they had been forced into a short-lived confrontation with the Yugoslavs in the Italian province of Venezia Giulia, over possession of Trieste, one of the first of several potential flashpoints involving the British armed forces. Troops of 24th Infantry Brigade were in fact destined to stay in the province until 1954; for obvious climatic and social reasons it was considered to be a highly desirable posting. In the Middle East there were garrisons in Egypt, Libya and Palestine; further east, forces were deployed in Aden, Abyssinia, Eritrea, Somaliland and the Sudan. There were still large garrisons in India, the jewel soon to be wrested from Britain's imperial crown; and in the Far East, in the wake of Japan's defeat, servicemen were needed in Malaya, Singapore, Hong Kong, North Borneo, Indo-China, the Dutch East Indies and in Japan itself. To complete the chain of command, there were also British bases in Jamaica, the British Honduras, Gibraltar, Malta and Cyprus. It was the largest garrisoning job ever undertaken by the nation's armed forces; the army had around three million men involved in the operation, but it was in chaos. Many of the garrisons and installations were beginning to be run down, and the nominal strengths of wartime divisions had been cut by men returning home to demob.

The Royal Navy still kept open its major overseas bases at Gibraltar, Malta and Singapore, and although the dinosaur fleets of the two previous world wars were soon to be a thing of the past, naval power and its associated stations were still essential for maintaining Britain's influence in the Middle East and the Far East. During the war the expansion of the RAF had taken it to most corners of the global conflict, and the return to peace saw some consolidation of that new strategic responsibility. In 1949 the Middle East Air Force (MEAF), with its headquarters in Cyprus, controlled bases in North Africa, Iraq, Aden, the Persian Gulf and East Africa. Malta came under the control of the Air Ministry in London. Many of the squadrons provided transport facilities with Hastings and Valetta aircraft, but even in peacetime large numbers of MEAF strike aircraft were kept busy. Lancasters of 38 Squadron performed maritime reconnaissance duties in the attempt to control illegal immigration by sea into Palestine; in Kenya, Lincoln bombers of 61 Squadron attacked terrorist camps during the Mau-Mau troubles of 1952–1955, and Vampires and Venoms of 6 Squadron flew strikes against rebel tribesmen in support of the Oman Trucial Levies during Britain's intervention in the Oman in the early 1950s. In the Suez Canal Zone alone, fourteen squadrons were deployed in 1951, giving a front-line strength of 152 aircraft.

East of Aden the RAF's presence was concentrated in Malaya and Singapore, with smaller contingents in Ceylon and Hong Kong. Eight squadrons were based in Malaya in 1948, consisting of Dakota transports, Mosquito reconnaissance aircraft, Beaufighter light bombers, Spitfires and Sunderland flying boats. The Far East Air Force (FEAF) was for a long time the haven of such World War II veterans, all of which continued to give good service until the mid-1950s. They were updated and increased during the years of the Emergency with the introduction of jet fighters and, more significantly from the point of view of military operations, sophisticated helicopters like the Westland Whirlwind. In Germany, the 2nd TAF in 1950 had a front-line strength of sixteen squadrons equipped with Vampires and Meteors; these were later replaced, first with Venoms and Sabres and then with Hunters and Javelins by 1956. By then the TAF's front-line strength had increased to twenty-five squadrons.

The world-wide presence of British armed forces in the postwar world was a double-edged sword. On the one hand, Britain appeared to have assumed again the mantle of Empire; on the other, the people of the old imperial colonies were starting to demand independence and voicing their resentment of a foreign military presence in their countries. From the very beginning, the newly-won peace was bedevilled by an atmosphere of rioting and civil unrest which was to continue throughout the fifties and sixties.

On 29 September 1945 British units entered Batavia (Jakarta) in the Dutch East Indies to help restore Dutch control which, it was claimed, would be welcomed by the local population. This assumption proved to be mistaken, as Indonesian nationalism had been nurtured during the Japanese occupation and Dr Soekarno and his supporters were in no mood to accept back their former masters. Against a background of clumsy diplomacy, followed by violent rioting, the British were forced to rush in additional forces including the 23rd Indian Division as well as naval and air support. During the consequent confrontation the British (and Indian) units carried out their peace-keeping role with a good deal of self-restraint which earned them the plaudits of both sets of protagonists. In March 1946 they were able to leave the country to Dutch reinforcements as fighting came to an end and the Indonesians were promised a measure of self-determination. Sixty British servicemen lost their lives during the operations and there were 2,136 casualties. Shots were also fired at British troops in Indo-China as Ho Chi Minh put in hand the violence which would disfigure the future of Vietnam. In both countries, peace-keeping operations were being carried out amongst a people who resented the presence of foreign armed forces: it was a grim taste of what lay ahead for the British soldier.

Elsewhere, there was violence in the mandate of Palestine where a large British garrison attempted with little success to maintain security and law and order in the Jewish homeland. In 1948 Britain gave up the unequal struggle and passed the problem over to the United Nations; that same year also saw the final British withdrawal from Greece, where a civil war between Royalists and communists had been raging since 1946. By then India and Pakistan had achieved independence after two years of bloody rioting, during which British army, naval and air force units had brought a semblance of calm into a maelstrom of religious and political hatred. The last British troops in Pakistan, the 2nd Bn. The Black Watch, left on 26 February 1948, and the 1st Bn. Somerset Light Infantry, *Ultimis ex Indis*, left Bombay two days later, thereby bringing to an end two centuries of British soldiering in the sub-continent. Four regiments of Gurkhas remained in the British Army, but for both sides, Indian and British, the parting of the ways was not taken without regret:

many British soldiers looked on India as the army's true home, and there were tears amongst the assembled Mahrattas and Sikhs as they bade farewell to the Somersets when they trooped their colour for the last time through the Gateway of India.

The end of the imperial connection with India should have heralded a new perception of Britain's role in the world. With India gone there was no longer any need to maintain a powerful presence in the Middle East, but first the Labour government and then successive Conservative governments clung rigidly to the Victorian strategy of protecting the imperial jugular through the Suez Canal. The Mediterranean, therefore, remained the nub of British global strategy, and it was to that end that large and expensive garrisons and associated naval and air force installations were maintained in the area between 1948 and 1959. Further east, the bases of Hong Kong and Singapore had an obvious strategic importance during the Korean War and the Malayan Emergency, but they were also symbolic of Britain's desire to maintain a presence in the Far East. There, inter-service co-operation was particularly strong, largely because the army and navy had to rely on aircraft both to support operations and to transport men. Helicopters had become essential battlefield weapons, and the planes of RAF Transport Command helped put an end to the boredom and occasional discomfort of long journeys by sea.

Gradually the continuing Cold War between the Soviet Union and her satellites in Europe, and the western powers as represented by NATO began to focus the thrust of British strategic thinking on West Germany, the home of BAOR and 2nd TAF. In time, the bases with their garrisons and associated training areas came to assume the function, if not the glamour, of those in pre-war India. For the fortunate few there was still the possibility of a posting to one of the more exotic corners of Britain's receding Empire – to places like Malta, Jamaica, Bermuda, the Bahamas, Khartoum, or to a plum posting with SHAPE in Paris. 'Join the Navy and See the World' had been a popular slogan during the inter-war years: paradoxically, conscript sailors were less likely to be posted abroad than their brothers in the army or the air force during the National Service period.

To move its servicemen around the globe, the armed forces relied mainly on its fleet of troopships which numbered 22 in 1948. By

1957 it had been reduced to 14 troopers and the fleet was phased out five years later, the last voyage being made by HMTT *Oxfordshire* which arrived in Southampton from Malta on 19 December 1962 with 1st Bn. Royal Highland Fusiliers. Many of the troopers were of European construction, having been requisitioned after the war. The *Empire Fowey*, which was employed on the Far East run and took many men to the war in Korea, had begun life as the Nord Deutscher Lloyd passenger liner *Potsdam* in 1935, and between 1945 and her last voyage in 1960 carried over 40,000 servicemen and their families. On the Harwich to Hook of Holland run, the *Empire Wansbeck* was the converted Danish minelayer *Linz*; in 1962 she became the Greek cruise liner *Esperos*, and her most recent transformation was as a ship blown up by the Danish underground in the BBC television series *SOE* which examined the wartime intelligence work of the Special Operations Executive. Other notable troopers included the ex-Cunard liner *Georgic*, the largest passenger vessel able to use the Suez Canal; the *Andalusia*, the fastest trooper on the Far East run; the *Empire Orwell* mainly on the Middle East run; and the elderly *Vienna* which transported troops to the Hook of Holland and the awaiting Green, Red and Blue trains for the journey to Germany.

The crossing between Harwich and the Hook of Holland was notoriously rough, and conditions on the troop decks where the bunks were triple-decked could be uncomfortable and claustrophobic. For many soldiers and airmen, especially those who had never been on a ship before, it could be an unpleasant experience, relieved only by the mixture of discipline and good humour administered by the ships' RSMs. (On the *Empire Wansbeck* this was RSM E. H. Smith, RA, known to one and all as 'Eat Horse Shit'.)

> They (National Servicemen) were generally well-behaved, though there was of course the odd one who tried to board 'under the influence' and had to be turned back. I remember one who didn't like the crowded troopdeck and complained bitterly that he couldn't find a bunk. The RSM told him he would sort one out when the ORs were all on board. This didn't suit, so the RSM asked him if he would like a cabin to himself. He fell for it and said yes, and was promptly shown into a cell with a wooden bed and pillow. Another man, on boarding, told the RSM that he couldn't do anything to him because he was being demobbed that week. He was marched ashore and left behind in the transit camp at the Hook of Holland to await the next sailing, four days later in his case.
>
> (3rd Officer David Cullum, *Empire Wansbeck*)

Once disembarked, the servicemen were divided up and issued with British armed forces currency ('Baffs') for use in Germany. They were then given breakfast. This was usually the first surprise. 'The bread was fresh and crusty,' remembers David McNeill, who spent two weeks on detachment at Bad Eilsen during a NATO exercise in August 1953. 'In Britain it was still the limp grey austerity loaf.' The next surprise was the standard of the transport which had been laid on for them.

> The trains were different too, spotlessly clean inside and out, and that was before a squad of Dutch cleaners came and washed the outside with long brushes while we waited to leave. An enormous electric locomotive pulled the train to the German border through quaint sparkling towns. It was a different world from the sooty, dilapidated, litter-strewn slums of fifties Britain. Everything was neat, clean and well-ordered and looked to us like the illustrations in a child's picture-book.
>
> At the German border, the electric locomotive was uncoupled and we got instead a huge, highly polished black German steam engine with red wheels. It was a treat for the train enthusiasts and most of us got out to have a look. The whole journey had been impeccably organised. As the train rolled through Germany we were called to lunch. Everything had been booked in advance and we were all treated like ordinary fare-paying passengers, with white-coated waiters serving a four-course lunch of a standard rarely seen in Britain at that time.
>
> (SAC David McNeill, RAF Coastal Command)

Other servicemen on the same run remembered throwing cigarettes (5p. for 20) to Dutch railway workers whenever the train stopped, and feeling, even in the mid-fifties, as if they belonged to an army of liberation.

Journeys by sea to the Middle East or the Far East were an entirely different matter. Both had to pass through the Bay of Biscay, traditional home of rough seas and high winds, and with conditions on some troopers reminiscent of the Victorian years many servicemen would have been glad to have disembarked at any port of call. The first respite was usually Valletta, Malta's huge naval base; and the Mediterranean with its azure skies, balmy nights and enticing smells was, on the whole, an experience to be savoured. For those going on to the Far East there was the heat of Suez and the Red Sea before the long stretch across the Indian Ocean. On a more sombre note, the voyage through the Suez Canal in the early 1950s also gave National Servicemen their first inkling that the British were not loved in every quarter of the

world. Whenever a troopship passed through the canal it became
the custom for Egyptian nationalists to mount noisy demonstrations against the continuing presence of the 70,000-strong British
garrison in their country.

Once east of Suez discipline would generally be relaxed, and
during the last stages of the six-week voyage men began to make
the most of the basic conditions. This was usually done in the best
traditions of British Army improvisation.

> There were about 1,500 men on troopship *Empire Pride* – our
> troopdeck was below waterline. At night a whole maze of slung
> hammocks, some on the floor, some on the mess-tables, a large bin
> in the centre for sickness in constant use all night. The heat and
> stench produced a putrid fug, especially in the tropics. My mates
> and I took to sleeping up on the open deck, a bit hard and you had
> to get up earlier as the lascars hosed the decks, but the air and the
> starlight were much sweeter.
>   (Rifleman George Savage, 1st Bn. Royal Ulster Rifles)

George Savage's draft was bound for service in Hong Kong
with the Royal Ulster Rifles, which had arrived there in October
1951 after war service in Korea. At one stage during the voyage
ship's gossip had it that the drafts would be diverted to join the
UN forces, but even that unfounded rumour and the discomfort
of the troopdecks could not dampen George Savage's excitement at being abroad for the first time in his life – 'quite an
adventure for an eighteen-year-old Londoner'. Others were
more fortunate in their mode of transport. When Trooper Brian
Wilkinson, 11th Hussars, went out to Malaya, his draft travelled
on board the old Cunarder, *Georgic*: 'an idyllic trip, just like a
world cruise for free'. Package holidays were a thing of the
future, and the chance to escape the confines of family and the
austerity of life in Britain turned most postings overseas into
something of an adventure.

Officers, of course, travelled first class and were frequently
unaware of the conditions their men had to endure. For them, the
journey out east was usually one long round of pleasure with
cocktail parties, excellent food and drink and ample diversions to
while away the time. Troopers also carried unaccompanied wives
and single women who rarely untouched by the spell of the
East and the glamour of a long sea voyage. 'When the weather
gets sultry, you gets your adultery,' more knowing stewards in the
officers' quarters would remark once the ship had reached the
balmy waters of the Indian Ocean.

As more sophisticated aircraft with longer ranges began to come into service it made tactical sense to use them as troop transports. The average voyage to the Far East took six weeks – on its last trip, the *Oxfordshire* left Singapore on 26 October 1962 and did not arrive in Southampton until 19 December – whereas a plane stopping at Rome, Nicosia, Bahrein, Karachi, Delhi, Calcutta and Bangkok on the London to Singapore run took only four days to complete the journey. Twenty Hermes IV aircraft carrying 65 men each were operated for the War Office by Airwork Ltd, and with their employment Britain was able to extend her strategic options in the Far East. For the first time, men could be rushed into the area should reinforcements be required, thus removing the need to maintain large and expensive garrisons in Singapore and Hong Kong at the end of the 1950s. The planes also introduced many young National Servicemen to the luxury of air travel at a time when it was otherwise prohibitively expensive.

The Handley Page Hermes IV, which had made its maiden flight in 1948, was ideally suited to trooping operations. It had a range of 3,500 miles and a cruising speed of 276 mph. Most of the machines operated by Airwork had been employed originally by BOAC on its South African services, and the standard of accommodation was consequently very high. As a concession to the niceties of international protocol, National Servicemen travelling by air to the Far East were issued with civilian clothes – suits, civilian, tropic, grey – at the London Assembly Centre in Tottenham Court Road, which were then returned when the plane reached Singapore. The suits were worn to prevent any embarrassment that might have been caused by troops overflying non-aligned countries en route, but to most men they only served to add to the illusion of luxury attached to travel by air.

Other companies involved in trooping by air were Skyways, Surrey Flying Services, Air Charter and Scottish Airlines, most of which used as their workhorse the venerable Avro York, a derivative of the wartime Lancaster bomber.

> Next morning I boarded an aircraft for the first time in my life. It was a York. It shook, it bounced, it dropped and rose in the slightest turbulence, but it was a wonderful experience. So far as I could find out, it was the first flight for all my group. We stopped at Malta where I had my first cup of tea with goats' milk. We took off into the Mediterranean sunset, a most memorable experience, and landed in Egypt in the early hours of the morning.
> (Signalman W. Findlay, Royal Corps of Signals)

Other aircraft used for troop transport included the Avro Tudor, the Dakota and the Vickers Armstrong Viking; all noisy, vibrating, Spartan aircraft, but in their day considered by first-time fliers to be the peak of luxury.

Service in post-war Europe generally meant a posting to Germany, but between 1946 and 1955 National Servicemen were also stationed in Austria with the force known as British Troops Austria (BTA). Until an international agreement could be reached guaranteeing Austria's neutrality, Britain occupied the southern zone of the country and one infantry battalion was stationed in Vienna for ceremonial duties. Despite some initial hostility from elements of the population, mainly ex-Nazi, to the allied occupation of their country, Austria was a popular posting. Unlike Germany, the country had not been completely devastated, food and drink were not in short supply and the Alpine landscape made a pleasing backdrop. Even Vienna, in spite of a plethora of shelled buildings in the city centre, retained something of its pre-war glamour, and within a few years of the war's end a visitor like the poet Stephen Spender was able to describe it as 'tremendously prosperous'. The climate was good too. In the summer months the garrisons at Graz, Villach and Klagenfurt were issued with tropical kit and, to complete the illusion, battalions like the 1st Royal Warwickshire Regiment adopted almost the precise routine they had followed in India before the war when its senior men had been juniors. As another of J. M. Lee's schoolfriends told him, it was an ideal posting.

> I am now stationed at what must rank among the best British stations in the world, namely, British Troops Austria. I am at Graz, the capital of the Province of Styria, the most easterly zone of the western powers in Europe.
> The barracks are centrally heated and have all mod cons. My own billet (although rather exceptional) has wardrobes, bedside lockers, and hot and cold water. It is a big room and there are only two of us in it. The food is every bit as good as that one gets at home, and the prices of everything (except clothes which are very expensive) is about half, and in many cases less than the English equivalent. This is mainly due to the unemployment that exists. Life has its bad side, of course. There are distasteful jobs such as guarding political prisoners and the young English recruit here tends to get drunk rapidly (beer 5*d.* per pint, double whisky 1*s.*, cigarettes 20 for 1*s.* and English brands at that) and of course, VD is rife.

Duties come pretty thick upon the average type but haven't affected me at all yet, for which I am of course grateful. I must say that I feel that if such barracks were built in England and if such amenities existed, there would be no need for National Service as all our forces would be Regulars – but perhaps that is wishful thinking.

To begin with, most of the men of the army of occupation in Austria were battle-hardened veterans, old soldiers with plenty of old soldiers' tricks. 'I remember that "rackets" were the in thing, selling cigarettes and other things to civilians,' recalls Lance-Corporal Arthur Franks, who served with the West Yorkshire Regiment in Austria for seven months in 1952. 'I remember that the regiment contained some real characters – long serving blokes who were into everything. In a sense it was unreal, too good to last.' As in other parts of the world, especially war-torn Europe, the black market was rife but in the lackadaisical atmosphere of Austria its operation frequently brought out the entrepreneur in the soldier. Military vehicles were requisitioned to convey illicit goods to and from the distant corners of the British zone and across the Alps into Italy and the port of Trieste. Surplus military equipment, particularly clothing, would be conveniently 'lost', and villagers in Styria and Carinthia seen wearing army-issue greatcoats and boots. Meanwhile, fresh vegetables and Austrian beer would appear on the tables of the BTA garrison in Graz. No posting to Austria was complete without taking part in at least one 'deal', even if it only entailed selling off water-bottle tops to the local vineyard.

The good times came to an end in 1955 when the last British unit in Austria, the 1st Bn. Middlesex Regiment, left Schönbrunn Barracks in Vienna on 17 September: to them had fallen the privilege of providing the guard of honour to the Austrian Chancellor during the independence ceremonies held on 27 July.

During the British occupation of Austria the Russian zone had been to the north, and the relationship between the two armies had mirrored events happening elsewhere. In the beginning, in the wake of the relief which greeted the end of war, British and Russian soldiers got on well together in spite of several misunderstandings over zone boundaries; by 1948 and the days of the Berlin Airlift, the atmosphere had become less congenial; and by the 1950s it was one of distinct antagonism, especially on the Yugoslavian border. The same was true of the position in

Germany, only there the confrontation was writ large and several incidents in 1948 almost spilled over into war.

The British zone of occupation was in north Germany and included the industrial Ruhr as well as the important port of Hamburg: governing the area and its people became the army's first task. In this they were assisted by 26,000 civilian administrators of the Control Commission, which worked in conjunction with the Military Government staff under the direction of a senior officer – first, Lieutenant-General Sir Ronald Weeks, Montgomery's deputy, and then Lieutenant-General Sir Brian Robertson, the son of Field Marshal 'Wullie' Robertson. During the early months of peacetime the British pursued a vigorous policy of non-fraternisation. 'You are about to meet a strange people in a strange enemy country,' warned an army handbook. 'When you meet the Germans you will probably think they are very much like us. They look like us except that there are fewer of the wiry type and more big fleshy types. But they are not really as much like us as they look.' Naturally, the outrage caused by the discovery of the concentration camps had excited public indignation in Britain and memories of the horrors of the Nazi regime were still strong, but the British policy of alienation made immediate post-war Germany a sullen and disgruntled colony. 2nd Lieutenant James Kennaway, 1st Bn. Cameron Highlanders, was posted to the 1st Gordons in Essen in 1948, and on his arrival was pelted by snowballs thrown by small undernourished children. 'They were waiting for me when I came out [of the station refreshment rooms], blue-eyed, fair-haired children, hungry children, and me with a three-course meal inside my belly,' he told his mother. 'And then on into the streets of the city where children, German children – but who cares? – were playing amongst the rubble. One little boy tripped over a boot, then picking himself up, brushed his knees and ran on. Now, that could happen anywhere and it wasn't the fair, curly hair, almost as white as the snow, nor the look of hope in his face that caught my eye. It was the boot. The boot still had a foot in it.'[12]

Not that conditions were bad for the army and air force of occupation. On the contrary, the armed forces and the staff of the Control Commission enjoyed a high standard of living: their quarters were in the buildings which had remained unscathed and the provision of duty-free luxuries meant that most enjoyed a relatively pleasant posting as far as living conditions were concerned.

The camp (RAF Lüneburg) was the height of luxury after being in Nissen huts in Britain. We were in German Airforce barracks and they were solid brick-built buildings with two storeys; the place had central heating and all the rooms were double-glazed. The toilets were fantastic as were the baths and showers and we were billeted two to a room with a chest of drawers and a wardrobe each.

(Corporal John Inglis, RAF Regiment)

The front-line operational bases of the RAF in Germany following the signature of the NATO agreement were in Celle, Fassberg, Gütersloh, Wahn and Wunstorf, with back-up bases west of the Rhine at Wildenrath, Geilenkirchen, Brüggen and Laarbruch.

BAOR had been created in 1946 out of the British forces occupying Germany, and initially it was composed of two divisions, the 7th Armoured ('The Desert Rats') and the 2nd Infantry. Increased Soviet belligerence forced Britain to add the 11th Armoured Division in 1950 and the 6th Armoured Division two years later, and to form 1st Corps with its headquarters at Rheindahlen, five miles outside München Gladbach. A field force was established in West Berlin with its headquarters in the former Olympic stadium. Within BAOR, National Servicemen could expect to serve at one of the garrisons at Osnabrück, Detmold, Lippe, Soltau, Dortmund, Hildesheim, Celle, Münster, Falling-bostel, Hameln, Minden, Menden, Hohne, Sennelager, Lipp-stadt, Padeborn, Rheindahlen or Lübbecke. The barracks were of three standards: 'Kaiser' barracks built before World War I, 'Hitler' barracks dating from the 1930s, and the more recent prefabricated 'Ophumane' barracks built throughout the 1950s.

All garrisons were self-contained units, and even after the policy of non-fraternisation had been ended it was still difficult for British servicemen to come into contact with the local population. As a result facilities had to be provided for off-duty recreation: the Army Kinema Corporation provided recent releases of popular films; the British Forces Broadcasting Services, founded in 1942, was an acceptable alternative to the BBC World Service, with its British Forces Network Germany broadcasting a cosy mixture of record request programmes and military gossip; and the ubiquitous NAAFI made every posting a home-from-home. There were possibilities, of course, to visit the local towns, but these were often restricted by language difficulties – few National Servicemen bothered to master more German than the necessary '*Zwei Bier, bitte.*' Trouble between service-

men and the local population was a niggling problem during the
1950s and 1960s, although most of the tension amounted to little
more than coldness towards British servicemen in pubs and cafés
and to the occasional 'English go Home' daubed on barrack
walls. Occasionally, however, the suspicion entertained by the
Germans towards the army of occupation erupted into violence.
In 1962 fighting between the men of the Cameronians and local
youths in Minden earned all Scottish soldiers the somewhat
unenviable nickname of '*Giftzwerge*' – 'poison-dwarfs'.

For their part, most National Servicemen found a posting to
BAOR or to 2nd TAF something of a let-down. Life tended to be
restricted and monotonous, and although the forces did their best
to keep morale high with military and sporting competitions and a
full timetable of training exercises there were lengthy periods of
inactivity and boredom. (Berlin, with its active night-life and the
artificial gaiety of its citizens was an exception.) Also, to some
National Servicemen there seemed to be a contradiction in the
conditions of their posting: although they were an army of
occupation (later of defence) in a defeated country, the conditions outside the bases seemed better than those at home.

> The streets and buildings in Germany and the Netherlands were
> clean and in good repair, the people were well-dressed and
> confident and the food seemed plentiful and of high quality. The
> first thing that struck me after only three weeks away was the
> drabness of austerity Britain. There were still bomb-sites in
> London overgrown with rosebay willow herb, the buildings were
> sooty and dilapidated with unrepaired war damage everywhere,
> and the people seemed tired and shabbily dressed, off-hand and
> dispirited. In contrast to the fast, clean and efficient trains and the
> huge lorries with trailers even then thundering along the auto-
> bahns, transport in Britain seemed to consist of dirty, slow trains
> and grinding, congested traffic. The Continent seemed even then
> to be on the road to the kind of lifestyle we are only used to now.
> (SAC David McNeill, RAF Coastal Command)
>
> I remember we went into Lüneburg just before Christmas 1951
> and it was quite amazing the things they had in the shops. On a
> Saturday there were market stalls in the streets and they were all
> displaying German sausages and fancy bread and all sorts of
> foodstuffs we had never seen before. I can still picture those stalls
> on a Saturday evening about 4 p.m. when it was getting dark and
> they were lit up with paraffin and Tilley type lamps and even with
> big candles. The smell of sausages and big German cigars is
> something I'll never forget.
> (Corporal John Inglis, RAF Regiment)

With financial assistance from the Marshall Plan, the massive American aid programme aimed at revitalising western Europe, Germany had taken rapid strides towards economic recovery. There was, too, the tradition of clearing up quickly after a war: for centuries the so-called 'cockpit of Europe' had been the site of all the major western European conflicts.

In 1955 the Federal Republic of Germany was permitted to become a full member of the NATO alliance, to rearm and thereby to make a full contribution to western defence. Its arrival on the strategic scene relieved pressure on BAOR's manpower difficulties, but to still French fears about the possibility of a German military resurgence it was agreed that the strength of the British forces in Germany should not fall below four divisions.

During this period the role of the allied forces in Germany had changed from that of an army of occupation to that of defence against eastern bloc aggression. The wartime alliance with the USSR had been shattered in 1948 by the blockade of West Berlin and the subsequent airlift during which the city was supplied by RAF and USAF transport aircraft flying round-the-clock missions. By cutting all land routes from the west into Berlin in June 1948, the Soviets hoped to induce the allies into removing their presence from West Berlin. The situation was retrieved by flying in supplies on a large scale. Between then and May 1949 the allied aircraft flew in a daily average of 7,000 tons of essential supplies. 130 RAF aircraft took part (later augmented by two squadrons of modern Hastings aircraft) as well as numerous aircraft flown by civilian charter operators. 18 RAF and 10 civilian aircrew lost their lives during the course of the operations.

The confrontation of the Berlin Airlift brought the USSR out into the open as a possible aggressor, and focussed the need to garrison Germany as the West's first line of defence in any future European war. To Gunner Gregor McIntosh, service with BAOR as a National Serviceman could be gently mocked with the standard army joke, 'We are guarding the Eastern Frontier against the might of the Russian Empire'; but that task, as all soldiers acknowledged, required constant training and battle practice.

> Most of the time we never knew just what was happening. Can you imagine digging no less than five slit trenches in the space of about three hours on the same evening and all in about a two hundred yards area? Of course, it always seemed to rain and the best protection I found was a tin hat and gas cape. Another bind – a

twelve-mile tactical withdrawal march, always in the dark. 'Keep
on the grass verge, don't lose the man in front. Here, Jock, your
turn to carry the mortar (32 bloody pounds).' That was the night I
fell asleep while marching. When you finally reach your destina-
tion, it's 'All dig in before you rest.'
                        (Corporal C. W. Phelps, 1st Bn. Gordon Highlanders)

In addition to the garrison towns of northern Germany the
army made its presence most felt on Lüneburg Heath, which
became the main training area for the British forces in the
country.

On Monday 3 March 1952 we went on our first exercise as a
squadron with all our equipment. It was called 'Exercise Har-
dener'. All I remember about it was that it was b— cold . . . We
only stayed away till the Wednesday but it felt like eternity. At
nights we slept in the rear of the trucks in full uniform with our
issue blankets piled all over us. On the day we were returning to
Lüneburg the CO told us we all had to smarten up and wash and
shave. We were in a wood somewhere and the cooks boiled up
water and each of us got a mess-tin of hot water to wash and shave
in. It was bitterly cold to say the least, and without exaggerating by
the time you walked the length of the convoy and back to your
vehicle the water was cold and beginning to ice over . . . We had
one Pilot Officer who stripped to the waist and shaved to set an
example to the men. When we got back to the camp he developed
pneumonia and had to be flown back to England for treatment and
we did not see him again for two months.
                        (Corporal John Inglis, RAF Regiment)

Lüneburg Heath was the home of 'schemes' or manoeuvres
during which units were tested in realistic battlefield situations for
service anywhere in the world. Having lost India as a training
ground, the Army soon discovered that Germany – despite its
drawbacks – provided an acceptable alternative.

Of all the postings on offer to National Servicemen between 1945
and 1956, the Suez Canal Zone has left the most indelible mark.
If you fell into the waters of the Sweet Water Canal*, you were
told on arrival at Ismailia, you were more likely to die from
poisoning than drowning. The fly-blown, sand-strewn military

*The Sweet Water Canal, or Tur'at As-Suways Al-Hulwah, was completed in
1863 to provide drinking water to an otherwise arid area. It was cut from the
delta to Wadi Tumelat and a southern branch ran to Suez. In an oasis near Suez
are the Springs of Moses which Moses is supposed to have made miraculously
sweet.

bases with their lack of facilities were forlorn and disagreeable, the climate was vile and the local population hostile. It was without doubt the least popular posting for any serviceman, National Service or otherwise.

> The objective was to 'protect' the canal from those who might want to take it over – and this principally meant the Egyptians themselves. Militarily and economically, the canal was of immense importance to British imperialism. Its control and protection were possible only with the force of a conscripted army. Thousands of young men spent two very uneventful boring years in unbearable camps guarding the canal. It was a soul-destroying experience and one which conscripts hated. To them it seemed a pointless experience – mostly spent in boring daily routine duties which were utterly meaningless.
>
> (Private Charles Lubelski, 1st Bn. West Yorkshire Regiment)

> In Egypt everything was restricted – most places were off-limits, including Cairo. Everywhere we went it was with armed guards. It was dirty, very hot and sometimes unpleasant. Mostly it was boring and monotonous – confined behind barbed wire with regular guard duties.
>
> (Lance-Corporal Arthur Franks,
> 1st Bn. West Yorkshire Regiment)

To understand why the British should have found themselves in such a God-forsaken strip of land as the Suez Canal Zone, the National Serviceman had to dig back in the history books to the year 1882 and the British military intervention in Egypt in support of the Khedive, the Sultan of Turkey's viceroy. Originally Britain was only to have stayed for six years, but using a variety of guises it remained in virtual control of the country until 1936 when Egypt was granted independence. Even then, the British grip was not entirely loosened: a garrison 10,000-strong was permitted to guard the Suez Canal, Britain's route to her imperial possessions in the Far East and the real reason for her presence in Egypt. During World War II Egypt became a vital military centre for the war in North Africa and the Middle East, and a staging post for war in the East. By its conclusion most Egyptians felt that the presence of a foreign garrison in their country was an affront to their national dignity, and at the end of 1945 the Prime Minister Nokrashy Pasha put pressure on the British government to revise the 1936 treaty by removing her troops from Egyptian soil. Rioting broke out in Cairo and Alexandria, and the first British servicemen were murdered.

The British response was to move its garrisons out of the cities and to take up residence in the Suez Canal Zone. To that end, GHQ was established at Fayid on the eastern shore of the Great Bitter Lake, and the military camps and air bases at places like Tel-el-Kebir and Abu Sueir were hastily reinforced and put on the alert. By 1950 the British garrisons were locked in the Zone, ostensibly guarding the Suez Canal but in effect protecting themselves and British possessions from the outraged nationalists. The Zone had long been known as 'The Graveyard of the British Army': for the 54 servicemen killed there between then and the final withdrawal in 1956, the nickname was all too literal.

> I recall being very depressed at Christmas 1953 as I received no letters or parcels from home – later I received a charred label and a note to say that the mail truck had been blown up and the contents destroyed. On reflection it was a small price to pay in comparison with some of my colleagues who suffered severe injury, death or who knows what. I still find myself wondering about the two Royal Signals who just disappeared while out checking lines – what their parents thought and whether to this day they know what happened to their sons. Due to lack of press coverage it came as a bit of a surprise on disembarking at Port Said to find the train heavily guarded by armed troops – we were totally unaware that there was anti-British feeling in Egypt.
> (Lance-Corporal Bob Downie, Royal Army Ordnance Corps)
>
> Patrols were sent out to guard cables against terrorist attack. On one patrol, of which I was not part, the officer in charge placed his bren guns and ordered the gunners to open fire if anyone should cross their line of fire. He took the remainder of the patrol away, got lost and led his men in front of the bren guns. As instructed the gunners opened fire, one or two men were killed and the battalion goalkeeper had a testicle shot off.
> (Lance-Corporal R. Dulson, 1st Bn. The Cheshire Regiment)

The arrival of the British forces in the Suez Canal Zone, far from appeasing the Egyptians, only served to give notice to nationalist leaders that Britain was susceptible to pressure. On 15 October 1951 the new Prime Minister, Nahas Pasha, formally abrogated the treaty of 1936, thereby destroying the legal right of the British forces to remain in his country. Rioting broke out again, servicemen and their families were attacked and Egyptian labour was withdrawn from the British bases. Much of the violence was fermented by the *Bulak Nizam*, paramilitary auxiliaries who quickly mastered the hit-and-run tactics of guerrilla warfare. Following several months of ambush and murder, the British retaliated on 25 January 1952 when forty auxiliaries were killed after a pitched battle in the streets of Ismailia. The Egyptian response was to burn down British property in Cairo, but by then the end of the violence was almost in sight.

With the prospect of the British taking over control of his country, King Farouk dismissed Nahas Pasha and restored some order by outlawing the *Bulak Nizam*. Six months later Farouk was himself deposed and replaced by a military council under Major-General Mohammed Neguib: the way was left open for both sides to negotiate a handover of British power. By then, too, Churchill's government was aware of the impossibility of maintaining a huge garrison – now 70,000 strong – without Egyptian support, and steps were already in hand to rehouse the British military presence in the Middle East in Cyprus. In April 1954 Neguib was succeeded by Colonel Gamal Abdul Nasser; agreement was reached on 19 October that same year, giving Britain 20 months to quit the country; and the last British garrison troops, 2nd Bn. Grenadier Guards, left Port Said on 24 March 1956. It seemed to everyone that after 74 years the British link with Egypt had finally come to an end.

During the lengthy negotiations, which almost foundered on dented British pride, outright violence more or less came to an end but the sense of hostility never evaporated. British bases became the targets for terrorist raids and it was virtually impossible to prevent the succession of break-ins and thefts. For the National Servicemen, therefore, to whom a posting to Egypt might have meant long hot days guarding filtration plants along the Sweet Water Canal, there were also frequent moments of tension and danger.

> Movement out of our own area (Abu Sultan) was severely limited and so we saw little, if anything, of the country apart from the sand and the odd garrison town like Fayid or Moascar. Single vehicles were not allowed out of the main gate, there had to be at least two, one of which had to act as armed escort, and every vehicle had to have an escort riding shot-gun. If on foot there had to be at least four of you – one of whom had to be armed. Jeeps had to have a wire-cutting attachment at the front to prevent decapitation by wires stretched across the road. The tactic of cutting-off the last vehicle of a convoy by a 'taxi' or other vehicle was well known and consequently steps were taken to prevent overtaking in this way. Escorts and guard duties were carried out with loaded weapons ready for immediate use.
>
> (Lance-Corporal Bob Downie, Royal Army Ordnance Corps)

With the local population sullen and hostile, the towns in the Zone were generally out of bounds unless an armed guard were present, and as a result servicemen had to manufacture their own entertainment within the bases.

> There were good points – you could swim daily, we played cricket all the year round and we weren't short of money. To begin with we had a NAAFI run by Egyptians. I remember that they were sacked and replaced by Greeks – from then on the NAAFI was first-class with excellent meals and ice-cold beer. I had some good friends and these friendships lasted for many years. I had no real complaints, just the usual gripes all young lads have.
>
> (Lance-Corporal Arthur Franks,
> 1st Bn. West Yorkshire Regiment)

Towards the end of the British occupation restrictions were lifted, and parties of servicemen were permitted to visit Cairo and the archaeological sites on the Nile. Others made their way to Port Said, traditional home of the tout, the postcard seller and the hawker.

> One chap fell victim to a classic con trick. An Arab came along and asked if anyone wanted to buy a watch; it looked good and the price was reasonable. The Arab was paid and off he went down the road, then the buyer suddenly realised that the watch had stopped and that it would not start again. Some of the men, sten guns at the ready, raced after the Arab who was caught and brought back again. He offered the money, took back the watch and promptly disappeared. The buyer was so relieved to get his money back that he put it in his pocket; then, realising that the Arab had hopped it rather quickly, took the money out of his pocket to find that he had a top note and a bottom note and pieces of paper in between. We sure learned some things the hard way.
>
> (Signalman R. G. Jones, Royal Corps of Signals)

Depending on your perspective, Port Said was either the historic crossroads of Empire or the 'arsehole of the world'. P&O liners en route to Bombay and Singapore passed through it into the Suez Canal, allowing their passengers to be amazed by the antics of the gully-gully men conjuring chickens out of thin air or the small boys diving into the murky waters below the ship for baksheesh. Ashore, in the shady houses in the town's alley-ways, generations of soldiers had fornicated and drunk themselves into oblivion, usually being swindled in the process. The Eastern Telegraph building and the Casino Palace Hotel were regarded in their own way as imperial symbols; and yet, for all that romance, Egypt and the Egyptians were regarded as something of a joke by the British. 'King Farouk, King Farouk, 'ang 'is bollocks on a hook,' sang the soldiers: few servicemen knew why they were in the Suez Canal Zone or why their presence there was so unpopular. Yet, paradoxically, the reasons usually unfolded during their posting – the demonstrations and the terrorist attacks were difficult to ignore – and it was in the Zone that most National Servicemen came to terms with the fact that Britain's imperial influence was on the wane. No other posting, perhaps, brought home the message that Britain's withdrawal from Empire would be dictated by the vocabulary of sandbag, roadblock, barbed wire and rearguard action.

The first inkling had come in Palestine, where between 1945 and 1948 Jewish terrorists waged a hard-hitting and eventually successful guerrilla war against the British, throughout the troubles holding down two divisions – the 6th Airborne and 1st Infantry – as well as two maritime reconnaissance squadrons, four fighter squadrons, a photographic reconnaissance squadron and a transport squadron.

In November 1917, under the terms of the Balfour Declaration, Britain had promoted the principle of creating a national home for the Jewish people in Palestine; the League of Nations had ratified this proposal by entrusting the mandate of Palestine to Britain, but Arab dissent in the 1930s had persuaded the British government to give its ear to the Arab cause. (Palestine contained 600,000 Arabs and only 55,000 Jews.) Jewish immigration was restricted and a British military presence established in Palestine to deal with civil unrest and to provide a strategic reserve for the Middle East.

At the end of the Second World War, the continuing restrictions – only 1,500 Jews per year were permitted to enter Palestine – finally persuaded Jewish nationalists to stage a military offensive against the British. For two years the Jewish secret army, the *Haganah*, and its extremist factions, the *Irgun Zuai Leumi* and the Stern Gang, waged a ferocious guerrilla war against the occupying British forces. The King David Hotel, housing the British secretariat in Jerusalem, was blown up on 22 July 1946; other outrages included the kidnap and murder of British personnel, an endless stream of assassinations, and the destruction of aircraft at RAF bases. In all, 223 officers and men, several of them National Servicemen, were killed during the three-year period of 'aid to the civil power' (as the British termed it), or the war of liberation (the Jewish point of view). In

ber 1947 Britain announced that she would hand over the
to the United Nations, but between then and the final
al in June 1948 units of the British Army remained in
country in a vain attempt to keep apart Jews and Arabs, who
were by then engaged in a bloody civil war.

One problem facing the British in Palestine after the war was
that their moral stance was difficult to maintain. Many of the
British troops there had fought in Europe against the Germans
and were loath to act the bully against the Jewish people, many of
whom were concentration camp survivors. For their part, Zionist
organisations were able to put tremendous international pressure
on Britain, and the photographs of Royal Navy gunboats turning
back illegal Jewish immigrants aboard rickety tramp steamers did
nothing for Britain's standing in the world community. Ideally,
Britain would have preferred to see Jew and Arab live in
harmony and then to have established in Palestine its Middle East
headquarters to watch over the Suez Canal. To that end,
arrangements were made to build a huge installation at Gaza
which would have housed the units from Egypt, but the handover
to the United Nations put paid to those ambitions.

For all servicemen stationed there, Palestine was an unwelcome posting. 'I looked upon it then as an unpleasant duty and
though I was frightened, we all were,' recalls Lieutenant
Alexander Dunbar, 1st Camerons, attached to 1st Argyll and
Sutherland Highlanders in Lydda and Jaffa in 1947. 'We were a
hundred times better off, though, than our immediate seniors
who had had to fight in a six year war.'

The young conscripts in Palestine had ample cause to be
frightened. The *Irgun* was a brutal enemy which used ruthless
tactics to achieve its aims. One example of its methods will stand
for many. On 5 April 1948 a platoon of the 1st Highland Light
Infantry was patrolling the system of tunnels and catacombs
below the Holy Sepulchre in Jerusalem when a booby-trap bomb
exploded, killing 2nd Lieutenant Alasdair Hilleary, a National
Service officer. 'His was the course of the brilliant comet,' wrote
his friend 2nd Lieutenant James Kennaway, 'snuffed out by some
underhand Jew. Never let anyone talk to me of sympathy for the
Jews: I have never felt more like murder in my life.'[13] Feelings
like those were also part of the British problem. At first, revolted
by the exposure of the Nazi concentration camps, most ordinary
British people felt an overwhelming sympathy for the Jewish
plight in Palestine: but three years of outrage and hardship had
whittled down the original emotion to numb resignation or even

outright hatred. Although British forces were supposed to be in Palestine in aid of the population, the harsh reality of the situation ensured that they were virtually at war with the Jewish terrorists.

With their ambition of maintaining a military presence in the Middle East at an end in Palestine and Egypt, Britain looked again at her bases in Cyprus, the Mediterranean island which had been in her possession since 1878. Disraeli, who had engineered the transfer at the Congress of Berlin, had been captivated by its acquisition and had sold it to the British public as the romantic isle where Aphrodite had dallied with Adonis, and where in later years one of its governors had smothered his wife Desdemona in a fit of jealousy. More realistically, the War Office regarded Cyprus as a second Malta, a strategic base in the eastern Mediterranean which could guard the Levant and, more importantly, the Suez Canal: in that role Cyprus had long been regarded as a beautiful and sleepy posting where the bases had all the atmosphere of holiday camps.

No sooner had Britain announced that her Middle East Command would be moved to Cyprus, than she found herself embroiled once more in a terrorist war waged by those inhabitants hostile to her presence on the island. The majority of the half million Cypriots were Greek, and the announcement of the establishment of Middle East Command coincided with an upswell of popular opinion that Cyprus should come under the rule of their Greek motherland. This movement towards *Enosis*, or union with Greece, was given substantial moral and political impetus by Archbishop Makarios, and between 1955 and 1959 it spilled over into violence as Greek Cypriot guerrillas formed themselves into the National Organisation of Cyprus Fighters (EOKA) under the leadership of Colonel George Grivas. During the EOKA emergency, 105 servicemen and 50 policemen were murdered in addition to 240 civilians, 26 of whom were British.

As was the case in other troublespots, the services did little to inform their men about why they were involved in the fighting, or why the local population was antagonistic to their presence. While stationed at the British Military Hospitals at Nicosia and Dhekelia in 1959, Corporal Peter Davies, RAMC, experienced a mixture of 'Anger and fear. Anger that you were in a situation you did not understand, and fear that you might not get back home.' Later, his feelings turned to bitterness when he realised that the lives of National Servicemen were being risked in a political game which could never be solved by force. At the height of the disturbances, as in Egypt, servicemen were not allowed out of camp unless they had an armed escort, and all the quarters on the military bases were always heavily guarded. Eventually the continuing terrorist warfare led to intercommunal fighting between the island's Greek and Turkish populations, and Britain turned over the problem of internal security to the forces of the United Nations.

Yet for all the difficulties of those four years of violence, Cyprus, with its beaches and its golden climate, had much to offer young soldiers and airmen. Even under the watchful eyes of armed guards the beach was still the beach and the waters of the Mediterranean still warm and inviting. Despite the violence and the threat of sudden death in the narrow streets of the five principal towns, large elements of the population remained on friendly terms, and throughout the EOKA emergency the military authorities preached the doctrine of integration not confrontation. Because the terrorists concentrated their efforts on the urban areas, the countryside retained an air of calm where servicemen could live in conditions of some safety – even at the height of the troubles.

A feature of Cyprus life was its transitory nature. Small camps of about half-a-dozen men, comprising, say, a battalion's 'Rear Detail', dotted the island, and the RAF in particular spawned several tented villages, Cotswold effigies, like the one belonging to a signals unit at Cape Gata near Akrotiri.

> We were in a small unit and we all lived in tents. I remember that there were about four rows of these things and we constructed front gardens and built timber walls round the sides so we only had tented roofs. I worked for a big shipping company before National Service and they sent out fitted curtains for my tent. It was quite spectacular.

> (SAC John Murphy, RAF)

Another feature of service life on the island, especially for hard-up National Servicemen, was babysitting. Several hundred service families lived there, and even though conditions could be dangerous the authorities still went to considerable lengths to lay on entertainments for the families of its Regulars.

> One could volunteer to act as a babysitter for the families and this I did. Once a fortnight a vehicle would take us to our respective family and pick up the lady of the house and take her to the

meeting point. In return for babysitting I was left food to cook myself a meal, 20 cigarettes and a bottle of whisky to help myself from. Also I was allowed to have a hot bath – a luxury after cold showers.

There was an English farmer locally and I took orders and delivered poultry from him at Christmas.

Entertainment was more available, cinemas, cabaret shows, the beach, and I did see some of the island, although, looking back I realise I didn't take advantage to explore the island more fully.

(Lance-Corporal R. Dulson, 1st Bn. Cheshire Regiment)

Dogs, too, were an important ingredient of domestic life in Cyprus. As had always happened in other parts of the world, servicemen away from home befriended local strays, and dog-ownership gave a warm reminder of the affection the men had left behind in civilian life. Soldiers took stray animals 'on the strength', almost as if the love and tenderness they were able to bestow on the beast compensated for the conditions of life both had to endure. Because dogs will normally return devotion with interest they were popular pets with servicemen on Cyprus; because the islanders did not hold dogs in any special regard they were never in short supply, and no base was without its share of soldiers' pets. Occasionally, when the military dog population got too large or there was a rabies scare, the authorities would clamp down and order the Military Police to go on a 'dog hunt'. The rounding-up and the shooting of their pets upset many men, who felt doubly aggrieved if the MPs turned the round-up into a full-scale hunt with whoops and tally-hos, terrorising the already frightened beasts. When the dogs were ordered to be destroyed at Cape Gata, John Murphy and his fellow airmen took retaliatory action which bordered on mutiny.

There was a decision taken that stray dogs should be rounded up and destroyed. What is a stray dog to one person is inevitably someone else's pet. All these dogs roamed around the place and there must have been thirty or forty of them, but they were all fed and they all had names. The MPs duly arrived one day to shoot the dogs. Then the unit turned out and formed a human barrier between the police and the dogs which were all smuggled off and hidden in the undergrowth. It developed into quite a riot. The unit was wrecked and it ended up with the signals room being burned down and the CO's office being totally destroyed by one of those great mobile fire extinguishers from the Motor Transport Section. We actually put the radar off air but the whole thing was hushed up.

(SAC John Murphy, RAF)

Because feelings were running high the RAF authorities took no action, and presumably a security blanket was thrown over the whole affair. Yet during the course of the riot RAF Middle East Command lost the services of its fighter control for the eastern Mediterranean and thousands of pounds' worth of damage was done to the radar equipment. Incidents of that kind were extremely rare but it is easy to see why the affair was hushed up. By 1959 National Service was beginning to run down and was extremely unpopular at home in Britain. Any severe punishment meted out to the young RAF conscripts for their part in the 'Dogs of War' incident, as it had become known, would have created the kind of press publicity both the Air Ministry and the War Office was anxious to avoid. Besides, man's best friend was involved in the incident, and as things turned out the dogs also benefited. Stay of execution was granted and they were allowed to take their chances with the local population.

Between 1945 and 1969 Britain retained a military and air force presence in Libya, which had been won from the Italians during World War II by means of military conquest. With its principal bases at Tripoli, Tobruk, Benghazi and El Adem, Libya was regarded essentially as a training area, although towards the end of the British occupation military units were used more to bolster the regime of King Idris than for any strategic purpose. Elsewhere in the Middle East the RAF maintained a fighter base at Amman in Jordan between 1948 and 1957, and when Cyprus failed as a base in 1959 thoughts turned briefly to using Kenya in that role. For those few National Servicemen posted there after the Mau Mau menace had been defeated, Kenya was an idyllic setting. 'The posting of our Signals unit to the outskirts of Nairobi for my last ten months of service was of course the highlight,' remembers Signalman Peter Smith who was based there in 1961 with 602 Signals Troop, Royal Signals. 'At weekends we had trips to the gameparks. Some colleagues climbed Kilimanjaro for their holidays whilst I chose the coast at Mombasa.'

Kenya became independent in 1963, and with other countries taking the same path Britain's military involvement in East Africa was confined thereafter to the occasional aid to the civil power (Tanzania, January 1964, for example) or assistance after natural disasters (Kenya, October 1964). By the mid-1960s, though, Britain's military presence in Africa was limited to Libya (eventually evacuated 1969–1970) and her imperial holdings there and in the Middle East were at an end.

After World War II the British forces continued to maintain their major bases east of Suez in Malaya, Singapore and Hong Kong. The reasons for that presence were twofold: defence of the colonial territories and Britain's trading interests, and as a contribution to the stability of the area. The beginning of the Malayan Emergency in 1948 and of the Korean War two years later put the Far East forces on a war footing, and British servicemen were to be involved in fighting of one kind or another in the area until 1966 and the end of the confrontation in Borneo.

For a large number of National Servicemen a posting to the Far East spelled danger, discomfort or death on active service; but for many more, Malaya and Singapore – the two territories which contained the largest military bases – the posting meant Tiger Beer, sexy hostesses in exotic nightclubs, a hint of eastern promise and recreation areas of outstanding natural beauty.

> The city [Kuala Lumpur] itself is safe for Europeans and they are indeed the ruling class here [he wrote to J. M. Lee]. The public buildings are very dignified and well designed and even the railway station looks like an oriental palace. It is in fact the most beautiful city I have seen. The native quarter, populated by Chinese, Malays and Tamils, is much the same as in most eastern cities – picturesque, colourful, hot, smelly and romantic. I realise now that I did a wise thing by volunteering for the Far East. I would not miss this opportunity of seeing the world for any price. Many of the things at which I used to sneer in exotic novels, the things which I thought existed mainly in imagination, I now see at first hand. Bananas, coconuts, melons, monkeys, lizards, fireflies, deserted palm-fringed beaches, all make life seem one long unbelievable holiday.
>
> (SAC Graham Mottershaw, RAF)

Britain had come into possession of her colonies on the Malay peninsula through a series of treaties signed with local rulers between 1874 and 1910. (Singapore, the island on the southern tip of the peninsula, had been in British hands since 1819 when it was acquired by the impetuous merchant adventurer, Stamford Raffles.) Known first as the Straits Settlements (Penang, Province Wellesley and Malacca), the Malayan states of Perak, Selangor, Negri Sembilan and Pahang joined them in federation under

British suzerainty in 1896, giving up their independence in return for British support and investment in the country's tin and rubber industries. Malaya quickly established itself as one of the wealthiest components of the Empire, and Kuala Lumpur, its capital, became one of the great imperial stamping grounds, a city of handsome white buildings built in a strange mixture of English and Moorish architectural styles.

World War II marked the beginning of the end of Britain's imperial hold on the Malay peninsula. In January 1942 the Japanese army bicycled down through Malaya, bombarded the 'impregnable' fortress of Singapore, crossed over the Straits of Johore, and within a few weeks of the invasion had trounced Britain's imperial forces. The promises to the Malayan people of British protection fell in ashes, around 100,000 servicemen went into brutal captivity and British influence in the area was never to be the same again. In 1945 the British did return to Malaya, and through a series of new (and unpopular) confederations attempted to go on as before. But it was too late: there was now a determined nationalist opposition to their presence, resistance which soon broke out into armed rebellion. During the war, Malayan opposition to the Japanese invaders had been headed by the Malayan Communist Party (MCP) and its Malayan Peoples Anti-Japanese Army (MPAJA), which had received substantial supplies from the British. Once hostilities against the Japanese had ceased these same men turned their weapons against the British as the Malayan Races Liberation Army (MRLA), and in 1948 a State of Emergency was declared. The violence did not finally come to an end until 1960.

In spite of the dangers attendant on living in a country in which attacks on civilians and military personnel were an everyday fact of life, Malaya was not an unpopular posting, even amongst units whose task was waging war against the MRLA. Malaya had an agreeable climate – hot and humid all the year round – the people were generally friendly and not undisposed to the British servicemen, and there were ample opportunities when on leave to enjoy such luxuries as swimming on deserted tropical beaches or sampling new and exotic food. Malaya also provided the setting for two of the best novels of the National Service period, Alan Sillitoe's *Key to the Door* and Leslie Thomas's *The Virgin Soldiers*, both of which involve (in different ways) a sexual relationship between a National Serviceman and a local Chinese girl.

Trooper Brian Wilkinson, 11th Hussars, thought Malaya 'a

beautiful country and the memory of it can never be forgotten. At times it was like one long holiday and despite the difficulties, you can put up with a lot at eighteen, especially when the climate's good.' Few National Servicemen would disagree with that assessment, although a hint of resentment does mar some memories of the local British population.

> I was angry when the British planters and their families adopted a superior attitude towards us. It was annoying that all our efforts went unsung in this country, despite our superiors telling us time and time again that 'we were to be good ambassadors for our country'.
> (Corporal David McMurray, Royal Army Service Corps)

Although the Japanese had dented the imperial legend in the Far East, the post-war British colonial caste still had a good conceit of itself. In Kuala Lumpur, Robinsons was a good substitute for Harrods; cricket was played on the Padang in Singapore as if it were Lords; and the clubs and hill stations still aspired to the manners of pre-war Anglo-India. In such a society the ordinary soldier did not enjoy a particularly high status and so the military authorities contrived to keep their rank and file distanced from the patrician English community. It was a case of Kipling's 'Tommy Atkins' all over again. (Even in wartime Calcutta, Firpos, a fashionable English watering-hole, maintained its policy of refusing entry to 'Indians, dogs and private soldiers'.) Little wonder that when they came to write of their time in Malaya, novelists Alan Sillitoe and Leslie Thomas painted in such detail a picture of forlorn National Servicemen seeking love and affection amongst the hostesses in the dancehalls of Singapore and Muong.

For the officers, it was all rather different.

> I enjoyed the magic carpet of S55 choppers taking us out of the filth and swamp to a Mess dining-in night the same evening. I enjoyed meeting planters who had survived the Jap period . . . I took duty officer in Sellerang Mess on the occasion of the SEATO conference and entertained the delegates (French secretaries) and wondered why my French was becoming most fluent. I discovered a friend (a mess waiter) was lacing my soft drinks all evening and I suddenly found the world went sideways just before I took my staff parade. I was roused in the early morning by a corporal who was in my Scout troop at school, just in time to change into greens from Mess kit. Very near thing!
> (2nd Lieutenant A. D. S. MacMillan, 1st Bn. The Royal Scots, attached 1st Bn. King's Own Scottish Borderers)

While stationed in the Far East, regiments tended to make special attempts to preserve such rituals as Guest Nights and dining-in nights. Officers would don number 1 dress uniforms or patrols, the regimental silver would be displayed and local worthies would be entertained in a style which even post-war austerity had done little to tarnish: the most sought-after invitations were those given by Messes offering traditional Sunday curry lunches with fiercely spiced Indian and Malaysian dishes. (Entertainments of that kind were not offered by regiments on active service in forward bases.) In return, officers were invited to the clubs and spent time with local planters and officials, thereby cementing the traditional links which existed in all postings between the Mess and local society.

In no other garrison was this more the case than in Hong Kong where 12,000 officers and men watched over British interests. Ostensibly the regiments stationed in the New Territories were there to prevent a possible Chinese invasion, but so remote was that possibility – except during the Korean War – that a posting to Hong Kong was considered something of a luxury. Its very Englishness inspired confidence, from the spire of the noble church of St John's to the racecourse at Happy Valley, from the seat of power at Government House to the stately mansions on the Peak, from the busy warships in the harbour to the Indian-style bungalow barracks at Queen's Hill camp. And in the background lay the mysteries of the Orient, the bustle of the Chinese quarter, the sampans and the rickshaws and the new sights and exotic smells. Military life there was unhurried and well ordered, duties were light and training kept to a minimum. In no other posting did officers come into so little contact with their men or could the relationship between the two be so undemanding.

> Our platoon officer was a 'Wild West' fanatic and always had us playing at '7th cavalry' with himself as John Wayne. On one occasion as we trained on a hill above a Chinese village he said, 'There's Apaches down there . . . extended line! Fix swords!' (In a rifle regiment that's a bayonet.) 'And . . . Charge!' And so we charged down the hill following him through the village emitting appropriate yells much to the alarm of the Chinese villagers and livestock who fled indoors. We all felt quite foolish at this later.
> (Rifleman George Savage, 1st Bn. Royal Ulster Rifles)

With time hanging heavy on their hands, men either took advantage of the sporting and recreational facilities available to them and took their leaves in neighbouring countries, or they stayed in camp and moped, unable to come to terms with their temporary service in a strange land. Those who took the former option rarely regretted their attitude to service life abroad.

> The Hong Kong posting was in some ways idyllic – swimming was a regular pastime. There were opportunities to travel and I took three-and-a-half weeks leave on a ship to Japan. Sporting activities were encouraged and I represented the regiment in cross-country running.
>
> (Gunner John Shepherd, Royal Regiment of Artillery)

> Although nearly always broke we managed some trips to Kowloon to see the sights, nosh-up, visit the cinema and to purchase small gifts to send home. We warned each other of the perils of the brothels . . . 'Blobby nob stops demob!' And counted the days with one eye on the clock and one eye on the calendar.
>
> (Rifleman George Savage, 1st Bn. Royal Ulster Rifles)

Most National Servicemen – whether or not they had travelled abroad before – regarded an overseas posting as one of the more tangible benefits of their service life. In some cases they might have been involved in fighting and encountered death and violence for the first time in their lives, in others they might have had to endure a vile climate, antiquated barracks and long days of boredom; but there were many compensations. While stationed abroad, far from the moral confines of home and family, they could be more independent and act differently; drink and cigarettes were generally cheaper, the night life in some places more exotic, and many admit that an overseas posting, especially in the Far East, provided them with their first sexual experience.

In those innocent days, too, few questions were asked about Britain's strategic role in the far-flung places of the world, and most National Servicemen did not ask why their presence was so unpopular or why outrage, terrorism and riot had become constant companions in once friendly colonies.

Chapter Seven

THE NATIONAL SERVICEMEN'S WARS: MALAYA AND KOREA

During the period of National Service not a year passed without British servicemen seeing action in one part of the world or another. Those years also saw 2,912 servicemen killed in action, 395 of whom were National Servicemen. In fact, it is a sorry statistic that in the period between the end of World War II and the present day (1986) only 1968 stands out as the one year in which no British soldier, sailor or airman has been killed in action.

To put that statistic into perspective, however, many of the incidents in which servicemen were killed were terrorist attacks on personnel or bases in countries where the British military presence was no longer acceptable, colonies straining to be free like Cyprus, Kenya and Malaya. As so often happened in Britain's imperial history, while the politicians talked, the soldiers endured the consequence of terrorist attack and murder, followed by low-level counter-insurgency operations, a facet of warfare in which the British Army soon began to excel. It came as little surprise to military observers in 1976 that when the Soviet Union published a survey of post-war 'Imperial Aggression' Britain was awarded prime place in its league of 'aggressors'. Even after the loss of India the habit of Empire died hard, and throughout the 1950s politicians – and a large section of the British people – still regarded Britain as an imperial power. Trade routes had to be guarded, treaties honoured and the colonies defended: all these required a military or naval presence. Later, when the imperial dreams were seen to be an illusion, those same servicemen had to cover the withdrawal from Empire, remaining in colonies as a kind of imperial gendarmerie as one outpost after another struggled its way towards independence.

Many National Servicemen found themselves caught up in

those outbreaks of violence, trying to maintain order in countries where the uniform they wore only seemed to goad further the population they were supposed to be protecting. During the same period, National Servicemen were also caught up in two major conflicts which turned into full-scale military operations: the counter-insurgency war against Communist terrorists in Malaya, which lasted from 1948 to 1960, and the British contribution to the United Nations' operations in Korea between August 1950 and July 1953.

The long drawn-out war in Malaya against the terrorists of the MRLA was regarded by British and by most foreign observers as the only example of a successful counter-insurgency campaign against terrorists in the post-war years. That it was so was due in no small measure to the part played in it by National Servicemen, particularly to those National Servicemen who served in infantry battalions. Nearly half the officers and men of the 1st Suffolk Regiment were National Service conscripts and while they were on duty in Malaya between May 1949 and February 1953 they gained a hard-won reputation for their expertise at 'jungle bashing', the infantry patrols into the jungle aimed at engaging the hard core terrorists.

> It would be impossible to imagine worse country in which to fight than this stinking, swampy, leech-infested secondary jungle, so different from the beautiful Suffolk countryside in which the majority of young National Servicemen had grown up. Four hundred yards of backbreaking sweat in one hour was good progress and ambushes were purgatory because the enemy, like wild beasts, could detect the slightest movement, so the attention of wasps, bees and above all myriads of mosquitoes had to be borne stoically. Day after day, month after month, the young soldiers would struggle their way through the jungle, reporting by wireless the now monotonous 'Non Tare Roger', nothing to report. But when action did come, it was all over in a split second. To succeed under these conditions, special duties of leadership, discipline and good regimental spirit were required. All these were forthcoming in the Suffolk Regiment and literally within months these young boys became jungle veterans.[14]

The regiment received that encomium from an admirer, Lt-General Sir Brian Horrocks, in 1969 after the Suffolks had been transformed into the 1st Bn., Royal Anglian Regiment; but their exploits in Malaya also speak for themselves. During their tour they accounted for 198 terrorists killed, one of whom was the noted terrorist leader Liew Kon Kim who met his end against a Suffolk patrol commanded by 2nd Lieutenant Hands, a National Service subaltern. For their part in the Malayan campaign the Suffolks were awarded 2 DSOs, 1 OBE, 1 MBE, 9 Military Crosses (one of which was awarded to Hands), 2 Military Medals and 1 British Empire Medal. Most of their time had been spent at Kajang, fighting in the forests of Selangor where their own losses were 12 killed and 24 wounded.

Most infantry regiments in Malaya regarded their tour of duty as their most gruelling post-war action. Not only did they have to accustom themselves to fighting a jungle war after training for combat in the European theatre of operations, but they had to engage a concealed enemy skilled at hit-and-run tactics. At the outset of their campaign the terrorists, led by Chin Peng OBE, had moved into the jungle where they had a secure base and could rely on support from many of the Chinese villagers. (Malays usually had to be coerced.) The geography and terrain of Malaya suited their purpose: it is largely a land of mountains and dense tropical forest, and the west and east coasts are divided by a mountain range where the highest peaks are 7,000 feet or more. The coasts and the jungle share the same tropical climate; it is generally hot all the year round, temperatures varying between 70° and 90° Fahrenheit. Rainfall varies more widely but is high everywhere, the average being about 98 inches a year. The wettest part of the peninsula, Maxwell Hill near Ipoh in Perak, scene of some of the hardest jungle fighting, receives 232 inches of rain a year. To make life even more difficult for the jungle fighter, the north-east monsoons hit the east coast between November and April and the south-west monsoons the west coast from May to October. The combination of heat, rain and dense tropical forest made Malaya a frighteningly strange battle-ground, one which tried and tested even the most hard-bitten veteran.

> There followed two weeks of arduous marching and back-breaking toil. Every day for two or three hours the rain beat down through the canopy of foliage two hundred feet above our heads. It soaked through our clothes, through our skins, into the marrow in our bones. It turned the soft sand-soil floor of the jungle into a treacherous slippery quagmire. Our route lay across the grain of hilly country. We had to climb each ridge, dragging ourselves up the steep slopes, using hands, feet and knees and every muscle in our aching bodies to maintain balance and keep moving upwards.

On reaching the top we would move along the ridge for a little way and then down the other side, slipping and sliding, clutching at every bush and sapling to prevent a headlong fall to the unseen raging torrent that crashed its way along the floor of the narrow valley below. On reaching the bottom, half-dead with fatigue, we must cross the stream, slowly feeling our way across the shifting boulders, hand in hand waist-deep in the madly rushing waters. And then, up again, over the next ridge. And at each step we had to fight the thick clinging undergrowth, hacking a way through with machetes while thorns tore at us.[15]

This description of a jungle patrol, written by Major A. F. Campbell of the Suffolks, is one that few National Servicemen who did a spell of jungle bashing in Malaya would fail to recognise. That these physically draining routines were necessary was due to the strategy of one man, Lt-General Sir Harold Briggs, who was appointed Director of Operations in Malaya in April 1950, 'to plan, co-ordinate and to direct the anti-bandit operations of the police and fighting forces.' To achieve those ends, Briggs integrated the efforts of the police and the military, and reorganised his intelligence forces to provide him with information about terrorist movements and infiltrate the communist cadre infrastructure. Then it was the task of the infantry to move into the jungle, to secure bases and drive the insurgents deeper into the inhospitable jungle. A 'food denial' policy was also instituted, but the main obstacle to the success of the Briggs' Plan was the support given to the MRLA by the Chinese inhabitants of the jungle.

The solution was the resettlement of villagers or squatters in other safe areas beyond the immediate war zone. Initially 410 new villages were built, but although a good deal of thought was put into the social and economic problems, the resettlement programme was the cause of much local offence and bad feeling. Villagers were seldom told about the plans for evacuation and their first inkling that a move was imminent was the arrival of police, soldiers and trucks to effect the eviction. National Servicemen soon discovered themselves in the unfortunate position of having to implement an unwelcome policy, one which created a good deal of resentment; certainly, the picture of armed British troops forcibly rounding up bewildered Chinese villagers did little for Britain's stock in world opinion.

Nevertheless, that component of the Briggs' Plan did help to break up local support for the terrorists in the jungle: by the end of 1951 some 400,000 Chinese had been resettled. What it could not do was break up the gangs themselves: with each successive British initiative they merely pushed themselves into the fastness of the jungle – hence the need for infantry patrols to flush them out, engage them in action and, if possible, kill them. On this level the war in Malaya was fought by the men who led the jungle patrols, and these were either Regular Army sergeants or Regular and National Service 2nd Lieutenants. It was recognised by the military authorities that two years was the absolute limit for most patrol commanders, and even Regular Army subalterns were taken out of the jungle after that period and posted elsewhere. The National Service subalterns were automatically withdrawn at the end of their service, to return to civilian life where, as 2nd Lieutenant Oliver Crawford of the 1st Bn. Somerset Light Infantry recalls in his memoirs, *The Door Marked Malaya*, jungle bashing became a distant dream.

> Life was reduced to physical details – the softly tigerish padding of jungle boots, the pain of hands ripped by thorns and of shoulders aching under heavy weights, the warm pleasure of a bellyful of rice and meat in the evening, the tedious heat of blind sweaty hours at night before one could sleep.

An infantry patrol in the jungle demanded strength, stamina and determination of its members, and only the very fittest were able to stand up to its rigours – it was for that reason that most jungle bashers were in their early twenties. A National Service subaltern usually had a young Regular sergeant at his side, and at least one other NCO would be a jungle veteran; the other members of the patrol, the radio operator, the Bren gunner and the riflemen, would be predominantly National Servicemen and this was to be their war.

The first thing that struck most young soldiers seeing the jungle for the first time was its frighteningly large scale. The trees, forming an unbroken canopy, often reached two hundred feet into the sky; their leaves could be as large as warriors' shields; and all around the base, crazy patterns of creepers and roots constructed walls that were well-nigh impenetrable but for brute force and razor-sharp parangs or machetes. Underfoot, rotting leaves and undergrowth provided a soft mushy surface frequently traversed by meandering streams which turned what footholds there were into a spongy swamp. Many National Servicemen have likened the experience to entering an undersea world in which the only illumination was green light filtering slowly from above to the depths where they toiled below.

Had the terrain all been flat, progress might have been simpler, but the Malayan jungle had layered itself over hills and into river valleys, up creeks and through ravines. Pilots flying over it in Auster observation planes or Valetta transports thought it looked like a huge green carpet, carelessly folded with many bumps and creases; but in their airborne chariots they were the lucky ones. Down below in the hidden depths the infantrymen were doing well if they covered four hundred yards in an hour's marching. Relying on compass bearings and largely featureless maps, the infantry patrols boxed the jungle day in and day out, following leads given to them by informers or putting their trust in the instincts of their Iban scouts*, always hoping to engage the enemy. This in itself was no mean feat: at the end of the campaign it was estimated that one kill was made for every 1,800 man-hours spent on patrol. Although additional supplies were parachuted into specially cleared dropping zones, thus allowing patrols to stay in the jungle for two or three weeks, each man still had to carry five days' worth of supplies in a 60lb. load, made up of spare clothes, rations, mosquito net, poncho, groundsheet, ammunition and first aid kit. In addition he carried a parang, the short .303 rifle developed for use in Burma during World War II, and wore a specially designed lightweight jungle-green uniform and bush hat, this last item being particularly vital as it was often the only means of identifying friend from foe in the dark of the jungle.

To cope with the conditions the National Serviceman not only had to be fit, he had to be stoical too. Trench foot was a common and unpleasant problem in footwear that was never completely dry; a variety of insect bites, sores and cuts plagued his body, making equipment straps a painful burden; and each hour he lost bucketloads of sweat. Unless he was prepared to look after himself, to take regular draughts of salt water and to tend sores and cracked skin, he quickly became a burden on the rest of the patrol. Added to all those hardships were the dangers of the jungle itself: hornets which could beard a man and paralyse him, snakes which could kill, and beautiful, innocuous-looking plants which left a painful rash on exposed skin. At the end of the day in the damp twilight there were twelve hours of darkness during

*Dyak trackers from the Iban tribe in Borneo who served with jungle patrols of the British Army. Their fearsomely sharp knives and deadly blow pipes made them formidable opponents; a Cameronian officer said of them, 'They knew all about the jungle and were expert trackers; their skill was uncanny when tracking, and when the scent was hot, they went faster than any hunting dog.'

which the denizens of the jungle set up a torrent of noise – yaps, screams and howls – which could test the nerves of even the most hardened veterans. And at night-time, when resolve could be at its lowest ebb, the patrol had to remember that fighting took precedence over personal survival. National Service subaltern 2nd Lieutenant John Comyn, 1st Gordons, recalled it as a time when the slightest sound could make men jump.

> It was pitch black (no moon) and you couldn't see your own hands – still less the man in front of you, so you had to hold onto his equipment. By the time we had found the rest of the platoon the guide had really lost his bearings and we were backing along a track making a hell of a noise – I was horrified, but there it was. Suddenly a torch shone on us from another track about five yards away only. We stopped dead and pushed safety catches forward expecting an ambush . . . But the guide whispered 'Kampong Guard' – a sort of local Home Guard to keep the bandits out of the kampongs of Malay coolie lines. I had not previously thought any KG would have been efficient enough to come and investigate a noise.[16]

The expansion of the kampong guards' scheme into a militia force numbering 200,000 had been set afoot by General Sir Gerald Templer, a serving soldier who had been appointed High Commissioner in January 1952. He succeeded Sir Henry Gurney, who had been murdered in the previous year in a terrorist ambush on the road between Kuala Lumpur and Fraser's Hill. Templer insisted that the Malayan contribution to the war should be increased, and under his guidance the police force was strengthened and a sixth battalion added to the Malay Regiment. Also, between 1952 and 1954, the period of his leadership, the armed forces in Malaya became more multi-racial in character with regiments from East Africa (1st and 3rd King's African Rifles) and Fiji (1st Fijian Regiment) added to the eight Gurkha battalions already in service. Templer also had at his disposal the 22 SAS for long-range jungle penetration, and units of the Royal Air Force supplied him with a jungle support and air strike component, as well as with helicopter and observation services. It was in Malaya that the helicopter came into its own by showing its potential as a troop carrier and casualty evacuator. Bristol Sycamores of 194 Squadron were particularly useful in these roles, as were the later deployments of the larger Westland Whirlwinds of 155 Squadron.

Under Templer, too, more emphasis was put on intelligence work and on winning the confidence of the civilian population. So successful were the police in this latter respect that many terrorists surrendered and turned informers. (Another Templer innovation was to call the enemy 'terrorists' or 'CTs' [Communist terrorists] in preference to the earlier term, 'bandits'.) Few British soldiers ever ceased to be amazed by the rapidity of these conversions: men who had been fighting in terrorist gangs one day would willingly surrender and then lead British patrols to the hide-outs of their erstwhile comrades. But in spite of Templer's confident assertion that 'the answer lies not in putting more soldiers into the jungle but rests in the hearts and minds of the Malayan people', the jungle warfare had to continue.

In all, Templer had at his disposal 24 infantry battalions, 2 armoured regiments and a battery of field artillery. One of the infantry regiments which served in Malaya during his period as High Commissioner was the 1st Bn. Somerset Light Infantry, a typical example of an infantry unit which had been forced to accustom itself to the new art of jungle fighting. It had taken over from the Suffolks in southern Selangor early in 1953, and during the course of its three-year tour in Malaya it was principally a National Service battalion – 90% of all lance-corporals and 50% of all corporals were National Servicemen, one of whom had the rare distinction of being promoted to the rank of sergeant. The majority of the subalterns were National Service officers, and at the campaign's end the regimental historian Kenneth Whitehead gave full credit to the part played by the conscript element in the battalion:

> No one would wish to, nor could, belittle the value of National Servicemen in Malaya and elsewhere. It was true that they caused more work, produced wasteful overheads, resulted in periodic inefficiencies and many headaches for the Regular cadre; but this cross-section of the nation were splendid and enthusiastic men who helped to make a happy and successful battalion. The National Service officers, with their Regular sergeants at their elbows, were particularly successful leaders. Military crime was practically non-existent, so willingly did all work together. And of course the National Servicemen paid the price, as did others, of casualties: some killed in action, or as the result of lamentable accidents and others dying through illness.

At the end of 1954 the Somersets relieved the 1st Royal Hampshire Regiment in the jungle hills of Pahang, where they were involved in one of the few pitched battles of the war. During an attack on a terrorist camp, Major Haigh of C Company found that he was fighting a much superior force which was prepared to hold its ground instead of following the usual tactic of melting away into the jungle. Only his ingenuity in pretending to command a superior force saved the Somersets, and after a fierce firefight the terrorists were beaten off. Most battles, though, were short-lived and unexpected affairs as 2nd Lieutenant Oliver Crawford discovered when he had his first experience of combat shortly before the end of his National Service.

> I was badly shaken. Those few cries had been like a bucket of cold water in my face. I was awake, gasping with shock. This was real. This was happening. We were shooting people. We were killing them. At first I had been living from second to second, automatically, but now I was awake. We had worked for this for months. This was raw savage success. It was butchery. It was horror.

By Malayan standards Crawford's episode was a common enough experience. His patrol had been attacked by terrorists and during the resulting fire fight two enemy, one a girl, had been killed. The following morning the platoon had to carry the corpses off to the nearest police station for identification, a gruesome exercise which left Crawford and his men feeling like murderers.

The counter-insurgency war in Malaya involved relatively few men in actual combat, but those who did find themselves in ambushes or terrorist attacks found them harrowing experiences. Fear marched hand in glove with infantry patrols – fear of the enemy, fear of death or injury, and the individual soldier's fear that he might disgrace himself or let down his comrades. This last fear often haunted National Service subalterns, nineteen- or twenty-year-old youngsters facing combat for the first time and knowing that the lives of their men depended on their ability to cope in a crisis. 'I found being in charge of 30 men when in the jungle extremely difficult,' admitted 2nd Lieutenant Michael Radford, 1st Bn. Queen's Royal Regiment, who was in Malaya in 1956 and 1957. 'I felt too inexperienced and young and not ready for command.'

> The most terrifying part of 'jungle bashing' was being on night ambush. On occasions two of you were placed in a forward position, and on change of guard, one of you was left on your own in isolation for some time. It seemed to rain most nights and the trickle of water on the dense foliage was most unnerving. On many occasions in this situation at two or four in the morning I imagined

that bandits (CTs) were about the break through and knife or kill me. This more than anything else stands out in my memory.

(2nd Lieutenant J. M. H. Radford,
1st Bn. Queen's Royal Regiment)

In spite of those natural fears the patrol commander had to keep his anxiety in check, to conform to the basic battle-field rule that the commanding officer must suppress his own emotions, thereby providing his men with an example to follow. According to Major-General Frank Richardson, an experienced medical officer, the physical symptoms of fear are due to 'rapid involuntary muscular action designed to warm up the body for the anticipated activity'; in themselves they do not signify cowardice or an absence of backbone. Once that lesson had been learned by young patrol commanders they usually found the concept of combat easier to understand, although it was a stock of knowledge which could be easily overdrawn. Officers and men who saw frequent action in which their comrades were killed or wounded discovered that their morale was eaten away by the new fear of being mutilated, or badly wounded and left behind in the jungle. For that reason most infantry battalions kept a strict check on the rotas of jungle patrols, and men who became careless or nervous due to the strain of prolonged jungle warfare were usually relieved, sent on leave and then given a spell at a 'soft' posting.

As was all too often the case in other 'emergencies' during the withdrawal from Empire, very few soldiers – officers or men – knew the exact reasons for their presence in the country. 'I always felt that we were not properly informed of the background to the emergence of Communist Terrorists in Malaya,' admitted Michael Radford. 'And in this respect when members of the battalion were wounded or killed, I was at a slight loss to really fully understand why they had to die and for what cause.' Nor was he alone: it was a rare senior officer who took the trouble to explain to his men the reasons for the British military presence, and it was only later that many National Servicemen discovered that their enemy had fought with Britain against Japan during World War II and was armed with British weapons. Most commanding officers put their faith in the old adage that it was the soldier's duty 'not to reason why', and simply informed their men that there was a job to do and that they had to do it.

To them, and to the majority of the servicemen in Malaya, the terrorists were an impersonal enemy which threatened the fabric of society and therefore had to be defeated. As such, they were only 'CTs' and their deaths were part of the battalion's 'bag'. The army's love of abbreviation and epithet helped to cloak the reality in other ways. Surrendered terrorists who became informers were SEPs (surrendered enemy personnel), whereas CEPs (captured enemy personnel) were merely prisoners. The jungle became the 'ulu', 'hard core' was the name for terrorist leaders, patrols practised IA or immediate action drills to sharpen their skills for combat, and at the end of the day in the jungle they built 'bashas' – shelters made out of groundsheets, bamboo and foliage.

To help underline the idea that on one level the war was an impersonal activity, each battalion kept a score of the terrorists it killed. The Suffolks topped the 'league' for British units with 198 kills, followed by the Cameronians with 125, but as with any competition its existence provoked rumours of sharp practice. John Baynes, a Cameronian Regular officer, remarked rather tartly in the regimental history that the Suffolks had achieved their score by forming special 'hit squads' – patrols of specialist jungle fighters – whereas his own regiment had used ordinary jungle patrols made up of a cross-section of the available personnel. Eventually the official tallying of kills was forbidden by parliament after visiting MPs complained that it was too barbarous a practice. The army continued it anyway.

That all battalions claimed large numbers of killed terrorists in comparison to their own losses was due entirely to the soldiers' professionalism and their ability to cope with jungle warfare – when the Royal Hampshires left Selangor in August 1956 they had 67 kills to their credit for the loss of 2 officers and 7 men, and their 'score' was by no means untypical. One reason for the unequal losses was that in spite of the misgivings initially held by the National Service subalterns, the British jungle patrols were superbly led. Much of the credit for their success must go to the Far East Land Forces School of Jungle Warfare at Johore: most of the instructors were tough and experienced Australian officers who made sure that their charges were well versed in the actual problems that would face them when they hit the jungle. They saw no reason to pretend that jungle bashing was anything other than back-breaking, relentless and dangerous work, and they drummed into the young subalterns the lesson that their first duty was to engage and kill a cunning enemy. Under their tutelage National Servicemen became experienced fighters, secure in their knowledge of such arcane mysteries as the direction of a firefight and the absolute necessity to control the killing ground. Then it was practice, practice and practice again, until the patrol commanders could look on the jungle as a second home and be alive to all its many dangers.

Despite the intensity and thoroughness of the training there were some disasters, and the Emergency, like any other war, claimed lives either because the enemy had the upper hand or because the British soldiers were careless. In October 1951 a company of the Royal West Kents was ambushed not far from the scene of Gurney's murder: 12 British soldiers and 3 Iban scouts died in a carefully planned and executed terrorist attack. The Gordons lost 7 men in a similar ambush in January 1952, and during the early part of their Malayan tour, when they were at their most vulnerable, the Green Howards saw six of their number killed in as many days during jungle operations in Pahang and Selangor. Some of these were National Servicemen and the casualties were high enough to cause disquiet in Britain. It was one thing for Regular soldiers to be killed on active service – professionals are, after all, encouraged to think of themselves as servants of the state – but peacetime conscripts were supposed to be different.

Many of the young men in the jungle patrols viewed the problem rather differently. They had been caught up in the drama of real warfare and had mixed feelings both about the Malayan Emergency and about National Service in general. It was not easy to forget the trauma of action in which men were killed or injured: those who survived realised that their lives had been changed utterly, that they had been forced to face great dangers but had come through the experience. There was also the feeling, strongly held especially by the National Service subalterns and junior leaders, that they had been allowed to do something useful for their country and that they were better men for it. 'I felt pride in the small police stations, immaculately kept, with the Union Jack flying over them,' remembers 2nd Lieutenant Alex MacMillan, a KOSB subaltern in Malaya in 1956 and 1957. 'I was thrilled by the cheers of frightened British residents in flats as we drove over the Causeway to put down riots. It was Mafeking again!' Many other National Servicemen have admitted that they went out to Malaya as boys and came back as men, and that they matured more quickly as a result of the tension and dangers they had to face during their tour of duty.

Not all the engagements in Malaya were matters of life or death. Men on jungle patrols could spend whole months without ever coming into contact with the enemy – the Gordons' posting in the Tampin area of Negri Sembilan was relatively quiet and therefore very frustrating for the battalion's senior officers – and for many the Emergency was a dull and repetitive war whose monotony was only relieved by guard duty and the occasional false alarm.

> The only time I heard shots fired in anger was one dark and extremely wet night when we were stationed in the southern sector of Malaya. It had been a fairly peaceful period and most of the regiment was either drinking in the NAAFI or in the Messes. Suddenly the guards started shooting, the tents emptied and men started running in all directions – because there were no trenches some ended up in the monsoon drains. It was only after order was restored that it was discovered that the sentries had opened up on a pack of stray dogs, mistaking them for terrorists. We suffered more casualties that night than in any other escapade and I was busy with the Medical Officers for hours afterwards patching up minor wounds and cuts.
>
> (Trooper Brian Wilkinson, 11th Hussars)

Brian Wilkinson served as medical orderly with the 11th Hussars in Negri Sembilan in 1954 and 1955, when the Emergency was beginning to be contained by the British forces. Prior to his conscription he had been a member of the Young Communist League, and remained a card-carrying member of the Communist Party throughout his National Service. Unlike his fictional counterpart, Brian Seaton – the hero of Alan Sillitoe's *The Key to the Door* – who let a CT go 'because he was a comrade', Wilkinson never had to fire a shot in anger against fellow communists; but he did find evidence of other kinds of subversion. The weapons hut of the 11th Hussars was managed by an officious corporal who made men queue up and sign for their weapons even during an emergency, and it was fairly common for National Servicemen on exercises or routine patrols to hide in the jungle and refuse to fire their rifles because they wanted to keep them clean for inspection. Minor aberrations of that nature will come as little surprise to the student of modern warfare. Avoidance of combat has been a regular feature of battles throughout the 19th and 20th centuries, and both World Wars have seen well-documented incidents in which each side's sense of self-preservation triumphed over their feelings of aggression. In Vietnam it was common practice for infantry or Marine patrols to construct mock ambushes in the jungle rather than engage the Vietcong. These ruses were generally accompanied by elaborate charades to cover the patrol's moves, such as the filing of careful reports, the counting of spent ammunition and, in extreme cases, the calling in of air strikes to hit non-existent enemy positions. It has, of course, also been a convention in all wars for soldiers to refuse to open fire for fear of drawing enemy fire themselves.

Any war, though, is bound to bring its quota of casualties, and many of those injured in Malaya still suffer today. Private William Skinner served with the 1st Bn. Seaforth Highlanders, the first infantry unit to see action in Malaya: shortly before he was demobbed in 1952, while attached to the Gordons, he was hit in the back and legs by terrorist bullets,' wounds that have left him permanently scarred.

> After doing two years' National Service I had to spend six months in a military hospital, but even after treatment I could not move my right leg and had to use crutches. The shrapnel could not be removed so I was shipped home on the *Empire Orwell* for further treatment. I had to make my way to hospital on crutches carrying my two kit-bags. Then I was discharged and sent home. I couldn't even work in a light job for six years and although I had seven further operations I still have pieces of shrapnel in my body. I am 50% disabled – when I was released from the army I got 16s. (80p) a week. Now I get £24.
>
> (Private William Skinner, 1st Bn. Seaforth Highlanders)

Not surprisingly, William Skinner believes that he would be 'better off today if it hadn't been for National Service'. On the whole, though, military medical support during the Emergency had been honed to a fine art and the forces in Malaya enjoyed standards of medical back-up second to none. For the first time, helicopters were used to evacuate the wounded to military hospitals where they received professional aid. Improvements in first-aid training, too, meant that minor problems encountered on jungle patrol, such as skin problems, stomach upsets or light wounds, could be treated without recourse to evacuation or endangering the safety of the rest of the patrol.

But however greatly the medical services had improved, there were still grave dangers and risks in evacuating the wounded: helicopters were always in short supply and the wounded still had to be transported on makeshift bamboo stretchers to the specially prepared jungle clearings. In the more remote areas the short endurance of the helicopter meant that evacuation by air still entailed a long and painful journey by road to the nearest hospital. RAMC patrols frequently ventured deep into the jungle to bring succour to the worst cases, a role in which National Service lieutenants, all trained doctors, came into their own. Not only did they have a first-class medical training but they were also young, fit and competent soldiers.

RAMC officers attached to infantry or armoured regiments quickly became important parts of the closely-knit life of a battalion on active service. In peacetime it was often the case that smart infantry or cavalry regiments would treat with condescension the presence of a corps officer in the Mess, but in time of war these officers (medical, padre, transport, and so on) had vital tasks to fulfil. The appearance of the 'medic' or the 'doc' near the scene of battle could mean the difference between life and death for the battalion's wounded.

> In the remaining twelve months before I was due for demob in October 1949 I had a varied experience of travel to the four squadrons of the 4th Hussars – taking me on two occasions across the notorious Gap Road (where the High Commissioner, Sir Henry Gurney, was tragically ambushed and killed in 1951). This road ran through the largest state – Pahang – to the idyllic tropical east coast at Kuantan. Subsequently we travelled in a humble 'convoy' of two 15-cwt. trucks and one jeep, but in July 1949 the convoys consisted of at least twenty vehicles. All officers were obliged to carry a Webley .38 revolver but as a non-combatant officer I was not offered any instruction in target practice. On these convoys we were also issued with that frightening weapon, the Sten gun. I was terrified that it would produce more self-inflicted or accidental wounds than ward off a Communist ambush. In fact, I treated more accidental wounds of this nature than wounds inflicted by the insurgents during my service. However, I was one of the lucky ones, but we were all saddened when one of our patrols was ambushed in the notorious Sungei Siput area on New Year's Eve in 1949.
>
> (Lieutenant H. M. White, Royal Army Medical Corps)

This was when a patrol of the 4th Hussars consisting of two officers and 16 men in two GMC personnel carriers and a 15-cwt truck was ambushed by a terrorist gang in Perak. It was a classic guerrilla action: the terrorists trapped the patrol on a twisting dead-end minor road. The troop leader, Lieutenant Michael Questier, showed great courage in concentrating the troop by backing his vehicle to the rear GMC commanded by 2nd Lieutenant Jon Sutro, who was under instruction. By then the surviving 4th Hussars had deployed on the road, but during further action Questier was killed, leaving Sutro in command. He regrouped the survivors and ordered the GMCs to drive through a hail of bullets to a defensive position further down the road. Though wounded, Sutro and a trooper summoned help by driving back through the ambush: he was decorated with the first Military Cross of the campaign.

During the Malayan Emergency, 134 officers received the Military Cross, which is awarded for acts of gallantry in the field by junior commissioned officers or warrant officers of the British Army. In time of war the decoration has a special significance, being an award for conspicuous gallantry shown by officers of platoon leader level, and the number of awards made to National Service subalterns is an indication both of the ferocity of the fighting and of the bravery shown by nineteen- or twenty-year-old patrol commanders. Typical of the kind of courage which earned the award of a Military Cross was the fortitude and enterprise shown by 2nd Lieutenant Ian Wightwick, 1st Cameronians, on 8 April 1953. While patrolling in the Labis area of Johore his party of ten men made contact with a CT encampment in dense, swampy, secondary jungle. Forming his men into an extended line with his Bren gun on the right flank, Wightwick attacked the camp, killing the terrorist machine-gunner in the first minute. Although wounded twice, Wightwick continued to direct the fire fight which lasted twenty minutes, and during that time he refused to allow his men to attend to his wounds. The official citation gives the reasons why his commanding officer recommended him for the award of the Military Cross.

> The pain from the wounds must have been intense yet 2nd Lieutenant Wightwick at no time gave into it and it was due to his outstanding leadership and example that this battle was brought to a successful conclusion. Three enemy bodies were recovered, many more were seen to be wounded and doubtless some of them died in the jungle. A large quantity of weapons, equipment and supplies were recovered . . . Throughout the operation 2nd Lieutenant Wightwick displayed an outstanding sense of leadership, devotion to duty and courage that were of the highest order. His personal example was an inspiration to his men and resulted in a most successful battle in spite of the odds of two to one against us.[17]

264 rankers and junior leaders won the Military Medal in Malaya for similar acts of gallantry. All National Servicemen there were presented with the General Service Medal and Malayan clasp, with its distinctive purple ribbon with green stripe – the medal had been established in 1918 to recognise the numerous actions which fell short of actual war. On the obverse of the National Service period medals was the effigy of King George VI or Queen Elizabeth II, and the reverse depicted a standing winged figure of Victory placing a wreath on the emblems of the two services (Army and RAF). Although it was

not an award for gallantry and was 'passed out with the rations' at the end of a tour of duty, most National Servicemen were pleased enough to receive it, however much they might have scoffed about it in public, claiming that the proliferation of medals only debased them. At the end of their service in Malaya the majority of National Servicemen still took their uniforms to the camp tailor to have the ribbon sewn on for the passage home.

By 1953 the policy of resettlement had come to an end, and later that year the province of Malacca was freed from Emergency regulations. The following year saw the states of Trengganu, Kedah and Negri Sembilan follow suit, with parts of their territories being declared 'white' or free from terrorist activity: with those declarations the Emergency in Malaya could at least be said to have an end in sight. Templer retired on 30 May 1954, and the task of the Army and the RAF for the following six years was one of retrenchment and mopping up. Some terrorist gangs were still at large in the jungle, and there were to be many setbacks and hardships before victory could be claimed, but the back of the war had been broken. The first general elections were held in July 1955, bringing Tungku Abdul Rahman to power; from Britain he wrung the promise of provisional independence by August 1957, and using that offer as a lever he attempted to bring the terrorist war to an end. Chin Peng's refusal to negotiate with the new Malayan leadership eventually dented his own support, and what remained of the terrorist offensive dragged on in piecemeal fashion until 1 August 1960 when the Emergency was officially ended. Independence, or 'Merdeka', had been granted three years earlier, in 1957, and in the intervening years terrorism had been stifled by police and Special Branch officers backed up by British and Gurkha infantry units and components of the SAS; but by then superior intelligence and not the jungle bashing of earlier years was winning the war for the Malayan government.

It was at times a brutal and bloody war, as any counter-insurgency war against terrorists is bound to be. Many of the murders of planters in remote settlements beyond the reach of help were sickening affairs, and the uncanny ability of the terrorists to mount successful ambushes, especially in the wilderness of Kelantan, was a source of constant irritation to the security forces. Gurney's murder also caused a good deal of bitterness and it has to be recorded that many unofficial reprisals were taken, and that not all the resettlement programmes were carried out with kid gloves. Much of the frustration was born of the soldiers' own fear about the enemy: because the CTs fought in the jungle, using subterfuge as their principal weapon, they became 'bogeymen' in the eyes of jungle patrols; hence the policy of no quarter adopted by many commanders. The most notorious example of frustration boiling over into outrage came early in the campaign, on 12 December 1949, when a patrol of the 2nd Bn. Scots Guards rounded up suspects in a settlement at Batang Kali north of Kuala Lumpur. The males were separated from the females, and under conditions that are still not altogether clear the Guardsmen mowed down 26 villagers as they attempted to escape. An official investigation conducted by the Attorney-General of Malaya, Sir Stafford Foster Sutton, concluded later that no blame should be attached to the Scots Guards patrol and its commander, a sergeant, and that they were merely doing their duty by preventing a mass break-out of possible terrorists. Most of the patrol members, drawn from a battalion with little jungle warfare experience, were National Servicemen.

Despite isolated incidents of brutality and heavy-handed reprisals – all carefully hushed up – the Malayan campaign was not completely disfigured by unnecessary violence or the total alienation of the population, as the war in Vietnam was to be. Victory was a slow and painstaking business, taking twelve years to achieve, and many reasons were put forward for the British success. Firstly, the fruitful wooing of the Malay population and the isolation of the Chinese terrorists provided the bedrock; then the determination of the colonial administration and the strategic planning of committed leaders like Briggs and Templer produced the necessary framework; the final strengthening came from the hugely successful counter-insurgency tactics worked out by the security forces. Air power was essential for supply, evacuation and limited strikes against jungle bases; ships of the Royal Navy gave close-range fire support along coastal strips; but the war was really won by the infantrymen of the jungle patrols who had to learn to live with a new, frightening and frequently hostile environment. That they managed to overcome those difficulties and to acquit themselves with honour was due in no small measure to the indefatigability of the National Servicemen.

In fact it is true to say that the average National Serviceman was of superior calibre to his Regular counterpart, which is no surprise at a time of full employment. They had, of course, one big advantage over the Regular: that of doing a worthwhile job, albeit in foul conditions, for a definitely limited period. The Regular was committed to the same job for a full three years – and three years of 'jungle bashing' is a long time.

That encomium from the regimental historian of the Somerset Light Infantry was not isolated praise; nearly all the Regular officers who fought in Malaya were quick to recognise the part played by the army and RAF National Servicemen.

An impression exists that some of the young National Service soldiers who fought in Malaya may have been poorly trained. (The book and film of *The Virgin Soldiers* helped to perpetuate this idea.) In some regiments there may occasionally have been found badly trained soldiers, but on the whole in the Cameronians there were very few. The general level of efficiency and training reached was extremely high, largely due to the tremendous enthusiasm of the young men. Over and over again the keenness of the 'Jock' was demonstrated. The number of men reporting sick was always low, and it was not unknown for men who had been told to go to bed by the doctor to be found leaving with their platoons the following day on long patrols, rather than miss out and be left behind by their friends. As the three-year tour neared its end in 1953 the skill of the average Cameronian soldier in the jungle was extremely high.

That is regimental pride speaking, but John Baynes's mention of Leslie Thomas's novel *The Virgin Soldiers* is the only sour note struck in a vivid and readable account of the Cameronians' tour of duty in Malaya between 1950 and 1953. In fact, it was not so much Thomas's novel which angered many National Service veterans as the subsequent film based upon it, which emphasised the 'truthfully tough, wildly sexy, hilariously funny' aspects of Thomas's novel. Although the novel is set in the fushionless depot of 'Panglin, safe on the island, ten miles from Singapore City . . . as peaceful as a suburb', and concentrates on the ribald antics of a Royal Army Pay Corps unit, Thomas did not ignore the war, the final section being a dramatic account of a terrorist raid on the military train from Penang to Kuala Lumpur. Thomas served with the RAPC in Malaya in 1950 and 1951 and much of the action in *The Virgin Soldiers* was based on his own experiences as a clerk in the military base at Singapore; hence the criticism of Regular and National Service infantrymen who fought a different kind of war. But as Thomas told a BBC radio audience in 1984, the fact the *The Virgin Soldiers* was a work of fiction did not preclude him from ignoring any mention of the harsher side of service life in Malaya.

There was a section in the Pay Office which was horribly called

'Death Cases' and it was the task of one person in that section to finalise the accounts of soldiers who had died or who had been killed in Malaya. It was a pretty grisly sort of thing – a sergeant was doing it before me. He went home and I said I would like to do it. I might say that they never promoted me to sergeant but I sat there at this little private desk and I did the job as well as I could. At the same time I used to write short stories and articles under the desk because, frankly, it took me one and a half hours a day to do the job. It was there that war came home to me because one of the accounts I had to deal with was of a soldier who had been killed. His paybook was included in the accounts; now, when you're on active service you're not supposed to carry your paybook but this fellow had. There was a bullet hole right through it, very muddy and very bloody. I put that incident in *The Virgin Soldiers* to show how the horror of war came down home to every soldier.

Literature has always been one of the measures by which man has gauged war. On the one hand, popular fiction has frequently glorified battle and presented combat as a heroic ideal; on the other, what might be termed anti-war literature has presented actual warfare as a beastly and unedifying business, something best avoided by the cultivated man. Between those extremes, military novels or memoirs are tested for their accuracy and usually criticised when too much attention is paid to scrim-shanking or skylarking. It was this latter fate that befell Thomas's novel: military purists protested that he devoted too much effort to sending up the vagaries of life at the depot while ignoring the active service life of the jungle patrols. Given the context of the novel this is not altogether fair, as the infantry battalions in Malaya all depended on the existence of a large strategic and administrative back-up; and during the years of the Emergency men at the military headquarters in Singapore had to gear themselves to the task of supplying, equipping, feeding and paying a large army, as well as making all the necessary arrangements for the transport of soldiers to and from home. In that respect the war in Malaya was as much a triumph of logistics for the administrators who had to work over a twelve-year period five thousand miles away from home base as it was of arms for the infantrymen. Again, many of the clerks, storekeepers or drivers who carried out lowly but essential jobs were National Servicemen.

In contrast to Malaya, bewilderment was the most common reaction of the young National Servicemen who fought in the Korean War: bewilderment on the part of British soldiers and sailors (the RAF did not serve in Korea) that they should have to fight in such a far-flung corner of the world, bewilderment about the identity of their enemy and the cause for which they had been sent to fight.

> I would say that we were totally ignorant of anything that was relevant to the war. I think possibly that at the time we were still thinking of it as a follow-on from the war [World War II] and that in a sense we were fighting for world peace. I think that was really caused by the fact that we were part of a United Nations force. Again, we felt there was a sort of togetherness against the communist threat, although even from that point of view we were still very mystified about why someone we were fighting on the same side with during the war, an ally, was now an enemy. We were certainly very naive . . . I don't think it was clear to us what was happening at the time. There was all this mystery about who we were fighting: was it the North Koreans or was it the Chinese? My initial reaction to the country was that it was a great place for a war.
>
> (Lance-Corporal Jim Laird, 1st Bn. The Black Watch)

British servicemen were sent to Korea to uphold the aims of the United Nations' commission, which had been established to supervise free elections in the country following the evacuation of Russian and American forces at the conclusion of the Second World War. (Korea had been annexed by Japan in 1910 and freed from her domination late in 1945.) However, following their withdrawal, the country had split in two along the 38th parallel, the north becoming a communist regime and the south a somewhat hastily organised democracy. It was the task of the UN commission to attempt to unite the two halves, a task which became impossible on 25 June 1950 when North Korea invaded its southern neighbour. Shocked by this naked aggression, America persuaded the United Nations to oppose the invasion – their argument in favour of armed intervention was helped by the absence of the USSR from the Security Council in protest at the UN's refusal to recognise communist China – and by the end of July America had four divisions in Korea and the US air force was hard at work trying to slow down the North Korean invasion. By August Britain had thrown in her lot with the United Nations, and the 1st Argyll and Sutherland Highlanders and the 1st Middlesex Regiment were in Korea as part of the UN force which was desperately defending the Pusan Perimeter, the last line of defence in the south-east corner of South Korea. As the war progressed, though, the reasons for the UN involvement blurred and the war became a stalemate of entrenched positions, artillery barrage and frontal attacks as the armies fought it out while the politicians argued.

Although smaller than the contribution made by the US forces, Britain played a signal role in the war in Korea which lasted until July 1953 when an armistice was eventually reached between the two warring factions. The RAF was not called upon to serve in Korea (although some pilots flew on attachment with Commonwealth or American units, and three squadrons of Sunderlands flew reconnaissance sorties from their bases in Japan) but ships of the Royal Navy patrolled the Korean coastline to prevent infiltration, and a carrier task force provided air cover for the battle ashore. In all, 16 infantry battalions fought in Korea, backed up by 4 armoured regiments, 8 regiments of artillery with engineering, ordnance, transport and allied support. By July 1951 they formed part of the Commonwealth Division which provided three infantry brigades for the UN forces – 25th Canadian (2nd Royal Canadian Regiment, 2nd Royal 22 Regiment and 2nd Princess Patricia's Canadian Light Infantry), 28th Commonwealth (1st King's Own Scottish Borderers, 1st King's Shropshire Light Infantry and 1st Royal Australian Regiment) and 29th British (1st Royal Northumberland Fusiliers, 1st Glosters and 1st Royal Ulster Rifles). It was a hard, bruising war with high casualties: 71 officers and 616 other ranks were killed in action, 187 officers and 2,311 other ranks were wounded, and 52 officers and 1,050 other ranks were listed as 'missing', of whom 40 officers and 996 other ranks were prisoners of war and eventually repatriated.

These statistics might seem small beer when compared to the American losses of some 33,000 killed or the total UN casualty list of 447,697 officers and men killed in action, but as novelist Eric Linklater noted in an official British government publication on the country's war aims, what the British contribution lacked in numbers it made up for in enthusiasm and experience.

> Our land forces were small in material strength but were endowed with all the aptitudes of their calling and that tenacity of spirit which is traditional in the British Army. Neither the Middlesex nor the Argylls could muster more than three rifle companies and there was no military principle to justify the despatch and committing to battle of two weak battalions that had neither their own necessary transport nor their proper supporting arms. It was the desperate plight of the Americans in the Pusan bridgehead that had compelled their sudden embarkation and as military principles

were overridden by moral need so were the difficulties of their strange campaign to be overcome by recruitment, as it seemed, from the regimental spirit to which they were heirs. In the months to come both the Middlesex and the Argylls – though nearly half of them were youngsters doing their national training – were to enhance the pride and reputation, not only of the Diehards and the 91st, but of all the Army.

Some 20,000 British servicemen served in Korea and of these roughly 10% were National Servicemen, the ratio being determined by a government ruling that all soldiers on active service in Korea should be over the age of nineteen. Nevertheless, National Servicemen did play a vital role in Korea, and of the infantry battalions which fought in the later stages of the war – such as 1st King's Own Scottish Borderers (KOSB), 1st Royal Norfolk Regiment and 1st Durham Light Infantry – around 60% of the men were conscripts. The Durhams, who served in Korea between September 1952 and September 1953, had just completed a stint in Germany with BAOR and their commanding officer, Lt-Col Peter Jeffreys, was moved to ask himself in his official report whether his untried National Servicemen would adapt to the new conditions and uphold the fighting traditions of the regiment.

> Before going into action I was apprehensive that the qualities of toughness and self-assurance would be lacking in the very young men we had brought. Of their enthusiasm, discipline and general military efficiency I was certain . . . but could they compare with the confident, mature Australians with whom we were brigaded, and with the brave, resourceful, expert field craftsmen that their enemy, the Chinaman, had proved himself to be?[18]

The answer was not long in coming and was contained in the same document.

> I need have had no qualms . . . the battalion quickly settled down to war and the youthful National Serviceman changed in a few short weeks to a mature, self-reliant, imperturbable fighting man. He never, in all our time in the line, lost the form he had found.

Like other men who served with the UN forces in Korea, those National Servicemen of the Durhams, like National Servicemen of all units of the Commonwealth Division, fought their war over a malodorous, nearly unheard-of peninsula, almost as far away across the globe as it was possible to be. For many, the warfare was to be reminiscent of the fighting their grandfathers had encountered at the Somme; the climate was loathsome, too, the winters bitterly cold and the summers hot and wet, and they were to fight an enemy who asked for, and offered, no quarter.

Most of the action seen by National Servicemen came after October 1950 when the Communist Chinese committed themselves to the North Korean cause with an army of 'volunteer' fighting troops over half a million strong. Three actions from the many fought by British Army units between then and the war's end typify the contribution made by National Servicemen to the war in Korea: the Glosters' defence of Hill 235 during the Battle of the Imjin River in April 1951; the KOSB's fighting evacuation of the Maryang-San ridge a few months later, during which the regiment won 12 gallantry awards including one VC and four DSOs; and the stand made by The Black Watch and the Duke of Wellington's Regiment at the Battle of the Hook in May 1953.

At the end of July 1950, at the time when the American 24th Division was hanging on for grim death in the Pusan Perimeter and the war looked like going North Korea's way, the Glosters (1st Bn. Gloucestershire Regiment) received their orders to join the 29th Independent Infantry Brigade* and to prepare for embarkation to Korea. At the time they were some four hundred men short of their full complement, and their muster was reduced further by the government's age ruling and the Brigade's instruction that any National Serviceman bound for Korea had to be a 'volunteer'. (One National Serviceman, Private Albert Hawkins, an eighteen-year-old, 'put his age on' and went to Korea with the Glosters.) Reservists were called up to fill the gap and men who had signed on for 'seven and five' (seven years with the colours, five with the reserves) found themselves in the unenviable position of temporarily abandoning home and family to fight a war in a country few knew existed. Although the disruption to their domestic lives must have been a severe shock, these veterans provided a stiff backbone: most had fought in World War II, and their experience of actual warfare was to be invaluable to the young National Servicemen and Regulars.

When they arrived in Korea in November the Glosters were first assigned to anti-guerrilla operations in the Sibyon'ni area

*On paper, the 29th Independent Infantry Brigade consisted of the Glosters, Royal Northumberland Fusiliers, Royal Ulster Rifles, 8th King's Royal Irish Hussars, C Squadron of 7th Royal Tank Regiment, 45th Field Regiment Royal Artillery, 170th Independent Mortar Battery, 55th Squadron Royal Engineers and full technical and administrative back up. Its one shortage was men.

north of Kaesong before being caught up in the disastrous American retreats of January 1951. By that time General MacArthur's – Commander-in-Chief UN Forces – successful landings at Inchon in the north had relieved pressure on Pusan, and the war had turned into a highly mobile series of battles and retreats as the American and North Korean forces battled to gain control of the North Korean heartlands and to bring the war to a speedy conclusion. By Spring 1951, though, the UN forces – now commanded by General Matthew Ridgeway – had been badly mauled by their Chinese opponents and had taken up strong defensive positions astride the 38th parallel. The Glosters, together with their fellow units of 29th Brigade, found themselves responsible for a nine-mile sector of the western front along the Imjin River, a rocky area of hills and deep valleys offering little usable cover. They held the left of the line with the Fusiliers in the centre and the Royal Ulster Rifles in reserve. On the Glosters' left was a South Korean unit (1st ROK Division), the 25-pounders of 45th Regiment RA provided artillery support from the centre, and on a high flank on the opposite bank of the river Brigadier Tom Brodie, the 29th's commander, had deployed a Belgian battalion. The position covered the main highway south to Seoul, a traditional route taken by invading armies, and it was here that the Chinese decided to attack in strength on the night of 22–23 April 1951. The Glosters quickly discovered that their enemy was unlike anything they had encountered before.

> When the Chinese waded across the shallow Imjin River on Saturday night the brunt of their attack fell upon this battalion (1st Glosters). Cut off, and surrounded, without food or water, it fought for 80 hours. The Royal Northumberland Fusiliers on their right went to their help – still with the roses in their helmets with which they had been celebrating St George's Day – but the Chinese drove in between them. Throughout Monday night the Chinese attacked on every side, screaming, blowing bugles, ringing bells and clashing cymbals. But the Gloucesters held them and fought back, not giving an inch of ground.

The sparse language of the official communiqué – issued a week later due to the needs of wartime censorship – masked the harsh reality of the plight which faced the men of the Glosters. The night attack was followed by an equally bloody assault on the battalion's company positions, and gradually the ferocity of the Chinese attack forced them to retire from their forward positions into the relative security of the summit of Hill 235, formerly occupied by Headquarters Company. It was there that the Glosters made their last stand, cut off from their friends and surrounded by an enemy which had driven a wedge between them and the other two battalions of 29th Brigade. A few months after the battle, 2nd Lieutenant Edmund Ions, 1st Border Regiment attached Royal Ulster Rifles, surveyed the scene of the action and heard from the officers of his adopted regiment a lurid description of the problems they had faced trying to cope with the unorthodox Chinese attack.

> The main Chinese tactic was the 'human wave' technique of assault. Their vast numbers allowed this, and the Chinese force in the April battle was estimated at 60,000. If the front line was gunned down, the next 'wave' simply stepped forward in its place, and so on . . . Their infantry could march twenty miles a day on only a bag of rice. They attacked at night, filtered round to the rear of their enemy's position, then made an unearthly din with bugles and klaxons to create panic among the enemy's soldiers. There was nothing in British tactics manuals on these battle techniques.[19]

To their consternation, the gunners of 45th Field Regiment, RA, had discovered that the 'human wave' refused to be broken even by well-aimed shellfire, and although they were firing more rounds per minute than had been used at Alamein they could not halt the inexorable advance. The same fate befell the 170th Independent Mortar Battery which had given the Glosters loyal fire support throughout the battle. On the morning of 25 April Brodie ordered the remnants of the Fusilier and Rifle battalions to withdraw and, realising that any attempt to relieve the Glosters was out of the question, he ordered their commanding officer, Lt-Col Fred Carne, to 'break out' with what remained of his regiment.

It was a situation the regiment had faced before in the course of its long and distinguished history. At the Battle of Alexandria in 1801 the Glosters had been engaged in a bloody fire fight with a French regiment when they were simultaneously attacked from behind. The rear ranks had promptly turned to face the new threat, and in recognition of their valour that day the Glosters had ever since been permitted to wear a small replica regimental badge on the back of their head-dress. To the officers and NCOs the tradition of fighting 'back to back' was a vital part of regimental *esprit de corps* and every Gloster had been taught to take a special pride in the story. As Captain Anthony Farrar-Hockley, the battalion Adjutant, later recalled in his book *The*

Edge of the Sword, the remaining men on Hill 235 refused to waver even when it became clear that the odds were stacked so highly against them.

> I look round the small body of men in the trenches. Some of them are young men, hardly more than boys; some of them men in their late thirties: most of them are somewhere in between. I see that it is a good lot of faces to be in a tight corner with; reliable faces; the faces of old friends.

In fact, many of the men were of other regiments and had been drafted into the Glosters for the duration of their tour of duty in Korea; but even so, the ideals of Alexandria and of other battles in the 'Slashers'' past were not without meaning to them. Field Marshal Lord Slim once remarked that 'the moral strength of the British army is the sum of all these family or clan loyalties. They are the foundations of the British soldier's stubborn valour.' Although it may appear eccentric or even an example of the herd instinct to the outsider, to the soldier the regiment was – and is – all-important, and doughty deeds from the past bestow the same heroic attributes on the men facing great danger in the present. Soldiers have frequently remarked that they found danger or death easier to accept in the spiritual, family mystique of their regiment. The Glosters were about to test that mystique to the full.

Of those who tried to break out to reach the 29th Brigade's lines only 5 officers and 41 men – mainly from D Company – made it. 19 officers (including the imperturbable Carne) and 505 men marched into Chinese captivity and two years of hardship and deprivation; of these 34 died. But the stand of the Glosters on the Imjin had not been in vain. The impetus of the Chinese advance had been halted and the brief respite had allowed American reinforcements to be rushed into the defensive area. Honours were heaped upon the Glosters: Carne received the Victoria Cross, as did Lieutenant P. K. E. Curtis posthumously; there were 3 DSOs and 6 Military Crosses as well as a large number of other awards, and the entire battalion – along with 170th Independent Mortar Battery – received the United States Presidential Citation. When the 'Glorious Glosters' returned home in December 1951 it was the signal for a good deal of public excitement and pride in the regiment. It was noted, too, by the regimental historian Tim Carew, that when the battalion reformed after its battering on the Imjin, 'few of the replacements were Glosters and even fewer Regulars – the majority were

National Servicemen originally earmarked for the Middlesex and Royal Ulster Rifles – but all were delighted and proud to be with the Regiment. Some of them, indeed, had contrived to get themselves on the wrong draft and were welcomed.'

During the summer a flurry of peace talks had suggested the possibility of a truce, but by autumn the political stalemate had again degenerated into armed hostility. In October the 28th Commonwealth Brigade took up new positions beyond the Imjin, successfully dislodging the Chinese from the gaunt slopes of the hills known as Kowang-San and Maryang-San. The ridges formed an arrowhead piercing into the enemy lines and it was there that the men of the King's Shropshire Light Infantry (KSLI) and the KOSB faced some of the fiercest fighting of the war at the beginning of November. Following a series of probing attacks the Chinese turned the full weight of their assault on the KOSB positions on the Maryang-San ridge. It was there that Private William Speakman, a Black Watch regular attached to the Borderers, won a Victoria Cross after leading one attack after the other on enemy groups on Hill 217. His conspicuous heroism and powers of leadership stiffened the resolve of KOSB's B Company, and against all the odds the Chinese assaults were beaten off sufficiently to allow an orderly withdrawal from the ridge.

To the right of the ridge the KOSB positions were held on a feature called the Knoll by two platoons from C and D Companies which had come under the command of 2nd Lieutenant William Purves following the wounding of the senior subaltern. Formerly a bank clerk from Kelso in the Scottish Borders, Purves was a National Service officer with a reputation for being quiet and retiring, but his effective defence of the Knoll allowed his men to retire in good order in the early hours of the morning on 4 November. Every wounded man from the two platoons was withdrawn from the ridge, and despite his own wound Purves personally oversaw the dangerous operation until all his men had been shepherded safely off the hill.

> The position on the Knoll held by 2nd Lieutenant Purves's platoon of C Company and 2nd Lieutenant Henderson's of D Company was obscure owing to communications being destroyed. However, at about midnight it was established that this gallant party was still holding out though running short of ammunition, that 2nd Lieutenant Henderson being wounded, 2nd Lieutenant Purves had assumed command of the two platoons. Surrounded on three

sides, the plight of this party was serious. 2nd Lieutenant Purves was ordered to try and fight his way out towards D Company who were now holding out on 'Peak', a foothill of Point 317. This unpleasant operation was brilliantly carried out under the very nose of the enemy on Point 317. This exploit was rendered even more remarkable in that 2nd Lieutenant Purves succeeded in evacuating all the wounded and the complete equipment of his platoon under heavy mortar fire.[20]

For his conspicuous gallantry and devotion to duty 2nd Lieutenant Purves was awarded the DSO, a unique and never-to-be-repeated achievement for a National Service officer.

The bravery shown by men like Speakman and Purves – and by the entire battalion – allowed the KOSB to complete a successful evacuation from the ridge at a low cost in lives. 7 Borderers had been killed and 87 wounded, but after the battle it was estimated that the Chinese 'human wave' tactics had led to their sustaining around one thousand casualties. At one point the men of D Company had run out of ammunition and been forced to hurl rocks and even beer bottles at the advancing enemy; on a more serious logistical note, the KOSB Mortar Battery fired a total of 4,500 rounds during the night-long engagement. Both the KSLI and the KOSB spent another eight months in Korea, fighting through a winter which saw the war along the 38th Parallel degenerate into a struggle of static defence reminiscent of the Western Front battles during World War I. From this period onwards the domination of No Man's Land became the crucial test of the war as the stationary armies probed each other's defences. Hardly a night passed without infantry patrols infiltrating the Chinese lines, testing the enemy's strength, collecting intelligence information and attempting the difficult task of capturing Chinese prisoners for interrogation. (This latter duty reaped few rewards as most Chinese and North Koreans managed to commit suicide before – and in some cases, even after – being taken.) Most of the patrols were led by young subalterns, many of them National Servicemen.

For the most part, as in any war, the patrols passed off without incident, but they were always hazardous affairs involving danger and discomfort in the night-time landscape of No Man's Land. Frequently a British patrol would meet its Chinese counterpart and men would die or be injured in the resulting firefight; there were occasions, too, when patrols wandered into their own side's minefields or found that shells intended for the enemy were in fact falling on them; and at all times there was the torture of bitterly cold winter nights or tense hours spent in damp paddy fields.

Typical of the many patrol actions undertaken by men of the Commonwealth Division was one involving soldiers of the Duke of Wellington's Regiment on 24 January 1953 from their position at Yong Dong near a camel-humped hill called The Hook, shortly to be the scene of the last great action of the war. The patrol of 15 was under the command of Lieutenant Rodney Harms, the assault group was led by 2nd Lieutenant Ian Orr, a National Service subaltern, and their target was the destruction of an enemy communications trench which had been discovered behind the Chinese lines. The operation had been meticulously planned, and the preparation bore fruit.

> On approaching the tunnel 2nd Lt. Orr heard excited Chinese voices and firing which indicated that the alarm had been given. Nevertheless, he boldly ran forward and placed himself in front of the entrance from where he could effectively throw a phosphorus grenade. Whilst in the act of throwing he saw a party of Chinese soldiers and immediately came under sub-machine gun fire. Not being satisfied that his first grenade had landed sufficiently far inside the tunnel, he again rushed forward in front of the entrance and threw another grenade. As the machine gun fire still continued he hurled grenades into the tunnel until the enemy was silenced. He then called forward a number of his group who blew up the tunnel with a prepared explosive charge. By his bravery and complete disregard for his own personal safety 2nd Lt. Orr was able to silence the enemy opposition, thus allowing the tunnel to be destroyed and ensuring the complete success of the mission.[21]

Both Harms and Orr were rightly awarded the Military Cross, but there were many other patrols which yielded equally useful results and yet went unsung. The Dukes had a larger than average quota of National Service subalterns, many of them attracted to the regiment because of its rugby-playing tradition* and their keenness and enthusiasm helped to make the battalion's night patrols particularly effective.

Lying next to the Dukes on The Hook were The Black Watch, who had repulsed a desperate Chinese assault in November 1952 during which one of their National Service officers, 2nd Lieutenant M. D. G. Black, had won the Military Cross and seven other officers and men had been decorated for gallantry. Black had been in command of an advance standing patrol which had

---

*Of their number 2nd Lieutenant D. S. Gilbert-Smith had played for Scotland and 2nd Lieutenant M. J. Campbell-Lamerton later captained Scotland and the British Lions. Lieutenant D. W. Shuttleworth, a Regular officer, had won his first English cap against Scotland in 1951.

taken the brunt of the first Chinese assault; cut off from the rump of his company, commanded by Major Angus Irwin, Black and his men had been reduced to hurling rocks and fighting off the Chinese with their fists, but his stand allowed the Highlanders to aim their counter-attack at his position and by dawn on 18 November the enemy had been beaten off. Throughout the battle – which came to be known as the First Battle of the Hook – Black had shown a cheerfulness which was out of keeping with his and his men's parlous position. Asked by Irwin if he was as carefree as he sounded, Black quipped: 'No. Never have been!' During the course of the battle The Black Watch lost 12 men killed, 67 wounded and 20 missing: the Jocks counted almost a hundred Chinese dead before they were sickened by the task of counting bodies.

At the end of January 1953 the US 2nd Division took over the Commonwealth Division's sector of the line, allowing the British infantrymen a brief breathing space after confronting the enemy continuously during the previous eighteen months. The armistice talks at Panmunjon were still dragging on, largely due to Chinese intransigence, and the stalemate continued – a state of affairs which dictated continued fighting to prevent either side gaining a tactical advantage. There were still several months of hard fighting ahead for the men of the Commonwealth Division and when The Black Watch and the Dukes, backed up by 1st Bn. The King's Regiment, returned to The Hook in May they were to be on the receiving end of the last and most fiercely contested action – the Third Battle of The Hook.

The three-week long struggle began on the night of 7/8 May when the Chinese began a series of probing attacks on The Black Watch lines in the forward positions on The Hook. Occupying a forward section position of the battalion's observation post was Lance-Corporal Jim Laird, a National Serviceman from Glasgow who had been in Korea for almost a year.

> I had just reported to the platoon officer and was told to make my way to the section position again on the right of the line. By the time I was out of the dug-out the shelling was very heavy and every now and then I had to make a dive for it. It was obvious that a major attack was coming in on The Hook and that we were enjoying the first round of shelling. I got back into my own section area where we were pinned down. It got even worse when a Centurion tank, normally dug into the hillside, came forward into its command position. As soon as it came in all hell broke loose, most of the shells were dropping short so it was very much a case

of staying where you were and keeping low. Something hit the back of the trench and I went out like a light.
>   (Lance-Corporal Jim Laird, 1st Bn. The Black Watch)

Jim Laird had in fact received a spinal wound which was to leave him permanently paralysed from the chest down and to change dramatically his future life. Once the bombardment had eased off – it was estimated that over a hundred shells had landed in his immediate area – he was taken to the regimental aid post, bandaged up and then flown out by helicopter to a nearby American Mobile Army Surgical Hospital (MASH).

> Although not in a state to remember a great deal at the time, my memory does have some very vivid flashes of recall such as evacuation from the collapsed trench and being taken by jeep to the Command Post, of being strapped into a stretcher under the blades of the helicopter, with a partially covering hood over my head and shoulders, and the enormous downdraught of the blades tugging at the blankets around my body. In my next moment I had arrived at the 44th MASH unit and was being examined by an American surgeon, Major Allan F. Kingman Jnr. of the USAMC who was the start of my good fortune, being one of the few who were aware of the then new attitudes and methods in treating a spinal injury casualty. This came about because of the policy to staff these front-line MASH units with leading, fully qualified medics who had been drafted to serve where they were sorely needed and greatly appreciated by all the more seriously wounded United Nations casualties who were evacuated into their care.
>   (Lance-Corporal Jim Laird, 1st Bn. The Black Watch)

From Korea Laird was airlifted to Japan, and then in June he made the long and exhausting journey home by plane back to Britain. After periods at the Wheatley Military Hospital in Oxford and later at Stoke Mandeville, Jim Laird began the long journey towards partial rehabilitation and the prospect of life in a wheelchair. He was one of the 2,498 casualties listed as 'wounded' during the war in Korea.

Intelligence reports suggested to Brigadier Joe Kendrew, the new commander of 29 Brigade, that the Chinese attack was but a prelude to a new and larger assault. To meet it he withdrew the exhausted Black Watch from their front-line position and replaced them with the Dukes who moved in on 12 May. The main attack came a fortnight later on the night of 28 May, and it was preceded by an artillery assault reckoned to be more intense than any mounted during the Battle of the Somme in 1916. During the following forty-eight hours the Dukes resisted the

Chinese assaults and the furious artillery barrage to keep The
Hook secure for the UN forces; their stoicism and devotion to
duty, even when facing numerically superior odds, won the day in
what will undoubtedly be the last full-scale defensive infantry
battle fought by the British Army. Of their conduct, Kendrew
said: 'My God, those Dukes. They were marvellous. In the whole
of the last war I never knew anything like that bombardment. But
they held The Hook, as I knew they would.'

Serving with the Dukes at The Hook was 2nd Lieutenant D. J.
Hollands, a National Service subaltern who went on to write
about his experiences in Korea in a novel published in 1956, *The
Dead, The Dying and The Damned*. Based on his time with the
Dukes, it followed the story of Able Company, the Royal
Rockinghamshire Regiment, and Hollands was to view the Third
Battle of The Hook from a different – and more jaundiced – point
of view to that held by many of his fellow officers.

> For a day they might be called the heroes of The Hook, but they
> were not heroes – the heroes of the nation were a bunch of men
> who had climbed Everest, or sportsmen, or filmstars; they were
> simply the latest edition of Tommy Atkins, the men who in time of
> peace were treated as the scum of the land, laughed at, sneered at,
> and generally held in ridicule by the public and who in time of war
> were taken for granted.

In his introductory note to the novel Hollands called the armed
struggle in Korea 'one of the most sordid and bloody wars in the
history of the world', and remarked that, in the latter stages at
least, the brunt of action was borne not by the high command but
by young National Service subalterns and infantrymen in the
forward command positions of the Commonwealth Division.

> Throughout the Korean War a constant stream of young National
> Servicemen were leaving this country and joining the United
> Nations Forces in their so-called fight for freedom. Very few of
> them knew why they were going and the majority of them did not
> care – until it was too late; they were simply doing as they were
> told as members of the British Army.

There were servicemen who questioned the validity of Britain's
involvement in the Korean War, and many returning National
Servicemen – especially those who had served as infantry soldiers
– felt bitter about the roles they had been asked to play. Not only
had they not understood Britain's motives for fighting; at the

war's end it seemed that nothing had been achieved, that a questionable regime had been established in South Korea under President Syngman Rhee, and that many men had died in vain defending obscure principles.

Other servicemen returning from Korea were critical of the level of training they had received prior to fighting an unknown enemy over difficult terrain. In the later stages of the war, subalterns joining Commonwealth Division units as platoon leaders were given intensive training at the Commonwealth battle camp at Hara Mura in Japan, but nothing could have prepared them for the actual shock of battle. As for the men they led, improvisation was usually the order of the day, as the anonymous writer to the *Red Hackle* observed after The Black Watch arrived in June 1952.

> Ten days was all too short a time to do even a tenth of the training we knew was necessary. We were surprised, too, that the Brigade Exercises were of a mobile nature, and not what we were to need in the immediate future. We had many lectures from the 'Old Boys' of the Commonwealth Division, and we very quickly learnt how to scrounge and to improvise. With the aid of our Korean porter company, we soon had a small parade ground and Company swimming baths. The Pipes and Drums played Retreat on the parade ground to a large gathering of officers the Sunday before we went into the line.

Most of the battalion's National Servicemen had only received sixteen weeks basic training at Fort George in Scotland, followed by a similar period in Germany. Consequently they had to learn by experience, and the *Red Hackle* wryly remarked that two days of rain showed the men that they still had 'a lot to learn about weather-proofing'. When they entered the line in July the battalion retained a number of officers and men who had fought in World War II, but seven years of peacetime soldiering had unlearned many of the lessons gained in combat. Like the other British units in Korea they had to fall back on the first tenets of basic training.

> There was no doubting that we were well disciplined. From Day One at Fort George we had been pressured and efficiently processed to run, stand still, jump, salute, obey without question – or take the consequences. We were brimming with an élite Scottish brand of *esprit de corps*, and this combination of élitism and pride was shown to be sufficient to allow us to be led onto the field of battle without any great doubts that we would stand and defend ourselves when required – without tarnishing the good

record of the Regiment. The battle training could be safely left to the hard school of bitter experience.

(Lance-Corporal Jim Laird, 1st Bn. The Black Watch)

In fact, The Black Watch was superbly led and its commanding officer, Lieutenant-Colonel David Rose, was an experienced soldier who exuded an air of calm authority which greatly impressed his younger untried officers during the heaviest fighting. That combination of obedience and discipline – both to their superiors and to the spirit of the regiment – also affected the men, and their conduct under shellfire or in hand-to-hand fighting was considered to be beyond reproach.

In spite of all the difficulties and dangers, and despite the belief held by many young men that the war in Korea was senseless waste, most veterans of the war are agreed that the role played by National Servicemen was vital to the needs of the Commonwealth Division. Brigadier Kendrew had this to say of them after the war:

> I must also pay tribute to the National Servicemen that made up sixty per cent of the Regular Battalions. These young men, mostly nineteen years old, adapted themselves to the art and hell of war and played a full part in writing their regiment's histories. Many of the platoons were led by National Service officers.[22]

The war in Korea officially came to a full stop on 27 July 1953 with the signing of a truce at Panmunjon, and the same armistice remains in force some thirty years later. 12,773 UN prisoners were returned after enduring varying degrees of deprivation and hardship (one British POW elected to stay on in North Korea); a demarcation line was established roughly along the 38th Parallel; and South Korea and North Korea went their different political ways. The United Nations command in Korea still has a token existence, and Britain still provides an occasional guard of honour to its headquarters at Panmunjon.

From a military point of view the war in Korea exposed many shortcomings in the equipment and weapons of the British Army, a lesson which would be more cruelly rammed home during the Suez invasion three years later. The realisation that Britain was no longer a first-class power with armed forces to match its pretensions began to dawn in Korea, and, just as in the Great War field officers could find no solution to the problems of trench warfare, so too did the military command in Korea find it impossible to cope with the Chinese 'human wave' tactics. The war was also extremely unpopular at home, especially in its final stages, and the evidence of the hardships and casualties endured by National Servicemen was a contributory factor to the ever-growing public dissatisfaction with conscription. Public opinion polls in 1949 showed that 57% of the population thought National Service worthwhile and 33% were opposed to it. By 1953, those figures had been reversed.

Chapter Eight

NO MORE SOLDIERING FOR ME

Many of the counter-insurgency methods used to such good effect in Malaya were employed in another colonial trouble-spot which faced an armed uprising from a disaffected section of its population. In October 1952 the Governor of Kenya, Sir Evelyn Baring, declared a state of emergency in the country following rioting and the murder of a prominent native leader, perpetrated by Mau Mau terrorists of the Kikuyu tribe whose homelands lay to the north of the capital city of Nairobi. Although the Mau Mau did not possess the same sophisticated command structure as the communist terrorists in Malaya, and neither did they have access to modern weapons, they were to prove obstinate opponents whose tactics consisted mainly of acts of terror and the ritualistic murder of those natives who would not support them. Their principal targets were white settlers in remote areas and Kikuyu tribesmen loyal to the colonial government.

At the start of the Mau Mau emergency, Kenya was an out-station of GHQ Middle East, and its only regular troops were those of the King's African Rifles. By 1956 when the emergency had been brought under control – it did not end formally until 12 January 1960 – Kenya had become a separate command, and eleven infantry battalions with supporting engineer and signals units had served in the country, often under very trying conditions.

> Fighting the Mau Mau is not a very dangerous job compared to the Korean War, but it is a strenuous business nonetheless. Despite the brutal attacks on their own people and on lonely European farmers and their families, the Kikuyu gangsters will not stand and fight a patrol of six armed soldiers, even at odds of 10 to 1. In fact, our chief difficulty is to inflict maximum casualties on first contact,

before the gang has dissolved into the thick jungle. We attack the
enemy in three different ways. Patrols try to gain contact with the
gangs in the forest which is termed a 'prohibited area'. Here we
can shoot on sight. These patrols are usually of 24 hours duration,
but sometimes longer, and they carry 'compo' rations and a
wireless set. If they make contact with a gang they follow up as
hard as they can, using native trackers.[23]

The Black Watch's experience of anti-Mau Mau operations was
typical of the methods used by the infantry battalions in co-
ordination with the Kenya police force and the specially raised
'Home Guard' units: forest patrols to locate enemy hide-outs,
followed by sweeps and drives to flush out the Mau Mau gangs.
These were rather different affairs from the jungle patrols of
Malaya, for although the forest areas of Kenya presented their
own difficulties of thick undergrowth, high altitude, wild animals
and ferocious insects, they were not so enervating or depressing
as the damp and dark of the Malayan 'ulu'. Further initiatives
included the designation of the Aberdare Mountains as a war
zone, or 'no go area', the infiltration of Mau Mau gangs by
Special Branch men, and the establishment of 'counter gangs',
groups of loyal natives or former Mau Mau men who had
betrayed their blood oath of allegiance and thrown in their lot
with their colonial masters. At the same time a rapid programme
of social and political reforms, aimed at improving the conditions
of the black population of Kenya, undercut much of the Mau
Mau support except in the remote areas of the Aberdares. It was
a long, drawn-out and frustrating campaign which few servicemen
enjoyed: at its end it was estimated that the security forces had
accounted for 11,503 Mau Mau casualties in return for the loss of
590 casualties of their own.

Not all of the post-war actions in which National Servicemen
were involved generated as much publicity as the wars in Malaya
and Korea or the civil unrest in the Suez Canal Zone, Cyprus and
Kenya. British troops had to deal with IRA-inspired disturbances
in Northern Ireland in 1948, and again between 1952 and 1956.
Aid to the civil power was given to the Gold Coast in 1948, to
Somaliland between 1949 and 1951, to Singapore and Hong Kong
in 1956 during a period of severe rioting in both cities, to Bahrein
and Togoland in 1957, to Jordan and Barbados in 1958, to the
Cameroons, Jamaica and Hong Kong again in 1960, to Kuwait,
Zanzibar and Belize in 1961, to Guatamala and British Guiana in
1962, to Zanzibar and Cyprus once more in 1963 at the beginning
of the Greek-Turkish confrontations.

Usually such operations involved riot control, coping with eruptions of nationalist ardour, holding the peace while the former colony eased itself into independence, or simply shoring up British interests. At other times, troops were called on to pick up the pieces after a natural disaster. In August 1951 the men of the 1st Bn. Royal Welch Fusiliers helped to clear up the streets of Kingston after a disastrous hurricane had hit the island of Jamaica; engineers were on hand to lend assistance after the Ionian islands were struck by earthquakes in 1953, and in 1961 British troops were again in Kenya, this time to aid the civil powers after the country had been hit by serious flooding. Nor were these isolated incidents: not a year passed during the period of National Service without British servicemen lending a hand in some corner of the world or another, unloading supplies, constructing airstrips or just simply passing out bars of chocolate to inquisitive local children.

Although it continued to be obvious that the armed forces – the army in particular – still needed large annual intakes of conscripts to meet their obligations, throughout the 1950s the subject of National Service and its usefulness – or otherwise – was never far away from staff discussions. Those senior officers who supported National Service regarded it not only as a measure designed to keep the armed forces up to strength, but also as a means of improving their quality. Writing in the *Army Quarterly* of April 1950, Lt-Col E. H. Tinker put the case for conscription.

> The attitude of the average man towards National Service must be that it is an irritating interruption to his career. Having said this, it is indeed possible that many enter the Army with an open mind, prepared to make the best of it, but also prepared to be critical if they consider their time is being wasted.

Against those pious hopes – National Servicemen complained at their peril – other officers argued impatiently that the army could never conform to its prewar status of being a closed family of professionals until the last temporary guests had departed from its ranks. At the War Office, too, some staff officers were coming round to the idea in the early fifties that National Service was only a temporary measure and that the army would soon have to face a future without conscription. In February 1952 Lt. General Sir John F. M. Whiteley, DCIGS, noted that Britain's eventual withdrawal from Empire and a possible decrease in international tension could lead to the armed forces being cut back.

I only mention this because it has dawned on me that we are now taking a number of steps which if we continue will make the Regular Army more and more dependent on National Service and perhaps we shall eventually find ourselves with a manpower structure which would make the removal of National Service extremely crippling. For instance, we are now aiming, and rightly in my opinion, to offer a life career in the Army. This we can do without anxiety because at the present moment the need for the Regular Army Reserve has virtually disappeared thanks to National Service. But if the latter was ever taken from us we should be seriously embarrassed if the long service offer is widely accepted.[24]

This was written at a time when the strength of the Regular Army had reached its postwar peak of 441,128 men, and when British involvement in Korea and Malaya required additional recruits; yet three years later most senior officers had agreed reluctantly that, however much conscription might be a military necessity, it was unpopular from a political point of view. A General Staff brief of 7 July 1955, written at the behest of the Cabinet, summarised the feeling that the nation's high command would have to take into account the fact that National Service had become decidedly unpopular with the British people: 'There are obvious military disadvantages to an early end to the call-up, but it is considered that this will probably be outweighed by political factors.'

The debate was not confined to the army. For every senior Royal Navy or RAF officer who wanted to see an end to National Service, there could be found one to argue that it had played a creditable part in bolstering those services' manpower. In the RAF especially, the presence of National Servicemen meant that routine and unskilled tasks could be left to the conscripts, thus freeing Regulars for more specialised and technical posts. This attitude was not lost on the National Serviceman of the late 1950s. When asked if his duties were useful or relevant to the nation's security, most would reply, 'Hardly!' Neither was this feeling confined to the RAF: while serving with the Senior Railway Traffic Office at Longmoor in Hampshire, Corporal Iain Colquhoun and his fellow sappers put their frustrations into song – popular, too, at other bases – which they sang to the tune of *The Mountains of Mourne*:

> *They say that this Longmoor's a wonderful place,*
> *But the organisation's a fucking disgrace.*
> *There's sergeants and corporals and lance-corporals too,*

With their hands in their pockets and fuck-all to do.
They stand on the square and they bawl and they shout,
They shout about things they know fuck-all about.
And for all that I've done here I might as well be
Shovellin' up shit on the Isle of Capri.

Partly, the dissatisfaction had economic roots. Not only did National Servicemen earn a good deal less than their Regular colleagues*, but many, usually those with trade qualifications, received less pay than they would have done in civilian life. They might have known that their jobs would be waiting for them on demob – a legal right they shared with the conscripts of World War II – but the two years of miserly pay was often a cause of irritation and, in some cases, genuine hardship. This was particularly true of men who had to make a financial contribution to their family at home, or to those, a minority, who were married and had wives to support.

Taking a wider perspective, National Service also brought with it problems to the British economy. The annual intake of 160,000 men meant a loss of double that number each year (taking into account serving men and those about to be demobbed), with the result that British industry faced acute manpower shortages throughout the 1950s, a period of relatively high employment. Equally badly hit were small businesses or family firms which could ill afford the loss, albeit temporary, of key members of staff. Then there was the problem of readjustment to civilian life, of keeping the boys down on the farm now that they'd seen Paree. At a meeting of the British Association for Commercial and Industrial Education, held in Edinburgh in October 1954, the industrialists present complained that young trainees returning to work after their National Service turned out to be more unsettled and poorer workers than deferred or exempted men. Later that year the General Council of the National Farmers' Union reported that of the total number of farmhands conscripted into the armed forces only 50% returned to their jobs once their National Service was over.

The problem of post-National Service employment was studied under the auspices of the Nuffield Foundation at the University of Glasgow in the mid-1950s, and the report's conclusions offered scant comfort to supporters of National Service (*In Their Early Twenties: A Study of Glasgow Youth*). Of the control group of

---

*They cost less, too. The Army calculated that the Regular cost four times as much to pay and twice as much to keep as his National Service counterpart.

346 ex-National Servicemen interviewed by Professor Ferguson
and Dr Cunnison, it was discovered that 21.1% experienced
difficulty in settling back into civilian life and work. Frequency of
job change was the most obvious manifestation of that sense of
dislocation, with 35% of the total admitting that they had
changed jobs at least once in the first year of their demob from
the services. This figure compared badly with the findings from a
second group of 222 men who had not done National Service, and
the trend towards a loss of skills in industry led the authors to
conclude that 'it must be a bad thing for the lads concerned and,
in the long run, for the country.'

In a prize-winning essay, published in the *Army Quarterly* in
October 1961 when the end of National Service was in sight,
Captain R. I. Raitt of the Gordon Highlanders put forward a
theory that one reason for Britain's slow progress towards
technological innovation in its industries was that each year the
country lost its brightest and best minds to military service. On
the other hand, he argued, West Germany – which did not
introduce conscription until 1955 – had in the same period laid the
foundations of its *Wirtschaftswunder*, the rapid progression from
post-war austerity to relative prosperity and economic stability.
His argument does not take into account the fact that in spite of
the wartime allied bombing offensive, Germany's economic
potential was still the highest in Europe, or that the country had
made excellent use of the aid provided by the Marshall Plan;
nevertheless, Raitt's essay did provide a thought-provoking
antidote to the oft-heard argument that conscription, *per se*, was
a good thing for the youth of the country.

Certainly, the most conservative supporters of National Service
thought its principal benefit to be that it instilled in young people
codes of discipline, dress and behaviour which they themselves
held; but by 1955 the battle for conscription was being fought less
on the grounds of its social usefulness than on its military and
economic effectiveness. The maintenance of large armed forces
after 1945 had become a costly burden and politicians from all
parties were starting to question the assumption that Britain
could afford to remain a world power.

In October 1955 a Gallup Poll revealed that 32% favoured
defence cuts more than any other form of economy, and earlier
that year, in April, the Labour Party had made a reduction in
defence expenditure coupled to a gradual phasing out of National
Service one of its commitments during the Spring General
Election. Although the Conservatives were returned to power –

under a new Prime Minister, Anthony Eden – some members of the new Cabinet, including the Minister of Defence, Selwyn Lloyd, admitted privately that National Service would have to go as it was now proving to be an expensive and inefficient liability. Even Eden, speaking at an election meeting in Rugby, was prepared to say that 'everybody wants to reduce the period of National Service'; his only reason for not wanting to do so immediately being his wish not to weaken Britain's position in the forthcoming disarmament talks with the Soviet Union.

As it was, Eden only waited until October before announcing that the strength of the armed forces would be reduced from 800,000 to 700,000, that there would be three instead of four registration dates a year, and that the call-up age would be increased, gradually, to nineteen. To his colleagues in the House of Commons he explained that the steps had been taken because Britain no longer needed a large strategic reserve – the building up of which had been one of the reasons for the introduction of post- war conscription in 1947–1948. At the same time, to speed up the transport of reinforcements, the government placed orders for Comet and Britannia aircraft to serve with RAF Transport Command.

By 1955, too, the armed forces were starting to tire of National Service. The RAF and the Royal Navy had already downgraded the status of their conscript airmen and sailors, and even in the Army, which required higher manpower levels, a body of opinion was questioning the usefulness of National Service. Firstly, it was now considered to be too wasteful as the continual intakes of raw recruits tied down Regulars in boring training routines; secondly, the end of National Service would encourage recruiting if Regular pay and conditions were improved; and thirdly, it was felt that two years was too short a term to train men and then use them to the best of their abilities. Besides, by the mid-1950s, National Service had become something of a military embarrassment, producing more men than were actually required for service at home: a committee under the chairmanship of Sir John Wolfenden, sponsored by the Army Council to examine popular claims that 'National Service manpower, and the National Service man's time during his service were being wastefully used', considered that large numbers of conscript soldiers were no longer required in the Regular Army.

> We have personally interviewed, often in private, many hundreds of National Service men. Our overwhelming impression is that, with few exceptions, the National Service man regards his two year

period of service as 'an infliction to be undergone rather than a duty to the nation'. It is this state of mind which encourages the National Service men to regard 'spit and polish', guard duty and prolonged drills as unnecessary impositions rather than as necessary elements in a scheme of training.

A similar conclusion had already been reached in the report of another research project, *Citizens of Tomorrow*, published by King George's Jubilee Trust in 1955. The Wolfenden report – *Report of the Committee on the Employment of National Service men in the United Kingdom* – went a stage further, though, and recommended that the Army should do more to place trained men in responsible posts, that there should be discussions with the TUC to assimilate military and civilian codes of training, and that many routine administrative tasks should be carried out by civilian labour. In other words, National Service was only useful to the nation if it gave a decent training and made the conscript soldier feel he was giving useful service to his country. The Army Council accepted the committee's report, although it was also quick to point out that defence cuts and lack of money would slow down any timetable of reform.

Another military argument in favour of reducing, or abandoning, National Service was occasioned by the introduction of nuclear weapons to Britain's arsenal. The first British atomic bomb had been exploded in the Monte Bello Islands on 3 October 1952, and thereafter the testing of similar nuclear devices continued in the Pacific and in Australia at regular intervals, lending confidence to a political belief that Britain might still claim to be a 'super power'. The test programme continued for five years, culminating in the dropping of Britain's first thermonuclear bomb from a Valiant jet bomber of 49 Squadron on 15 May 1957. This feat, plus the construction of the necessary bases at the Christmas and Malden Islands in the Pacific, and the massive monitoring operation, was a further factor in changing the direction of the government's defence policy towards a reliance on nuclear strategy – that is, the doctrine of dependence upon the deterrent powers of nuclear weapons. Such a policy would of necessity entail a reduction in manpower levels and the creation of smaller, more mobile and more professional armed forces. It was also felt that the introduction of nuclear weapons and their carriers would restore Britain's prestige and independence of action, both of which had been severely dented by the costly and disastrous military intervention over Suez.

*

With good reason, the Suez fiasco of November 1956 has been described as a watershed in British strategic thinking. Ostensibly, Britain's decision to use armed force against Egypt was born of President Nasser's nationalisation of the Suez Canal Company on 26 July 1956, thus forcing all users of the canal to pay tolls to Egypt instead of to the Anglo-French consortium which legally owned it; in reality, the conflict was caused by Britain's need to remain a key power in the Middle East. It was also fuelled by Eden's fear and dislike of Nasser, whom he compared to Hitler and Mussolini; and by the long shadow of British appeasement to the German dictator when he had seized the Rhineland, Austria and Czechoslovakia during the 1930s.

Relations between Eden and Nasser, never of the best, had been further soured the previous year, 1955, when Egypt had refused to join the Baghdad Pact, the alliance of Iran, Iraq, Pakistan and Britain aimed at strengthening the West's defences against possible Soviet aggression in the Middle East. This had been followed by a British refusal to supply Egypt with modern weapons: in reply Nasser had signed an arms deal with Czechoslovakia which provided him with modern Soviet aircraft and military weapons. In all his public dealings Nasser was nothing loath to appear violently anti-British, and in time Eden had come to believe that only by his removal could Britain restore her prestige in the Arab world. The seizure of the Suez Canal Company provided him with the motive.

The day after Nasser's proclamation Eden called together his Chiefs of Staff to lay down plans for an invasion and seizure of the canal in conjunction with French forces: these included, as a precaution, the call-up of some 20,000 'Z' reservists, many of whom were ex-National Servicemen, although, in the event, the invasion force was composed mostly of Regulars with a smattering of serving National Servicemen. The story of the Anglo-French military preparations has been told many times and a sorry tale it is, too. Britain had been strategically committed to a possible war in western Europe and to counter-insurgency or police actions in what remained of her world empire; in consequence most of the lessons learned during World War II about combined operations and seaborne landings had been lost. There were also problems with equipment. Warships and transports had to be taken out of reserve, there was an acute shortage of landing craft and the planes of the much-vaunted air transport fleet turned out to be useless for paratroop operations. In the end, the British paratroopers had to be flown in by side-loading Valettas while the more professional French employed rear-loading Nordatlas aircraft, and the Centurion tanks of the armoured units (1st and 6th Royal Tank Regiment) had to be transported to their ports of embarkation, courtesy of the removal firm of Thomas Pickford. Further problems were caused by the lack of training for airborne assaults by the men of 16th Parachute Brigade and 3rd Commando Brigade, many of whom had been engaged in anti-terrorist work in Cyprus.

While the Anglo-French forces laid uncertain plans, the politicians continued to talk in an attempt to bring world opinion round to their way of thinking. It was a vain hope. America was approaching a presidential election and the incumbent, Dwight D. Eisenhower, refused to lend his support to any aggression over Suez; on the other side of the fence, the Soviet Union bluntly let it be known that it would offer its support to Egypt in the face of any 'imperialist aggression'. In the event, a run on the pound – lack of American support caused British gold and dollar reserves to fall by £100 million – brought the whole sorry adventure to an end, but not before the Soviet Premier Bulganin had warned Eden that 'other means, such as a rocket technique' might have to be used against Britain.

The actual actions in which Anglo-French forces were involved took place in the first week of November after a successful Israeli attack on Sinai. (With British complicity, France had brought Israel, already threatened by Nasser, into the allied camp.) Following allied air attacks on Egyptian bases to wipe out the enemy air force, the Anglo-French paratroop forces landed on 5 November, seized their objective at Gamil without much difficulty and paved the way for a ponderous seaborne landing at Port Said. All resistance came to an end the next day, but by then the 'war' was over before it had really begun: American financial pressure had forced Eden to call a cease-fire and to turn the problem over to the United Nations. (Washington refused to support Britain's application to the International Monetary Fund for a loan to support the falling pound unless those conditions were met.)

British casualties in Suez were 22 dead and 97 wounded, but the greatest damage was done to her international standing. Egypt's neighbours in the Middle East had been outraged and the United Nations' Security Council had roundly condemned the Anglo-French action. To make matters worse for Eden's government, the reasons for the sudden cease-fire were widely known, and the subsequent withdrawal was a stunning public humiliation which marked the beginning of the end of Britain's position as a global power, a new and uncertain position which was bound to lead to a rapid rethinking of her military role. When Britain did come to revise her defence thinking in 1957, however, the changes turned out to be less radical than expected; but the one change of which the majority of the public approved was the decision to phase out National Service.

After Suez the protests against National Service had become more insistent. The Labour Party's Shadow Defence Minister, George Brown, spoke for many ordinary people when he declared his absolute opposition to conscription during a debate on defence in the House of Commons on 13 February 1957.

> It is National Service that makes the Army so costly, so inflexible and so immobile. We, on this side, believe that until a decision is taken on policy grounds to get rid of National Service, many of the other decisions that will raise the efficiency and purpose of our Services will never be taken.

The political climate was now right for an early end to National Service: the service chiefs, though, still had to be persuaded that Britain could meet her defence and strategic requirements with slimmed-down forces. The man responsible for making the change of direction, and for winning the armed forces over to the government's thinking, was Duncan Sandys, who became Minister of Defence in Harold Macmillan's Cabinet in January 1957. (Anthony Eden had resigned, on the grounds of ill-health, on 9 January.)

Sandys was a strong believer in the future of nuclear weapons and he also put great faith in Britain's ability to remain a 'super power' with her own carrier systems – he had been an enthusiastic supporter of the development of the Blue Streak rocket, and during his régime the Blue Steel 'stand-off' bomb added greatly to the strike capacity of the 'V' bomber force. His Defence White Paper (*Defence: Outline of Future Policy*, Cmnd. 124, 1957), released on 4 April 1957, based its argument on two principles: that defence spending was, and had been, too great a burden on the nation's economy; and that in a nuclear war no country could fight a major conflict with any hope of gaining ultimate victory. His doctrine of cutting the defence coat according to the available cloth resulted in a tailoring which took into account Britain's traditional role in world strategy. Its main points were:

1. Nuclear deterrent: thermo-nuclear weapons would be added to Britain's strike force and ballistic missiles would be added as they became available.

2. Conventional forces: the armed forces would be gradually re-equipped with modern weapons and World War II equipment (cruelly exposed at Suez) phased out.
3. Mobility: a new central strategic reserve would be created and RAF Transport Command strengthened. This would allow Britain to maintain bases in the Middle and Far East.
4. Home Defence: as it was expected that Britain could not fend off a nuclear strike, RAF Fighter Command was to be reduced and Anti-Aircraft Command finally phased out.
5. Manpower: conscription would be phased out by 1962, by which time service manpower levels would have dropped from 690,000 to 375,000.

Other measures included a cutback in the strength of Britain's forces in West Germany, the development of new supersonic strike and interdiction aircraft for the RAF, and the rationalisation of the Royal Navy's fleet strength. Sandys estimated that the overall savings in 1957 over the previous year's expenditure would be £180 million.

As the army would be the greatest loser when National Service came to an end, Sandys had to fight hard to convince service chiefs that a reliance on the nuclear deterrent and enhanced mobility would require smaller numbers of men. In 1956, a committee under the chairmanship of Lt. General Sir Richard Hull had forecast that the army's needs at any time would be a minimum of 220,000 men: under the Sandys' doctrine, the requirement for the early 1960s was 165,000 men. Even to achieve that latter aim without conscription, argued the army, would require new incentives, and one long-term effect of the Sandys' White Paper was the establishment of the Grigg Advisory Committee which advocated a steady improvement of living standards, pay and training related to equivalents in civilian life. It published its findings on 4 November 1958 and its principal recommendations were that service pay should be reviewed every two years, that pensions should be increased, that bad housing should be improved and that officers should be drawn from a wider social class. The committee also introduced the idea that officers should be retired early if their careers did not progress satisfactorily.

Despite those enhancements recruiting to the army was slow, and the Army Council argued strongly for the retention of National Service after 1962 if the minimum figure of 165,000 had not been reached. Critics of the ending of conscription, like Field

Marshal Lord Harding, CIGS, lived to see some of their worst fears fulfilled during the early 1960s when the army was stretched almost to breaking point. In 1962 9,000 National Servicemen had to be retained for a further six months due to a manpower shortage caused by the Berlin Crisis, and that same year sappers and craftsmen found themselves being employed as infantrymen during the early stages of the Aden emergency.

As one reason for the introduction of post-war National Service had been the maintenance of a large strategic reserve, there were also changes in the structure of Britain's reserve forces. After 1957 ex-National Servicemen were relieved of their obligation to train with the Territorial Army; by then, the strategic role envisaged for this reserve force had, in any case, been radically modified. Originally, the post-war Territorial Army had been re-created under Lord Montgomery's guidance as a regular volunteer force augmented by time-served National Servicemen of the Army Emergency Reserve: in that guise it would maintain 6 infantry divisions, 2 armoured divisions and an airborne division, but those plans had never been fully realised. In 1955 only 2 divisions were earmarked for service overseas and the remainder had been downgraded to home defence and civil defence work. Paradoxically, one reason for that change was manpower. Although National Service carried with it a liability for reserve service, hundreds of ex-National Servicemen simply refused to conform to regulations which were exceptionally difficult to enforce. (During the Suez crisis the army had been disconcerted to find that many emergency call up papers had been returned with the curt reply, 'Bollocks!' written on them.) Colonel George Forty, a TA adjutant between 1954 and 1956, knew just how difficult it was to encourage ex-National Servicemen to smile kindly on the aims of the Territorial Army:

> I know from personal experience how much the average National Servicemen disliked their part-time service and what lengths we had to go to just to ensure that they carried out their statutory commitments. More importantly, I know how much harm it did to the TA which was then, and always will be, firmly rooted in the principles of voluntary service, so that any form of compulsion was an anathema to any self-respecting Terrier.[25]

There were exceptions – for example, men in the REME who devoted their annual training to refresher courses or to learning new skills – but most ex-National Servicemen were lack-lustre about the TA, and many went to great lengths to avoid the annual camp. Those who did make the effort often discovered that it was largely a fortnight wasted.

> I had to put it off until September (annual camp) as I was a student. There were a couple of students in our group but the majority had only been able to change their time legally because they had been in prison at the time they were supposed to attend. Lots of fun really, but again, at Longmoor! I was the geographical expert but one had to be cagey with that lot. I fell asleep at Waterloo Station, so arrived late, and the duty corporals were tight-lipped in their duties. Trying to break the ice, I asked 'How did you get picked for this rotten job?' 'If it wasn't for bastards like you,' they replied, 'it wouldn't be crummy.' Then arrived in blazer and flannels, steaming drunk, the OC. After 20 minutes of argument, I finally admitted (an untruth) that, yes sir, I was pissed as a newt at Waterloo and that's why I'm late. At this, the OC grinned benignly, 'Look after this chap, fellahs!' and off he went.
> (Corporal Iain Colquhoun, Corps of Royal Engineers)

As the days passed, Colquhoun and his group were left largely to their own devices and found themselves being treated with a wary embarrassment by their Regular Army superiors.

> The officers and warrant officers, with one exception in this rag-tag tail end group, were all English, the troops Scots or Northern Irish. It was a positive pleasure to me to see a Warrant Officer issue a command, then wait, as his men emitted growling noises, look apprehensive, then say, 'Well, wait a minute, lads. There's another way.' I recall, too, one night at 1 a.m., playing cards in the billet when the orderly officer, off-stage so to speak, shouted for the fifth time, 'Lights out men. Put your lights out.' The Belfast lance-jack in charge bellowed in reply: 'I'll put your lights out you cunt if you don't fuck off and leave us.' Never heard another word.
> (Corporal Iain Colquhoun, Corps of Royal Engineers)

Bored men forced to spend fourteen days in an environment they detested posed disciplinary problems which could not always be dealt with under the same code of discipline that prevailed in the Regular Army in peacetime. In 1952 the War Office, alarmed by outbreaks of violence in Glasgow TA units, agreed that 'National Servicemen of bad character' should be forced to complete their reserve training with the Regular Army. When the men objected – four of their number had been charged by the civil police with larceny and assault with broken bottles – the matter was dropped, and from then onwards TA units with uncooperative ex-National Servicemen were quietly encouraged to do little to enforce their reserve forces' obligations.

The reduction in manpower recommended by the White Paper was also extended to the reserve forces of the RAF and Royal Navy: the Royal Air Force Volunteer Reserve was closed down, and in 1958 the Royal Naval Reserve amalgamated with the Royal Naval Volunteer Reserve. For many traditionalists, though, the cuts seemed hardest on the TA. Founded in 1907 as a secondary line of defence with part-time soldiers, the Territorial Army had fought with considerable gallantry in both world wars: under the Sandys doctrine its intended war strength was cut from 300,000 to 123,000 men. Those who supported the TA had long argued that it offered a valid alternative to conscription as, properly organised, it could provide the country with a real volunteer citizens' militia. In fact, its future employment was not finally settled until the late 1960s. The one palliative offered to the 'Terriers' was that TA units were excused the many cuts, amalgamations and changes of name which affected their Regular Army brethren under the new order. (The White Paper set in train a reduction of the infantry from 77 to 60 battalions, the armour lost 7 regiments, artillery 20 and the engineers 4. To avoid oblivion many infantry regiments chose amalgamation: some were sensible, such as the pairing within the Lancastrian Brigade of the King's and Manchester regiments; others less so, like the unpopular amalgamation of the Highland Light Infantry with the Lowland Brigade's Royal Scots Fusiliers to form the hybrid Royal Highland Fusiliers.) The final cut fell on the Home Guard which was disbanded in 1958.

By October 1960, the half-way point between the announcement of the end of National Service and its final phasing out, there were still 106,300 conscript servicemen in the British Army; but by then the old order had changed. The Regulars, especially the non-commissioned officers, had begun to think it hardly worth their while to train their conscript counterparts, and in a very real sense the National Servicemen became the services' poor relation – not just financially, because he had always been that, but in many other untold ways. For most National Servicemen who served between 1957 and 1963, though, money, or the lack of it, was the principal gripe.

> The one aspect of National Service which was annoying was the pay, which for the first 18 months was just a few shillings from which 7s. (35p) was compulsorily deducted and paid home. The pay only marginally increased as one gained promotion, which in

my own case was to LAC and then to SAC. The last six months of service were better as National Servicemen, certainly in the RAF, received the same pay as regular servicemen. As I was by this time in Germany where most items were cheap if bought on station, one felt like a millionaire. The low pay was the reason why many men opted to sign on as Regulars for a minimum period of three years. It was a matter of pride amongst the National Servicemen I knew to resist the carrot of the 'Queen's Shilling.'

(SAC D. J. Munro, RAF)

One of the National Service drawbacks, particularly at the beginning, was the shortage of money. My pay started at 25s. (£1.25) per week and after six months rose to 32s. (£1.60). However, in my last six months I drew over £7 per week which at the time was as much as my civilian pay – this was made up of trade pay, overseas pay and an extra 42s. (£2.10) for qualifying as a parachutist.

(Signalman P. H. Smith, Royal Corps of Signals)

Not every National Serviceman was able or prepared to volunteer for overseas postings or for the kind of additional duties which brought extra pay, and Peter Smith, who served between 1959 and 1961, readily admits that he was 'lucky' with his National Service which included a posting to Kenya.

Others, though, were less fortunate, and the years of the running down of National Service in Britain mark its least useful and unhappiest period. The 1959 General Election had returned the Conservatives to power under Harold Macmillan, ushering in the age of 'You've never had it so good.' New appliances in the home and factory provided easier working conditions and increased leisure time, and rising income levels meant that people had more money to spend. By 1961 the average weekly wage for men over 21 was £15 7s. 0d. (£15.35) and although retail prices had risen by 15% between 1955 and 1960, the products of the new technology – radios, record players, televisions, washing machines – were still relatively cheap in relation to the nation's spending power. (The introduction of hire-purchase had also made these products more generally available.) With the easing of financial restrictions and the arrival of increased leisure time – half-day working on Saturdays, for example, began to be phased out – British society commenced to throw off many of the restrictions which had been imposed during the Victorian period. The wider availability of cheaper wirelesses and gramophones aided the pop music revolution, clothes for young people became more colourful and less formal, student grants helped more young school-leavers go to college or university, holidays abroad became possible with cheaper travel and the relaxation of currency controls: all these changes offered a hint – for young people at least – that a new period of high-living was ready for the taking.

Excluded, albeit temporarily, from that new-found hedonism of the early 1960s were the National Servicemen with their weekly wages of £1 18s. 6d. (£1.92) – and in April 1961 there were still 78,300 conscripts serving in all the armed forces. The White Paper announcing the end of National Service (*Call Up of Men to the Armed Forces 1957/60*) had estimated that a total of 570,000 men would be the maximum requirement between 1957 and 1960, although the planners also admitted that one-third of that number would be liable for deferment. It also evolved a complicated timetable for the phasing out of National Service. Men born before 1939 would be called up in the normal way, as would those born in the first half of 1939. For those born in the third quarter of 1939, their call-up was deemed to be 'uncertain', whereas those born after 1 October 1939 were considered 'unlikely to be called up'. Men born in 1940 were informed that they 'need not expect to be called up', and 1941 or later was made the absolute cut-off date. Given the uncertainties of the timetable and the emergency of 1962 which kept conscripts in service until the Spring of 1963, mistakes in the call-up were always going to occur.

> It was at Wrexham (Regimental Pay Office, Western Command) that I remember talking to a Scots National Service corporal in the RAPC who was born at 5 minutes to midnight on the 30th September 1939. He was somewhat annoyed at this. However, I had a similar conversation with a GD man at Devizes late September 1959. He had been working in the mines at Stoke-on-Trent and had either got the sack or had left and was immediately called up for National Service. His date of birth was June 1940. I believe he questioned this and was told that he would be discharged. However he asked to stay on and was allowed to providing that he didn't contact the press on the subject. He was quickly promoted to lance-corporal with the Regimental Police. His name was Jeff Stanyer. A similar conversation in 1965 with the chap who was my Best Man at my wedding, ex-Trooper Bernard 'Mick' Cowlishaw, one of the few National Servicemen to serve in the Royal Horse Guards, revealed that he was born in November 1939 and had been called up in error. He served in Cyprus during the troubles there.
>
> (Private P. G. Smith, Royal Army Pay Corps)

The last registrations for call-up were made at the beginning of 1961. To maintain a degree of equality – and also to provide the forces with a reasonable balance of men – it was decided that trained men or graduates who had gained deferment before 1957 would be liable for call-up, but the same ruling did not always apply to those graduating or finishing apprenticeships between 1957 and 1961. School-leavers bound for university courses or trade training who were liable for National Service during that period often had unpleasant choices to make: should they opt for deferment in the hope that they would not be called up, or should they get their service over with before going to university? The problems of doing National Service as a graduate were by then well enough known.

The government of the day benefited from the decision to bring conscription to an end, for National Service had become an unpopular institution with politicians and the general public alike. The decision was also welcomed by most senior officers, although from a military point of view the phasing-out of conscription between 1957 and 1963 meant that several important strategic decisions had to be made. A reliance on voluntary recruitment forced the army to put its house in order, as conditions of pay, training and accommodation had to equal those in civilian life. The reductions in manpower also brought about a re-assessment of Britain's military objectives, resulting in a cutback to the NATO commitment, the closing down of obsolete overseas garrisons and the introduction and development of a modern arsenal. In these ways the termination of National Service marked the end of Britain's claims to be a global power, for without large armed forces it simply could not maintain the post-war chain of bases and the massive overseas military presence.

With the ending of National Service, the ceremony of demob began to lose much of its significance. In the hey-day of National Service, with thousands of men signing off, approaching demobilisation was the signal for a succession of parties as the countdown towards release began. There was hardly a National Serviceman who did not own a demob chart, the one essential guide to length of service. Some were relatively simple affairs with blocks of dates to be crossed off; others were calendars with elaborate designs featuring military insignia or satirical cartoons and kept in prominent positions; a few were carefully concealed private diaries; but they all had one thing in common. Along with his service number and his group number, the demob chart was the National Serviceman's most sacred item. It differed from a normal calendar in that it had 730 days (a day extra in case of the leap years of 1948, 1952, 1956 and 1960) numbered in reverse order, numbers which were deleted each and every morning as its owner counted off the days left in the service of his sovereign.

Demob day was a day to savour. Civilian clothes, hardly worn since the owner was eighteen, were put on again (that is, if they still fitted the growing young man), kit was returned to the stores, rail warrants issued along with the prized Certificate of Discharge, the Army's AB 111. All at once it was time to put away martial thoughts and to pick up again the strands of a young life. Most of the new civilians were still under 21, old enough to have served their country but still too young to be able to vote in its affairs. For them, a new dawn was breaking.

> Demob was almost unreal, like being in a trance. The military train took me (only passenger) to Liss, thence by BR to Haslemere, Waterloo and home to Scotland. I stopped at London, saw a film, *The Blackboard Jungle* with its opening music of 'Rock around the Clock'. Much as I hate rock music, I still like that one, and I still have a 78 record of it.
> (Corporal Iain Colquhoun, Corps of Royal Engineers)

Iain Colquhoun had spent most of his two years serving with the Senior Railway Traffic Office, RE, at Longmoor in Hampshire, where in 1953 the barracks had been 'filthy draughty hulks without doors, with broken windows stuffed with cardboard, no hot water ever, the usual complete absence of plugs in the sinks, too few WCs, no curtains, metal beds and lockers, and two fireplaces per billet of 20 men, only one of which was to contain a fire at any given time.' There, he had risen to the rank of corporal in the Railway Traffic Office, hence the use of a military train to take him to Liss and freedom. For him and for many others, the last scoring off on the chart was a signal for rejoicing; others were more detached when the great day arrived.

> On demob day the long-awaited 'early breakfast' didn't taste so good as I had expected and the joy of release was less strong. I was not called upon by the Adjutant to sign on, nor to give the apocryphal answer, 'Just give me three minutes, sir. One to get back to the block, one to pack and one to get out of here.'
> (Corporal Tony Carter, REME)

Like Iain Colquhoun, Tony Carter had also reached the rank of corporal, and when he was demobbed he was serving at Watchfield near Shrivenham in Wiltshire. He had disappointed his superiors by turning down the opportunity of being considered for a commission, but he had discovered other compensations: while at Watchfield he had been permitted to 'live out', cycling each day to the camp from his home in Swindon. His group, or demob number was 49.16, one which remained imprinted on his memory throughout his service, to be relished while telling less fortunate newcomers: 'Get some in! Get your knees brown!'

Those National Servicemen who had served abroad had a very different transformation from military to civilian life.

> I recall my leave-taking of Abu Sultan and the days spent in the transit camp in Fayid – the thrill of my first trip in an aeroplane. This was a Hermes chartered in London to take VIPs to Egypt to negotiate the British withdrawal from the Canal Zone. Rather than return empty they filled it with troops and I was one of the fortunate few. Being a civilian aircraft it had to fly the civvy air-routes so after picking us up it had to return to Cairo for customs clearance etc. – that's when I saw the Nile. We wondered what good fairy had granted someone's wish – in-flight lunch served with free drinks by beautiful stewardesses – a flight over the real desert, the magic of flying at 30,000 feet glimpsing blue seas and unknown lands far below one minute – then flying through the cotton-wool world above the thick clouds – circling round and round Rome as we spiralled ever closer to the airfield with the lights and illuminated fountains giving a fairy-tale-quality to the whole thing – then another surprise – a set dinner in the airport restaurant where the water carafes turned out to be full of white wine – then onward and upward – a last-minute change in flight plans – no, we weren't going to land at Nice after all but it was a clear night and we could see France and its glorious cities twinkling below – suddenly we are at London airport, through customs onto the BOAC bus, then, thump, back to earth or rather beneath it – some hell-hole they called Goodge Street Transit camp down in the bowels of the London subways. Dante's Hades must have felt, looked and sounded just like this and if that wasn't enough – all the bed bugs we thought we had left behind in Egypt seem to have beaten us home. I couldn't get out of there fast enough and back to the fatigues at the Regimental Depot at Feltham.
>
> (Lance-Corporal Bob Downie, RAOC)

From Feltham, Bob Downie went back to his native Aberdeen where he experienced some initial dislocation and difficulties in readjusting to the tenor of civilian life before starting work in an

insurance office. Like many other National Servicemen who had
spent time in the Middle East, he had acquired a cheap suit for
demob – the famous demob suits given to World War II servicemen had been discontinued in 1946 – but when he got home he
discovered that it was 'a little too advanced in style' for the
conservative tastes of Aberdeen in 1955.

For those who were denied the benison of a flight home and had
to travel by trooper, demob was usually more about the arrival
than the journey.

> It was towards the end of my tour of duty at Amman that I was
> approached by my CO from Baghdad about signing on in the army.
> I must admit I was very tempted and I feel that if he could have
> assured me of staying out in the Middle East I would have stayed on,
> but, alas, he could not, so I turned him down. But I was quite glad
> that I did not sign on because once I arrived back in Blighty and
> stood on the platform at Euston Station we came down to earth with
> a bump. There we stood, six bedraggled looking tramps, looking
> like extras from *Ice Cold in Alex*, with a pint of lovely Black and Tan
> each when two spotless looking young MPs bore down on us. They
> started shouting the odds but fortunately for them we were on our
> way for demob. We were tired after spending two weeks in transit
> camps in Egypt with very little sleep due to poor facilities so we told
> them to get their knees brown, plus a few other suggestions.
> Eventually they hustled us onto a train for Newton Abbot, our final
> camp in uniform.
>
>   (Lance-Corporal Griffith Roberts, Royal Corps of Signals)

While at Newton Abbot, Griff Roberts extracted a measure of
revenge by impersonating the camp chaplain wearing a borrowed
officer's uniform and reversed collar. Once all the new Royal
Signals' recruits were safely in their billets he would emerge to give
them a late-night lecture on clean living and the notorious diseases
to be caught from lavatory seats abroad. Impersonating an officer
is a serious offence, but Regular officers and NCOs tended to turn
a blind eye to pranks committed by their 'demob-happy' charges.
Certainly, very few National Servicemen wanted to be demobbed
with a bad Certificate of Service, and for many the days before
demob were spent hustling together bits of lost equipment and in
some cases purchasing odd bits and pieces from local army surplus
stores. Having been told on their first day in uniform that 'You
must pay for what you lose!' few men were anxious to have their
demob ruined by the presentation of a large bill.

> On my last weekend in Germany I went with the Squadron Shooting
> Team to Sennelager which was an all arms training centre. I went in

the advance party and I signed for 12 billets for the team. I dealt with an Army corporal who looked about fifty and he had three rows of medal ribbons on his chest. He told me everything had to be accounted for and I was responsible for all breakages and losses. It was a bitterly cold weekend and there were solid fuel stoves in the billets but nothing to light them with, though there was coal. Some of our more enterprising companions solved the problem by taking the drawers out of the wardrobes and chopping them up for firewood.

On the second day at the Firing Camp one of the members of our team had violent toothache and I had to take him in my jeep to the nearest RAF camp about thirty miles away to get a tooth out. We found the camp OK, and I met another chap who had been on my initial square-bashing course. I left my chap in the Medical Centre and I went to the NAAFI for a cuppa with the airman I knew. On my way back to the Medical Centre I was suddenly stopped by a Land Rover with two RAF policemen. It turned out I had gone down a one-way street in the camp and they booked me for it. I said, 'What happens now?' They told me that they submitted a report to their CO, who would forward it to my CO, who would have me up before him and if I pleaded Guilty I would be fined. I asked how long it would take and they obligingly said my CO would get the report in two weeks. I hadn't the heart to tell them I was bound for the UK the coming Wednesday.

Next day back at Sennelager, when we were leaving, the old sweat pointed out that I was six drawers short and that I was responsible for them. Nobody felt like contributing cash towards them and I certainly was not going to be the only one. I was therefore told that he would submit a report to his CO who would forward it to my CO who would have me up in front of him and fined. How long would all this take? Oh, about two weeks. Should I tell him I was UK bound on Wednesday? No fear, he was enjoying it all too much. I never did hear from the RAF Police or the Army about their drawers.

(Corporal John Inglis, RAF Regiment)

Another RAF man, SAC Malcolm Burrill, was ordered to buy a new set of best blues prior to the inspection by a visiting Air Commodore of his camp at RAF Patrington in West Yorkshire. Two years of regularly being pressed had made his uniform threadbare, but with demob beckoning he was unwilling to spend £8 on clothing which, in all probability, he would never wear again. Minutes before the inspection and the prospect of being put on a charge, his saviour was the unlikely sight of a dustbin on fire. Grabbing a fire extinguisher he doused the flames, making sure that as much foam as possible found its way onto his uniform. The hero of the hour was excused the parade and Burrill's service record remained intact.

Most National Servicemen left the services with fairly favourable statements on their Certificate of Discharge – in the RAF, the Assessment of Conduct, Proficiency and Personal Qualities ranged from Exemplary to Poor – and were usually content to have been regarded by their COs as having been satisfactory recruits. Not so ACI James O'Donoghue who was demobbed from RAF Leuchars in Scotland with a discharge which left little doubt about his attitude to service life.

> O'Donoghue [wrote his CO, Flt.Lt. B. Gunn] is an electrical assistant and works in the electrical section. As such he is of little technical use in the electrical or technical flight.
>
> He is not a willing worker and has to be continually supervised, always expecting concessions to be made in his favour and is not popular with his fellow workers.
>
> I consider he will be no loss to the service and the RAF will not suffer should he be given a premature release. Technically he will not be missed and no replacement will be requested.

James O'Donoghue holds several records as a National Serviceman, not all of them honourable. He was the last recruit to be conscripted into the RAF (although not the last to be demobbed), a prominence he was anxious to avoid from the minute he arrived at his reception camp. On his first day at RAF Cardington he was put on a charge and then took twenty weeks to complete his basic training. Thereafter, he was put on fourteen more charges and did a total of 180 days 'jankers' as he graduated through RAF Bridgnorth to RAF Leuchars, where he was eventually given early discharge. To celebrate his return to civilian life he poured weedkiller on the garden he had been ordered to tend during the latter part of his service career. For him, and for many others who had bucked against the system, demob could not come quickly enough. Even those who had avoided charges and conformed to service discipline were not always unhappy when their National Service came to an end.

> When the great day arrived it was like flying to the moon, to wake up and realise that here was the end of my National Service. It was almost too good to be true that I was on the verge of returning to normal civilised life with the freedom from that beastly uniform, morning roll-calls, parades and cookhouse food, from brainless NCOs and other moronic airmen, and from that aimless patrolling in the dead of night. My only regret was saying farewell to certain

fellows who had served me as good friends, for it seemed unlikely that I should see the majority of them again.

(LAC B. J. Tipping, RAF)

Brian Tipping was another serviceman who had been permitted to 'live out', in his case while serving as a clerk in Equipment Accounting at RAF Stafford between 1951 and 1953. In addition to that privilege he had made life more bearable by selling his nightly fire picquet duties at 7s. 6d. (37p) a stretch, or £1 15s. 0d. (£1.75) a weekend, and he took part in the well-recognised skive of organising an office rota to enable each member to have an extra Saturday off, the others answering the absentee's name at roll call. Yet in spite of all those 'benefits' which helped to make service life bearable, he still felt that his National Service had been 'a colossal waste of time as well as being a most unsettling intrusion upon the course of my life.' He began counting the days to demob from his arrival at RAF Padgate for basic training, and his demob chart was an ingenious affair, laid out like a large crossword puzzle with blocks shaded in red and blue to denote time spent at camp and at home.

Malcolm Burrill, the hero of the flaming dustbin, was one of the few National Servicemen who did not keep a demob chart. Although he believed that much of his work as a radar operator was time wasted, he regards National Service as a major factor in deciding his future career as a teacher. When demob came, he met it with mixed feelings.

> The latter months were happy times, with release and civvy street just around the corner; two years away from home had made me an independent man; I had done a fair amount of travelling around Britain and had come into close contact with youths from just about every part of the UK. The social life had also become very special; I was earning a reasonable amount of money in the latter months and being invited to a constant succession of demob parties.

(SAC J. Malcolm Burrill, RAF)

Generally speaking, the better the National Service experience, the less willing was the conscript soldier, airman or sailor to loosen his service ties. Men who had experienced the closed family relationship of the infantry regiment, for example, often found demob a disruptive experience and worried about losing friends of some eighteen months' standing – a long time when one is twenty. Alexander Robb, 1st Seaforth Highlanders, admits that 'I missed my army pals very much after demob.' And he was not alone – many other infantrymen looked on demob as a time of parting, especially if they had shared intense periods of active service or service overseas with their fellow men. Similarly, men who had done their time in the Royal Navy often felt ambivalent about leaving the senior service and soon found that they missed the camaraderie of the mess deck and the *esprit de corps* which accompanies the crew of a sea-going warship.

By April 1963, only the army retained a small number of National Servicemen – 2,600 in all. According to Ministry of Defence records the last National Serviceman to be discharged was Lieutenant Richard Vaughan of the Royal Army Pay Corps, who was demobbed on 16 May 1963, having left his unit in Germany nine days earlier and been allowed to meander home to claim the distinction ahead of Private Fred Turner of the Army Catering Corps, who had been demobbed on 7 May. Some units held special demob parades when their final National Servicemen left them in 1962 and 1963, and the luckier men were presented with mementoes of their time in uniform. When those last National Servicemen were demobbed they made news, too, and photographs of bizarre leave-takings became standard newspaper copy – one National Service Military Policeman was led to the ferry at the Hook of Holland handcuffed to his jeep.

Meanwhile, those young men of Britain who had served their country as conscripts breathed a collective sigh of relief. With their discharge the demob chart became a relic of the past, along with all the other paraphernalia of the National Serviceman's jargon – the AB 64, parts I and II; WOSB; drawers, cellular, green; RTU'd; best boots; OCTU; the schoolie; POM; fire picquets; spiders; your walking-out finger.

Chapter Nine

THE END OF AN OLD SONG

Although many politicians doubted that the Army could be manned on a purely regular basis – the 1957 White Paper had made provision for re-introducing National Service should manpower shortages make it necessary – recruiting turned out initially not to be a problem. 1962 was a bumper year. 36,607 men and boys joined up as Regulars, followed by a further 30,388 two years later; and by the end of the 1960s the Army's total complement of men and boys had never fallen below a quarter of a million. Frequently, though, shortages of equipment and an absence of trained men in key areas meant that some operations had to be run on a shoestring; nevertheless, during the run-down of National Service the three armed forces coped with a selection of diverse operations, including the uprising in Muscat and Oman (1957), civil unrest in Gan (1959), riots in the Cameroons (1960), assistance to the Amir of Kuwait (1961), and the extended confrontation in Borneo (1962 onwards). At times it seemed that the icing was spread extremely thin on the cake of Britain's military obligations, but once the decision had been made to do without conscription it was left to only a handful of senior officers to make increasingly feeble calls for its re-introduction. The possibility of bringing back National Service has been raised several times since 1963, but as a serious political issue it has never been a front-runner.

With the ending of National Service Britain joined Canada, Australia, India, Pakistan, Mexico, Iceland, Ireland and the United Arab Republic as the only countries which did not have some form of conscription as a means of raising men for their armed forces. Of the other major countries of the world, France, Turkey, Denmark and the USSR still maintained a universal obligation to military service; Switzerland, Sweden and Israel, for

example, based their armed forces on citizens' militias; and other
nations like the USA relied on a mixed system of conscripts and
volunteers. Countries which continued to rely wholly or partly on
conscription did so either on historical grounds or from
present-day military necessity. France and the Soviet Union
regarded it as the one sure means of defending the nation-state,
of keeping intact its political values and of manning garrisons
within their territorial possessions; whereas West Germany and
Belgium, for example, used conscription to meet their NATO
obligations. By turning its back on National Service, Britain
joined the select few nations which in 1960 relied on the voluntary
principle, and as a consequence, in the words of historian Correlli
Barnett, 'the army and the nation began to drift apart, as the
army became a closed "family" small in numbers'.

It was the family relationship which was the first to suffer in the
post-National Service years. Because an obligation to military
service had existed in Britain since 1939, few families had not
been affected by the nation's flirtation with its armed forces.
Fathers and sons had a common bond in their military service,
military terminology and slang were acceptable within the family,
and the armed forces were not the closed societies they were to
become. But by the late 1950s the times were changing. In the
first ten or so years after the war, society had changed little and
the immense effort required to put Britain back on its feet bred a
rough kind of solidarity. Those same fathers and sons united by
their National Service also shared the same dress, appearance
and tastes. Most young men still aped their elders, and it was not
until the pop revolution of the late 1950s that they discovered
leisure patterns which reflected their growing independence.
George Melly has called the movement a 'revolt into style', and
with it came radical changes in dress, behaviour and opinion: for
many young people growing up in the early 1960s it was almost as
if a safety valve had been released. In this perspective, the
freedom from conscription was also one of the reasons for the
rapidly mushrooming youth culture.

As National Service began to fade into memory, attitudes to it
became blurred and overlaid with a thick veneer of personal
emotion. In the process, many of the facts were forgotten. For
example, few National Servicemen can recall seeing coloured
servicemen of African, Indian, Middle Eastern or Caribbean

origin. Partly this can be explained by the fact that in 1950 there were only around 100,000 coloured people living in Britain: it was not until the mid-1950s that immigration from the Caribbean reached any significant proportion – 132,000 between 1955 and 1957 – and the figures went on rising until 1961 (136,000). Legislation aimed at controlling immigration was not introduced until 1962 with the passing of the Commonwealth Immigration Act, which provided an annual quota system. From the evidence of contemporary opinion polls the British people were generally in favour of immigration control, and the integration of white and coloured communities seemed to be never more than a pious hope. This was certainly true of the armed forces; one of the reasons why there were so few coloured National Servicemen was that the services, especially the Army, did not want them.

The position of coloured servicemen had been discussed by the Ministry of Labour and National Service as early as November 1949, shortly before India became a republic. Many Indians resident in the United Kingdom had retained their Indian citizenship, and it was unlikely that the government of India would allow them to be conscripted into Britain's armed forces; others had United Kingdom citizenship under the terms of the British Nationality Act of 1948, which entitled Indians and others from the old empire to become British subjects. It was here that the difficulty lay, and the report (*Liability to Military Service of Indian Citizens in the United Kingdom*) concluded that any call-up of Commonwealth citizens would result in 'a good many unwanted persons being conscripted, including Asiatics and Africans who are difficult to absorb and are not much value in the UK forces.'[26] The findings of the report were never made public, but it was agreed that wherever possible Indian and Pakistani recruits should be regarded as temporary residents or engaged in educational programmes, thus making them eligible for deferment. A further 'unofficial' solution was put forward by Sir Harold Wiles, Deputy Secretary within the Ministry, who suggested that the problem could be solved locally by 'simply omitting to call them up, even though they are still legally liable. The services would lose nothing of value and I have said that administratively it would be quite practicable.' Wiles went on to record his misgivings should such a system be put into practice officially, on the grounds that it was unfair to those who did National Service, but the message did seep down to local offices

of the Ministry of Labour and National Service with the result
that Asiatic-sounding names were quite often removed from the
register.

During World War II coloured servicemen from the empire
had fought alongside their white comrades, often in separate
units – many of the first post-war Caribbean immigrants were ex-
servicemen – and amongst frontline troops and serving men there
were few racial tensions. It was impossible, though, for a
coloured officer to command white troops and the Army was
determined to enforce that provision during the National Service
period. A draft Cabinet Paper drawn up by the Army Council in
1946 (*Post-War Regulations respecting the Nationality and Descent for entry to the Army*) recommended not only that the
wartime regulations be kept, but that they should be extended
with a recommendation that 'Men not of pure European descent
should not be allowed to enlist in UK regiments or corps of the
Regular Army.' Questioned by the Army Council on the same
subject, the Air Ministry replied that they would not debar
potential recruits because of their colour. The Admiralty was
more cautious, but stated that racial considerations would come
into play only in the most sensitive areas. A total colour bar was
out of the question in the Army and was never given serious
consideration, but the bar on coloured officers remained in force
throughout the National Service years. The Army Council's
report concluded:

> To sum up, the enlistment of coloured men into the Army, and *a
> fortiori*, the grant of commissions in the British Army to them,
> constitutes, in the view of the Army Council, a threat to the
> discipline and well-being of the Army which might be a very
> serious matter in time of war.[27]

If the Army Council's attitude seemed xenophobic, even racist,
then it was probably little different from that held by the country
as a whole. Initially, there had been a mixed reaction to the post-
war immigrants who had mainly settled in London, the West
Midlands and Yorkshire. One school of thought regarded immigration as part of the price to be paid for Britain's involvement
in Empire; others looked on it as a pool of cheap labour; but
amongst ordinary people in the areas concerned there was often a
good deal of resentment. The first race riots occurred in Notting
Hill in 1958, but even before then there had been numerous
examples of racial discrimination and discord over housing and
employment. Racial differences, too, were accentuated when

immigrants wanted to keep alive their own languages and customs, but the major difficulty was that immigrants usually settled in less advantaged areas with existing social problems. By the end of the 1950s racial friction had become a problem that was obviously not going to go away.

Another subject which was taboo in the armed forces was suicide. It forms the heart of David Lodge's National Service novel, *Ginger, You're Barmy*, in which a young and ineffectual Catholic conscript called Percy Higgins is literally bullied to death, thereby transforming completely the lives of those closest to him. Although Lodge has admitted in an afterword to the novel that the story is fictional, he also states that there is scarcely 'a minor character or illustrative incident or detail of setting that is not drawn from the life.' As many National Servicemen knew, part of that life included suicide.

> When on basic training (No. 2 Training Bn. REME, Honiton) I used to go to the local village Scout troop. On returning one night I climbed into bed just before lights out. In the bed opposite me was a Scots lad who had never been away from home before and he was having difficulty in making his bed. It was usually all on the floor in the morning. 'Lights Out' was blown, voices shouted, 'Put the lights out, Jock.' He looked at me and said, 'Do you know, if I had been in the Scouts when I was young, I wouldn't be in this mess now.' He put the lights out and walked out through the billet door but someone shouted to him, 'Put your pumps on – the grass is wet.' So he came back, put on a pair of plimsolls, then went out again. We didn't see him again – he went up to the railway line at the back of the camp and jumped in front of a train.
>
> (Craftsman Donald Greaves, REME)

No statistics are available for the incidence of suicides amongst National Servicemen, but they were probably little different from comparable figures for university students during the same

Group	Population Yearly average	No. of Suicides	Annual rate per 100,000
Cambridge	5,950 men	13	21.8
Oxford	5,250 men	16	30.5
7 British Universities	15,000 men	10	8.5
England Wales age 15–19	1,302,000 men	331	2.8
England Wales age 20–24	1,394,000 men	767	6.1

period. In 1959 the *British Medical Journal* produced figures which showed that undergraduate suicides in England and Wales were well above the national average between 1948 and 1958.

The report concluded that undergraduates at the Oxbridge colleges were at most risk because of their sudden social and domestic isolation, whereas the majority at the seven (unnamed) British universities either lived at home or near enough home to maintain close contact with their families. No conclusions were reached about the mental health of those who attempted suicide, but other reasons suggested for its prevalence amongst the university population included the strain of work, unhappy love affairs and anxiety over personal finance. Dislocation either from family life or from the childhood social group, however, was considered to be the principal reason for student suicides.

If those figures are extended to National Service, the annual suicide rate seems more likely to resemble the rate for the seven British universities than for the Oxbridge colleges; i.e., around 8 per 100,000 a year. The *British Medical Journal* had been quick to point out that the Oxbridge results were artificially high in that both universities were larger than average, and because the college system broke the undergraduate population 'into a number of self-contained, somewhat isolated communities'. In fact, most National Service suicides seem to have happened during basic training when recruits like David Lodge's fictional character Percy Higgins broke under the strain of being back-squadded. Certainly it was during those first weeks of service that military life was at its most intense and young men felt most isolated from the civilian lives they had left behind.

> Outside the station we got into the backs of RAF lorries and were taken to the camp [RAF West Kirby]. I can remember that as our feet touched the ground the shouting and screaming started. We were allocated billets and then had to try to find our kitbags which were all over the place. In some of the cupboards we found small nooses, left by the last lot of incumbents. Stories abounded of blokes committing suicide but I don't know if they were true.
>
> (SAC John Dinning, RAF)

Often the stories of suicides were just that – rumours put about by nervous young men pitched suddenly into a new and disturbing environment – and although John Dinning came across plenty of violence in his RAF career, he never heard of an actual suicide. When they did occur the authorities' usual response was to sweep the matter under the carpet. The normal remedy was to give the men a 48-hour pass to get over the incident, and it was not uncommon for witnesses of suicides to be given postings elsewhere. Suggestions have also been made that some suicides were recorded as 'accidental deaths'. If that did happen, it was presumably done to protect the feelings of relations, for until 1961 survivors of suicide attempts were liable to criminal prosecution and suicide itself was considered to be an act of gross impiety.

Whether the armed forces' subterfuge in such cases was reasonable is a moot point. Cosmetic accounts of suicides had obvious attractions to service chiefs nervous of attracting adverse publicity, but there was always the danger that unpleasant facts might be covered up, too. Stories abound of tyrannical NCOs driving their soft young charges to despair and eventual suicide, but no prosecutions were ever brought. In the wake of a suicide those close to the deceased will always question the reasons for the victim's unhappiness; and in such circumstances the bullying corporal will often appear as the prime suspect.

All too often, however, the reasons were more prosaic, if no less understandable. Men receiving 'Dear John' letters often felt suicidal. Usually their mates talked them out of their depression, and in the case of married men sympathetic COs were known to award a 48-hour pass to allow them 'to sort out the problem'. Disgrace was another motive.

> Whilst at ATDU Gosport, one of the airmen was charged with theft from one of the huts. Originally placed in close arrest, on the day of the station sports he was put on open arrest to enable as many personnel as possible to attend the sports.
>
> His body was found next day on a nearby railway line. He was from some remote West Country village and on the following Saturday I found myself detailed with an NCO to accompany his body home.
>
> (LAC Byron T. Denning, RAF)

Having collected the coffin, it was placed in an ordinary goods wagon at Fareham Station – 'the van smelled as though its last use had been to carry boxes of fish' – to go to Salisbury where it was to be attached to a West Country express.

> We had a travel document for A/C2 'H', marked 'deceased', and this had to be shown to the ticket inspector. We arrived eventually at 'C' junction and the van was unhitched to await the local train to 'W'. This was run on a single track and when the train arrived from 'W' the engine picked up our van and filled in an hour or so until its return journey was due by doing the shunting of milk wagons at the local creamery.

It was an incongruous situation. A gloriously sunny afternoon, the Sergeant and I watching a cricket match in a field adjacent to the station, and A/C 'H''s body being shunted around the creamery goods yard.

(LAC Byron T. Denning, RAF)

That was not the end of Byron Denning's bizarre experience. When they eventually arrived at the deceased's unmanned village halt, there was no undertaker or anyone else waiting to meet them, and ahead loomed the possibility of spending the night alone with his sergeant and the Union Jack-draped coffin.

We waited for what seemed ages, and I for one visualised only too clearly the possibility of spending a night on a deserted platform with a corpse, when along came a car. It turned out to be the deceased's uncle. He had taken the front passenger seat out of the vehicle and somehow we managed to get the coffin into the car.

Hardly a word was said as he drove off and we both saluted the parting deceased. I caught the next train to 'W' and that night slept on the sofa in my uncle's house, draped in a Union Jack that still had a fishy smell.

(LAC Byron T. Denning, RAF)

Taking one's life as a means of avoiding disgrace has a long history in the armed forces and, for discredited officers at least, it was considered 'the decent thing to do'. Because the armed forces are a tightly-knit society with their own standards of behaviour and discipline, any transgression of the code is regarded as a greater personal disgrace than it would be in civilian life. The young A/C2 at Gosport was below average intelligence, a quiet, insufficient character who had been in trouble before and did not fit into service life. Fear of harsher punishment was probably one spur which drove him to suicide; another may have been a feeling that he was no longer worthy in the eyes of his fellow servicemen.

In his monograph *Le Suicide* (published in France in 1897), Emile Durkheim contributed a sociological solution to the problem of suicide. He argued that the incidence of suicide was relative to the state of social institutions such as the family, the church and the army; a certain number of suicides were always to be expected, but serious faults in a social structure would always lead to an increase in suicide rates. A large part of his thesis is devoted to the phenomenon of suicide in the armed forces, which he pronounced to be 'contagious' in the French Army of his day. Soldiers would become liable to commit suicide, he counselled, because they had been made to feel unworthy, or because they had come to think that they no longer conformed to the military code of personal honour.

The testing of British nuclear weapons was another matter not widely discussed during the 1950s – mainly because it was a matter of national security. British scientists had been involved in the development of nuclear physics since the beginning of the twentieth century, and a team under the physicist W. G. Penney had made a valuable contribution to the American Manhattan Project which culminated in the successful testing of the world's first nuclear explosion in the New Mexico desert in July 1945. The decision to use nuclear bombs against Japan a month later hastened the development of such weapons, and in the immediate post-war years the British government took the decision to develop its own arsenal. An Atomic Energy Research Establishment was formed at Harwell and steps were taken to produce stocks of plutonium 239 and uranium 235, the essential fissile materials for nuclear weapons. Development of the atom bomb also ushered in plans for new carrier systems, radar and electronics: these, too, helped pave the way for Britain's reliance on a nuclear strategy, which lay at the heart of the Sandys's White Paper of 1957. By 1952 the first bomb was ready for testing, and with the agreement of the Australian Government a test site was developed in the Monte Bello islands, off the north-west coast of Australia. On the first occasion, the device was placed in an obsolete frigate, HMS *Plym*, which was vaporised in the subsequent explosion. It was to be the first of five series of twelve tests in the Australian sub-continent.

The problem facing the British planners was that explosions of the nuclear weapons, especially of the high-yield devices, caused unacceptably large levels of radiation fall-out over a wide area – in 1954 an American test at Bikini Atoll had polluted vast tracts of the Pacific Ocean. It was agreed by the Ministry of Supply, the coordinating authority for the British tests, that a new test site would have to be found for exploding the more powerful thermonuclear weapons, and in 1955 they settled upon the remote Pacific islands of Christmas, Malden and Penrhyn. Before the sites could be developed the programme of atom bomb testing would have to be completed, and it was agreed that the wide open spaces of Australia should continue to bear the brunt. A third series of tests in May 1956, code-named Mosaic, again at

Monte Bello, was followed by a fourth series, code-named
Buffalo, at Maralinga on the Nullabor Plain in central Australia.
(In October 1953, two tower-mounted bombs had been exploded
at Emu in the Australian desert under the code-name Totem.)
The Buffalo series of four explosions included the first air-drop of
an atom bomb on 11 October 1956. The aboriginal name for the
test-site means 'place of thunder', and for the British observers of
the tests, like Major J. M. A. Tillet of the Oxfordshire and
Buckinghamshire Light Infantry, Maralinga had not been named
in jest.

> Suddenly the whole area was lit by a blinding flash of greenish
> white light much brighter than the brilliant desert sun. I noticed
> that my shadow, which had been out to my left, moved over to
> straight in front of me and other people appeared like ghostly
> shadows in this world of strange light which blotted out all colours.
> Almost at once we felt the heat on our backs and it was just like
> opening a hot oven door, like a hot iron being pressed close to the
> skin, like the blast of heat which is blown up from a fire if you put
> paraffin on it. We were miles away from this explosion at this time
> and this made the heat more remarkable. Later the blast arrived
> but it was the flash and heat which will remain longest in our
> memories.[28]

Throughout the series of tests – which culminated in the testing
of the thermonuclear devices in 1957 and 1958 at Christmas
Island, code-named Grapple – the authorities showed an alarming ignorance of the effects of radiation. According to the
Admiralty in 1954, it was considered safe for military personnel at
the tests to endure levels of radiation fifty times greater than
those acceptable today. The dose was set at 50 roentgens*, a level
which Admiralty experts considered safe 'without undue risk to
life.' The report, which was not released until 1984, concluded:

> If a man is well enough to carry on working, he can be re-assessed
> and told that although he may develop some temporary illness
> later, he is not going to die. This optimism may be misplaced
> occasionally but probably not enough to cause a serious break in
> morale.

Partly, the ignorance was born of ignorance. The scientists did
not know precisely either the short-term or the long-term effects
of a nuclear explosion. What happened during the detonation and

---

*Radiation doses are measured in units called roentgens. A dose of 25
received by a normal person will cause blood cell changes. A dose of 450 would
be fatal in most cases.

its immediate aftermath were understood, but men's reactions to the experience and the long-term effects of residual fall-out were only partially known. To this end, observers from all three services witnessed the Australian and Pacific tests from varying ranges. Protective clothing was often kept to a minimum and was not always suitable: surveyors monitoring the explosions at Monte Bello tore off their masks because they were so uncomfortable, and at Maralinga men worked in 120° of heat wearing only shorts and sandals. In both cases men were exposed to radiation fall-out. Following the Australian series at Monte Bello and Maralinga, men were ordered into the blast area without sufficient protective clothing and were exposed to radioactive dust. Many returned with radiation burns on the exposed parts of their bodies, to be reassured that these need only be treated with ordinary ointment. Others were exposed to high levels of radiation cleaning the Canberra bombers which had flown through the mushroom cloud to collect dust samples; these and other pieces of contaminated equipment were subsequently buried in the desert sands of the Nullabor Plain. According to Air Vice-Marshal Stewart Menaul, who was in charge of the Mosaic tests at Monte Bello, of the 20,000 men who took part in the British tests, many were National Servicemen, mainly airmen and sappers: 'The entire task Group was composed of volunteers, some of them National Servicemen, who were determined not to miss a unique opportunity to take part in a very important venture, with an interesting Australia tour an added attraction.'[29]

In fact, the exact number of National Servicemen employed on the nuclear tests is not known and, along with many other important papers relating to this period, the information has not been released by the Ministry of Defence. Those National Servicemen who admit to having taken part in the series are reluctant to talk about their experiences, and it was not until May 1983 that Defence Minister Michael Heseltine announced that the stories of the nuclear veterans were no longer covered by the Official Secrets Act. Many had become members of the British Nuclear Tests Veterans Association, which was established at the same time – May 1983 – to cater for the problems veterans had faced in the intervening years. One of the first aims of the Association is to monitor the health of servicemen who experienced the tests, and a longer-term goal is to gain suitable compensation for those who have suffered as a result of exposure to radiation and nuclear fall-out. Despite the accumulation of evidence which suggests otherwise, the Ministry of Defence continues to deny that there are health hazards associated with the tests, although in 1983 they bowed to the Association's demands and agreed to conduct a survey of all those who had taken part.

The tests caused disquiet in Australia too. The second Mosaic explosion at Monte Bello resulted in a radioactive cloud being blown across the country, and by 1957 opinion polls in Australia showed that 66% of the population wanted the tests halted. Discrepancies in the information regarding the Monte Bello and Maralinga tests, and suggestions that servicemen and native aborigines were exposed both to the blasts and the fall-out in the immediate area of the explosions, led to the establishment in July 1984 of an Australian Royal Commission to investigate the safety of the British nuclear tests of the 1950s. Under the chairmanship of Mr Justice James McClelland, it published its findings in December 1985: its principal finding was that the twelve major detonations at Monte Bello and Maralinga should not have been made under the prevailing conditions and that there had been unacceptable departures from safety standards. Although the report did not comment fully on the health of the participants it did find evidence to suggest that the safety of the aboriginal population had been disregarded, and that in some cases this amounted to 'ignorance, incompetence and cynicism'. The Commission recommended that Britain should honour an obligation to compensate victims, and should pay for 'the total cost of rendering contaminated areas safe without fences or patrols'.

Many of the men involved in the Australian series moved on to the Grapple tests in the Pacific, where an air-drop technique was to be used to test 'cleanly' the more powerful thermonuclear devices. (This involved a high burst from a balloon or a drop from a Valiant bomber, the weapon being exploded above the ground.) The logistics were the first and greatest problem. Christmas Island, the site of the main base, lies in the south-west Pacific some fifteen hundred miles north-east of Fiji, and although it had been exposed to occupation in the past, its airstrip and jetty facilities were fairly primitive. The first job, therefore, for the Joint Services Task Force was to provide the necessary facilities for the test team; the runway had to be reinforced and lengthened to take jet bombers and transport aircraft, a port and ancillary roads had to be constructed, and domestic accommodation had to be provided. All the materials and equipment for these essential tasks had to be shipped or airlifted out from

Britain, and the base was not fully operational until the beginning of 1957. A communications centre was also established on the neighbouring Malden Island, a small coral atoll, and two other islands, Penrhyn and Jarvis, housed metereological and observation stations.

> On the island itself [Christmas] there were several thousand soldiers and airmen – there was a six-month turnover of men and no one went back after their stint. None of the men knew why they were going until they reached their destination, and the detachments (of naval personnel) then spent several months on the island before tests started.
>
> Then commenced a month of rehearsals in which we [RAF personnel] were taken to the place where we would be on the day. No one asked any penetrating questions, we were all used to doing as we were told. We were taken through the exact procedure each time – but no one could have imagined what lay ahead when the bomb was actually exploded.[30]

The first British thermonuclear device – a bomb seventy times more powerful than the one which had devastated Hiroshima – was successfully tested on 15 May 1957 at a site above the ocean off the Malden Islands. To Wing-Commander K. G. Hubbard, the captain of the Valiant bomber which carried out the exercise, the sight was 'truly breathtaking . . . towering above us a huge mushroom-shaped cloud with the stem a cauldron mass of orange'. Altogether three megaton bombs were exploded at Malden, followed by seven tests (5 megaton and 2 kiloton) at Christmas Island. All the explosions were witnessed by servicemen on the ground or at sea in naval vessels, and their experience was rather different to Hubbard's.

> Thirty minutes before detonation the ship's company (HMS *Scarborough*) was instructed to change out of shorts and into denim trousers and long-sleeved shirts – this was our so-called protective clothing, our winter-work clothes. Then we mustered on the upper deck. We were made to sit with our backs to the direction of the blast with our hands over our eyes – we weren't even given sunglasses. The count-down came over the tannoy for sixty seconds.
>
> Then the bomb went off . . .
>
> Five miles away from the blast with our eyes closed and hands over our eyes, we could see all the bones in our fingers – it was like an intense X-ray. And people fifteen miles away experienced the same effect. Then the noise – like a clap of thunder magnified a hundred times. The tannoy had been switched into the Canberra overhead and we were told to stand up and look at the explosion.

> There was a sudden blast of hot air, as if you'd opened the door of
> a baker's oven. We were looking up at the cloud and that was
> when the wave hit you. The blast of hot air was so intense it
> stopped you breathing. I remember very vividly the looks on
> people's faces – highly disciplined men absolutely terrified![30]

In the aftermath of the explosion several men panicked and
wandered around dazed and bewildered. Some suffered from
diarrhoea; others found themselves temporarily deafened by
noise which they likened to 'a loud clap of thunder from gigantic
stereo loudspeakers'. Ironically, there were those, too, who were
fascinated by the terrible beauty of the mushroom cloud which
loomed above them and reached high into the stratosphere, but
in most cases fear was the dominant emotion.

> When we got to the road the blast effect came, it was unbelievable
> – I had expected a blast of wind. But there were two huge
> explosions in the air. It was so strong we were thrown to the
> ground. When I looked at the guy next to me his face was petrified
> with fear – like I felt. [30]

Afterwards came the cleaning-up operation – the blast had
killed much of the animal life in the area, and swarms of dead fish
and blinded birds had been washed up onto the beaches of
Christmas Island. There were no medical checks and all
servicemen present at the explosions, Regular or National
Service, had to sign the Official Secrets Act on their return to
Britain.

It is now known that some servicemen who were observers at
the 1953–1958 test series were discharged soon afterwards, a few
on psychiatric grounds, others suffering from physical illness.
Later, too, it emerged that a significant proportion of veterans
had begun to suffer from mounting health problems, including
cataracts, dizzy spells, skin disorders, arthritis and haemorrhag-
ing. In *The Lancet* of 9 April 1983, researchers from the
Department of Social Medicine in the University of Birmingham,
reported findings which lent weight to the belief that nuclear
veterans were more prone than other groups to die prematurely
from cancers of the blood. Of 330 cases investigated by them 27
were found to have died from leukaemia and other RES
(Reticuloendothelial System) neoplasms. By successfully testing
thermonuclear weapons, Britain may have gained the right to
join the USA and the USSR* as the third member of the so-called

*In 1953 the Cabinet had been informed by intelligence chiefs that the Soviet
Union had between 150 and 200 atom bombs.

nuclear club – but at a price to many of the servicemen who witnessed the explosions.

Operation Grapple was destined to be the last series of tests of British nuclear weapons – a minor series, code-named Vixen, involving nuclear triggers, took place at Maralinga between 1960 and 1962. The V-bomber force had become operational, thereby giving Britain a nuclear strike capacity; close links were developed with the Strategic Air Command of the United States Air Force; and to provide Britain with intercontinental ballistic missiles, the American Thor missile was deployed in East Anglia. It was at this time (1958), too, that the Campaign for Nuclear Disarmament (CND) came into being and provided a focus for those who were concerned about the sudden proliferation of nuclear weapons. It gained its support from a wide and influential range of the British people – opinion polls in 1960 showed that 30% of the population supported its aims – and it was especially popular amongst students and young people. So strong had the anti-nuclear lobby become, that at its annual conference in 1960 the Labour Party was able to adopt a resolution in favour of unilateral nuclear disarmament.

National Servicemen were young people too, and several have admitted that they accompanied CND's protest marches to Aldermaston when on leave. 'I wore a badge, went on marches, even read the *Guardian*. But never in the barracks,' is a typical comment from one National Serviceman who served between 1959 and 1961. This was not unique, but neither was it widespread. It was against service regulations for serving men to join political parties or groups, but these rules were not always easy – or indeed advisable – to apply to conscript birds of passage. As young men with strongly-held political views were hardly likely to suspend them during their National Service, officers usually adopted a policy of *laissez faire* and took the line of least resistance.

> Shortly after enlistment, while I was at Carlisle, I was put on a charge for having a dirty towel in the gym. When I was taken to the platoon commander, he said to me, 'You're a commie, aren't you.' I was in fact a member of the Communist Party and had been a member of the Young Communist League and said so, but instead of reprimanding me the officer entered into a political discussion. Later on, the same officer allowed me to take the *Daily Worker* although an officious corporal had taken it upon himself to ban it.
> (Trooper Brian Wilkinson, 11th Hussars)

Reading the *Daily Worker* was hardly likely to be a heinous offence, even though it was generally disliked within the Army. Its reporting of the so-called humane treatment accorded to UN prisoners in North Korea and China during the Korean War had been shown to be biased, and in most military circles it was regarded with contempt. Amongst some of the rank and file, though, it enjoyed a degree of popularity for its campaign to bring National Service to an end and to replace it with a year's voluntary service to the state. Those aims were shared by *Challenge*, the newspaper of the Young Communist League which enjoyed a reasonably large membership during the early 1950s, especially in the north of England. Because National Servicemen were only required to sign the Official Secrets Act and did not have to swear an oath of allegiance to the Crown, it was politically acceptable for Communist Party members to be called up. Some, like Brian Wilkinson, trod softly; there were others who were inclined to be less discreet. They were soon marked down as potential troublemakers.

> I was a printing apprentice (compositor) from 1949 to 1953. I got deferment in 1952 and decided to accept my call-up papers in September 1953. Like many young men I did not want to join the army. I regarded the armed forces as instruments of the state; they were the capitalist means of repression and I knew full well the activities of the military in various parts of the world. I was particularly dreading the possibility of being sent to Malaya. One of my comrades had been sent there and had had the most appalling experiences because he was known as a communist . . . During my basic training I talked to many conscripts about socialism and peace and it soon became obvious to the army that not only was I the only Jew in the regiment, but I was also a major source of radical thinking. So after training I was transferred to the Sudan.
> (Private Charles Lubelski, 1st Bn. West Yorkshire Regiment)

From the Sudan Charles Lubelski was posted to the Suez Canal Zone in 1955, at a time when more and more National Servicemen were beginning to question the need for a British presence in Egypt and Britain itself was preparing to pull out. The Regulars may not have thought twice about their presence in the country but politically-orientated conscripts often had different views.

> There were two YCL members in the regiment. A conscript had been sent to my battalion from Malaya because he was an active

communist – we became very close friends and tried to influence the other men in the company. A good friend from my YCL days in Leeds was also stationed on the canal not too far from me. He was an active communist and highly educated politically. He was also a skilled engineer and took great pride in his professional skills. He commanded great respect amongst his fellows and because of this his views were also respected. He received a good deal of communist literature and this was read by many men in his camp; he also held regular political meetings, always informal, but meetings nonetheless.

(Private Charles Lubelski, 1st Bn. West Yorkshire Regiment)

That was not the end of the matter. Charles Lubelski remained under suspicion, and from the Suez Canal Zone he was suddenly transferred to Cyprus where he remained until demob. Membership of the Communist Party – even if only suspected – was a serious matter in the eyes of the army's hierarchy. The Cold War had brought the Soviet Union into focus as a potential enemy and the Korean War had hardened attitudes towards communism. The defection to Moscow of Burgess and Maclean had rocked the establishment, and worse was to follow in 1961 when the Vassall affair confirmed evidence of Soviet communist infiltration into the upper reaches of power. Quite simply, it was rarely advisable for any National Serviceman to express his political leanings, especially if they were to the left. Only in the officers' mess, as Edmund Ions discovered at Eaton Hall, was it safe to voice one's views – and then only if they conformed to establishment thinking.

When we took cocktails with the staff officers at Eaton Hall once a week before dinner, the conversation tended to revolve around set subjects: public schools, and their united front against the Labour Government and all its works; the attractions of county pursuits and county people; the cricket season, travel in hot countries; the White Man's Burden; and now and then outright racism wherever particular nationals could be subsumed under the compendious term 'wogs'.[31]

Politics, though, have never occupied a high position in service life and officers were expected to hold right of centre establishment views. Left wing thinking, if acknowledged at all, was supposed to be the realm of the eccentric, like the elderly storekeeper in a REME workshop at Bordon who had been a member of the Communist Party and had fought with the International Brigades in Spain, or the romantic supporters of the

IRA in the Royal Ulster Rifles. Most conscripts, it would seem, put politics (if they had them at all) to one side during their period of service, and as National Service was seen as an imposition in the first place, the general political feeling was that 'we're all in it together so let's make the best of it'. Under those conditions, politics could wait for civilian life.

Given the variety of National Service life and the intensity with which young men experienced it, it is hardly surprising that it should have spawned a variety of books. Some of those belong to the genre of war fiction, such as Alan Sillitoe's *Key to the Door* and D. J. Hollands's *The Dead, The Dying and The Damned*, which are set, respectively, in Malaya and Korea. Both, too, chronicle the journey of a boy into manhood, and Sillitoe's novel in particular paints an evocative picture of a National Service-man, Brian Seaton, who realises that he has been transformed utterly by his experience. On the verge of demob, he can see the safety of his adult life stretching out in front of him.

> I'll see mam and dad as well. Look, dad, I'm back. I'm out of jail, finished, free, paid-up and ready for a hard job at the factory. Pauline, go and buy me a couple of pairs of overalls, an old jacket and a mashcan, a good pair of boots to keep the suds and steel-shavings out. What number bus do I need to get there spot on half past seven every morning? Don't try and tell me; I was born knowing it.

Alan Sillitoe, who served as an RAF wireless operator in Malaya in 1947–48, admitted that the experience gave him the first glimmerings of the novel and that several episodes – including the search in the jungle for the lost plane – were drawn from his own service career. Leslie Thomas also served in Malaya, and many of his National Service experiences found their way into his novel *The Virgin Soldiers*, which enjoyed a huge popular success, selling over one million copies.

However, the novel which most National Servicemen recognise as cleaving most closely to their experience is David Lodge's *Ginger, You're Barmy*, first published in 1962 and re-issued twenty years later with an afterword by its author putting into context his time as a conscript soldier in the Royal Armoured Corps. While admitting that the progress of his narrator Jonathan Browne resembled his own passage through National Service, Lodge also revealed that the novel was born of his dismay at the slow rate of change in British society, especially as it concerned the RAC 'which incorporated all the traditionally "elite" regiments of cavalry'.

> The anger behind *Ginger, You're Barmy* is, then, the anger of a bright, no doubt bumptious young man, who, having sensed exciting possibilities of personal self-fulfilment via education, found his progress rudely interrupted for two years by compulsory enlistment in an institution which he could neither identify with nor defeat. But if the novel is, to that extent, a personal settling of scores, I hope its anger is controlled, for I deliberately delayed writing it for some years after completing my National Service.

Like Lodge, Jonathan Browne was a graduate while doing his National Service, and it is through his enraged eyes that we view the traumatic events of basic training and the uncaring brutality which is visited upon his intake at Catterick. Here we meet Mike Brady, a fellow student from London University who bucks against the system, and Percy Higgins, the miserable Catholic boy who is hounded by the sadistic Corporal Baker. During their basic training everything is writ large – the brutality, the bullying, the coarseness – and the episode ends with Higgins shooting himself on the firing range after being back-squadded by Baker. The question of it being a suicide is deliberately fudged, the subsequent coroner's inquest revealing that Higgins had killed himself while attempting to shoot off his trigger finger, the traditional way out for the unwilling soldier. Thereafter, the novel becomes less engaged with the facts of National Service life and more concerned with Brady's attempts to bring Baker to book. The novel also traces to its conclusion the triangular relationship between Jonathan, Mike and his girl friend Pauline, culminating with Mike deserting and leading an IRA raid on an army camp, and Jonathan entering into an unsatisfactory marriage with Pauline. Both men have taken radically different attitudes towards their service and to the process of growing up, but it is left to Jonathan to put National Service into perspective – both for himself and for thousands of other young men:

> National Service was like a very long, very tedious journey on the Inner Circle. You boarded the train with a lot of others, and for a while it was very crowded, very uncomfortable; but after a while the crowd thinned, you got a seat, new faces got in, old faces got out; the slogans on the advertisements got tiresomely familiar, but you sat on, until, after a very long time, you got out yourself, at the station where you had originally boarded the train, and were borne by the escalator back into the light and air. It was natural, then, that as you approached your destination, you should try to

connect the end of your journey with the beginning, try to recall all
the shapes and forms of humanity that had shoved and jostled and
brawled and snored in the narrow swaying compartment.

What Lodge did for the Army's National Servicemen, Gordon
Williams also did for the RAF's National Servicemen in his novel
The Camp. Although this is engaged with life on an RAF base –in
this case a 2nd TAF operational base in Germany – many of the
characters, including the central figure of Ritchie Brown, are
National Servicemen and their experience is central to the plot.
The novel is also a chronicle of the lives of the men who people
the camp – men like Brown, the unwilling conscript, 'Harry'
Truman, the regular who remains happily unpromoted, Big
Chick, the hard man from Glasgow who takes on the authorities,
Squadron Leader Thribbit, the wartime bomber ace, and, ruling
over all their lives, Group Captain Rodney House, the martinet
who arrives to shake up the camp and instil a new sense of
discipline.

The tedium of bull and the senseless routines imposed by the
draconian camp commander came as a shock to critics unused to
the excesses of service life when the novel was published in 1966,
but Williams was careful never to go over the top. Rather, his
novel explains why men, cooped up in a sullen occupied country,
will become peevish and lay themselves open to heavy-handed
discipline. In such a situation the only release comes from nights
of drinking to get drunk in the Malcolm Club, or in senseless
violence.

> There were times when the whole set up got on top of you and all
> you wanted to do was stick it on some bloke or kick something or
> go on the biggest stinking booze-up of all time.

In speaking for the rest of his billet, Big Chick Divertie
becomes a focus for Williams's sympathies in the central section
of the novel, where his hard man act is shown to be but a veneer.
One of the most violent scenes in the novel takes place in a
German *Bierstube* where Chick and his armourer mates provoke
a brutally drunken fight with the local Germans.

If this is a sombre picture of National Service life, Williams
does not always dwell on the darkness and shadows. Zeldorf is an
operational base housing Venom fighters and, in a graphically
written chapter, one crash-lands with its undercarriage up; horror
is only kept at bay by the rough compassion the men bring to the
awful task of picking up the remains of the pilot's body. There are
animal pleasures to be found in playing football and cricket,

casual sex is always available in the neighbouring town, and although all the main characters are drawn individually, they emerge as a cohesive unit, a reminder of the camaraderie which exists in the closely-knit world of the billet. Williams, who served as a National Serviceman in the RAF between 1952 and 1954, is uniformly excellent on the background details and the detritus of service life.

Accuracy of detail is also a virtue of James Kennaway's novel, *Tunes of Glory*. Although it is not strictly a National Service novel and is more concerned with the conflict which arises when two men from different social and military traditions – Jock Sinclair, a hard-drinking Scot who has risen from the ranks, and Basil Barrow, a professional with an impeccable military background – vie with one another for the colonelship of a Highland regiment, Kennaway's novel is a tough and realistic picture of life in a post-war National Service infantry battalion. It is especially good on life in the officers' mess; and that is where the novel opens on a winter's night, 'while the National Servicemen wished they were home in their villas, and horn-nailed Regulars talked of Suez'.

> But it was warm in the Officers' Mess. Dinner was over, and the Queen had had her due. The long dining-room with the low ceiling was thick with tobacco smoke. The regimental silver cups, bowls and goblets shone in the blaze of the lights above the table, and from the shadows past colonels, portrayed in black and white, looked down at the table with glassy eyes. Two pipers, splendid in their scarlet, marched round and round the table, playing the tunes of glory. The noise of the music was deafening, but on a dinner night this was to be expected.

Campbell Barracks, the fictional setting for *Tunes of Glory*, is easily identified as Queen's Barracks in Perth (now demolished) where Kennaway did his basic training with 58 Primary Training Corps in September 1946. The 'first horrible hours in Perth' were a rude shock to him, but Kennaway, a product of Trinity College, Glenalmond, had been identified as potential officer material and made his way to Eaton Hall where he narrowly missed winning the Belt of Honour. Commissioned into the Cameron Highlanders, he served with the 1st Gordons in Essen and it was there that the idea for *Tunes of Glory* was born. Later, in 1960, it was made into a film starring Alec Guinness and John Mills in the roles of the contending colonels. At the time the War Office was chary about cooperation with a production which they felt showed the Army in a bad light, but so successful was the film that when it was given its Scottish premiere in Perth, The Black Watch used the occasion for a recruiting drive and the performance was attended by the GOC Scotland as well as by several officers in uniform.

Another National Service novel with an Officers' Mess background was Alan Burns's *Buster*, which was published in John Calder's New Writing series in 1961. Here, the central character, Dan Graveson, is commissioned into an artillery regiment, but his brother's death awakens a new idealism and he becomes a member of the Communist Party. Encouraged by a fellow traveller, a lieutenant in the Royal Army Education Corps, he commits a mutinous act by daubing buildings with peace slogans, and after attempting to politicise his men he is asked to resign his commission. As Burns makes clear, the rebellion is both naive and futile, and Dan is seen to be little more than the dupe of Lieutenant Gerson, his so-called mentor.

> Standing in the Officers' latrine, a week later, they decided to paint on the Ammunition Store: *Join the Movement for Peace*. It was in Gerson's phrase, 'the correct slogan'.
> Dan thought it was too long.
> Gerson said: 'It can't be helped. Those words are essential. There may be another comrade along to help us.'
> 'Another comrade!' Dan felt he had been knighted.

More telling in its condemnation of the futility of many aspects of service life during the National Service period is John McGrath's play *Events While Guarding the Bofors Gun*, which received its first performance at Hampstead Theatre Club on 12 April 1966. Set in an army camp in North Germany in 1954, this is a study of seven men – six gunners and an eighteen-year-old bombardier – who are trapped in a purposeless situation, guarding an obsolete bofors gun on a cold winter's night. Two of the gunners, Shone and Rowe, are National Servicemen, but it is the thirty-year-old Regular, O'Rourke, who cracks under the strain of the watch. He gets drunk in the NAAFI – a military offence which could earn him a prison sentence – leaving Evans the bombardier to decide whether or not to charge him. On the surface, Evans appears anxious not to charge O'Rourke because he does not want to be responsible for sending him to the horrors of a military jail: the real reason, though, is that he has been selected as a potential officer and does not want the charges to interfere with the prospect of attending OCTU. His dilemma is put in perspective by his mate Flynn, an older man: 'If he breaks the law, he must go to prison; and some poor bastard like you has got to send him there. Do I make myself clear?'

In the end Evans fudges the issue, but the main thrust of the play is not directed at a conflict between lonely soldiers or at the ideology of Cold War strategy as represented by the elderly bofors gun. It is directed at a situation which is so ludicrous that O'Rourke can only act accordingly and treat it as a mocking jest.

A similar problem is investigated by Arnold Wesker in his play *Chips With Everything*, which was first performed at the Royal Court Theatre on 27 April 1962 before embarking on a successful commercial run in London's West End. Set in an RAF camp during basic training, it focuses on two radically different recruits: Pip Thompson, a general's son who refuses a commission, and 'Smiler', an inept and clumsy airman who becomes a victim of the officers' and the NCOs' brutality. Under those conditions Pip emerges as a natural leader, the only man capable of questioning the RAF's code of discipline; as such he is a thorn in the flesh of authority but a hero to the men. The search for Pip's motives is a preoccupation for the audience and the reader as much as for the officers, but Wesker, who served in the RAF, has claimed frequently that the main theme of the play could apply equally to other settings in which leadership qualities are examined. Nevertheless, *Chips With Everything* is an accurate portrayal of life in an RAF billet, and Wesker's deployment of language reveals him as an astute observer of National Service life. He is especially good on the differences between the lives led by the officers and the lives led by the men, and Pip's emergence at the play's end as a natural member of the 'officer class' is Wesker's own comment on that particular social system.

As National Service drifted into memory, so too did novels about post-war service life become less concerned with the matter of conscription and more engaged with an idealised service life. The success of Leslie Thomas's *Virgin Soldiers* spawned a number of imitations, all bent on describing National Service as a time of licensed debauchery. Donald Hardcastle's *Men They Came*, for example, is set in the Suez Canal Zone and centres on the unlikely sexual relationship between a young National Service driver, Frank Harvey, and his commanding officer's beautiful, frustrated wife. Equally taken up with gratuitous sex and violence is Walter Winward's *The Conscripts*, which follows a Royal Marine Commando platoon from basic training to active service in Cyprus during the EOKA emergency: the story hinges on the improbable juncture that all the members of the platoon are National Servicemen 'with something to prove'.

Writing about National Service was not confined to fiction or

the theatre. In 1955 Peter Chambers and Amy Landreth edited
Called Up, a collection of sixteen essays chronicling the contemporary National Service experience. The general feeling of the
writers was that they were in favour of conscription: most were
agreed that although boredom and waste were constant companions during their National Service, it was not without benefit
either to themselves or the nation. A more critical note was
struck in *Two Years to Do*, David Baxter's narrative of his own
National Service; but a sharp contrast to his views can be found in
A Call to Arms, Edmund Ions' sympathetic account of his time as
an army officer during the National Service period. He enlisted as
a Regular on a five-year engagement in 1947, went to Eaton Hall,
and while there decided to take a Regular commission at
Sandhurst which he found to be 'more a place of education that a
residence for idle young gentlemen seeking a military career in
the British tradition of amateurism.' Commissioned into the
Border Regiment, he served with the Royal Ulster Rifles in
Korea and with his own regiment in the Suez Canal Zone.

By far the most revealing accounts of National Service,
however, are to be found in B. S. Johnson's *All Bull*, which
appeared in 1972. Although Johnson was no admirer of National
Service and considered it to have been 'tedious, belittling,
coarsening, brutalising, unjust and possibly psychologically very
harmful', the overall picture produced by his twenty-four
contributors is not all monochrome. John Lawson is particularly
good on his service in the RAF, which he regarded as a 'crash
course in growing up': his trade training at RAF Halton he
likened to being a student anxious to pass an essential examination. Also to the point is Ian Carr's graphic description of the
snobberies he encountered while a subaltern with the Royal
Northumberland Fusiliers. A graduate, he left the army with
some relief to spend 'two rich years bumming around in poverty'.
Jeff Nuttall provides an appealing portrait of life as a 'schoolie' at
Weedon; the only sailor, Richard Key, ended his career on a high
note as an officer on coastal minesweepers; and Bill Holdsworth
makes a good job of his role as the reluctant soldier; but the most
telling and the most personal account belongs to Nicholas
Harman, who served in Korea as a subaltern and was wounded
there. While on patrol with two fusiliers, he ran into a Chinese
ambush and was hideously wounded in arms, leg and chest. His
story, though ironically told and gently self-mocking, is a
reminder that many National Servicemen had to pay for their
service with injuries which changed the course of their lives.

Chapter Ten

SUMMER SOLDIERS AND SUNSHINE PATRIOTS

In 1980, twenty-seven years after he had finished his service as a corporal in the RAF Regiment, John Inglis revisited RAF Watchett in Somerset where he had served in the summer of 1951.

> I went on holiday to Devon and one wet day I persuaded the family that we should go to Somerset and visit Watchett. After a lot of grumbling they agreed and I have never been so disappointed in my life. Watchett was a dirty miserable little town with no atmosphere whatsoever. It was wet when we arrived and we could not find a decent place to eat. Yet all my memories of the place were rose-coloured and I had always fancied going back one day. We then drove up to see the camp – another disaster. It was no longer there. Instead it was a holiday camp and what had been our camp cinema – the Astra – was still a cinema under a new name for the campers.
>
> (Corporal John Inglis, RAF Regiment)

Similar fates had befallen other camps, the most tangible landmarks of the National Service years. Norton Camp near Worcester, the home of No. 6 Training Regiment, Royal Engineers, is now derelict, although in the midst of all the broken masonry and rampant undergrowth it is still possible to see the Nissen huts and wooden billets which were home to thousands of National Servicemen during their basic training. Catterick has been cut back from the sprawling garrison remembered by Royal Signals and RAC conscripts, and is now a compact modern camp. The 'Catterick Flyer' runs no more along the Darlington to Richmond branch line, which disappeared during the Beeching cuts to Britain's railway system, and Richmond's station is now a trendy indoor market. Draughty Fort George with its fine Adam buildings was for many years a museum housing the treasures of the Queen's Own Highlanders. It is now a regimental depot again.

With the ending of National Service, the armed forces no longer needed to maintain a large number of bases and those surplus to requirements were closed down and in many cases the land sold off. RAF Bridgnorth in Shropshire is an industrial estate, although one or two of the buildings still remain intact and the lay-out would still be familiar to anyone who served there. The RAF's bases in East Anglia remain in being, with names like Coltishall, Marham and Wittering retaining a familiar ring for many former conscripts. In Scotland, RAF Leuchars is still an operational base, housing three squadrons of air-defence fighters, charged with guarding Britain's northern watch. The architecture of the National Service years has largely disappeared from these modern bases, but still, here and there, the knowing observer can pick out the last remaining wooden billets and air-raid shelters of an earlier period. In other camps along England's east coast, the runways and crumbling buildings have become part of the landscape to be uncovered, perhaps, by curious archaeologists of the future.

> An enjoyable day at Upavon – pressganged attendance at a demonstration of glider-borne operations. Huge troop and tank carriers swooping, whistling, hedge-hopping in to land – a marvellous sight. And the remains of a Hamilcar have just been found in Wiltshire and removed for reconstruction. Almost prehistoric now – certainly a bygone age – and yet, so recent.
> (Corporal Tony Carter, REME)

Just as the camps have changed beyond recognition, so too do the National Service uniforms belong to another age. The khaki or blue worsted battle-dress blouses and trousers, the thick woollen shirts, the unyielding webbing and the stiff leather boots today look like remnants from the years of World War II – which, in fact, many were. The equipment and armaments have altered, too. Modern technology has brought rapid and ever-changing innovations to all aspects of the services' range of equipment – computers, electronics, communications, weapon systems, surveillance – and training is consequently more thorough and time-consuming. This is one of the principal reasons why the re-introduction of conscription has been a military non-starter in recent years: it would take too long and be too expensive to train short-service men in the new technology. The Tornado variable-geometry all-weather multi-role combat aircraft contains over one hundred computer boxes, for example, and the Challenger, the army's newest battle tank, four. Electronics also now play a vital role in sea warfare and the Royal Navy's Type 22 'Broadsword' class destroyer is armed with Exocet and Sea Wolf missiles attached to sophisticated radar and computer systems. It is perhaps in this area that the National Serviceman would notice the greatest change between his young self and the young military technocrats of today.

Other less tangible benefits of National Service have changed, equally irrevocably. Most men would claim that friendship – or more precisely, companionship – was an important ingredient of their lives as conscripts. In the enclosed world of the billet, with twenty men sharing a small space, there was no room for stand-offishness and everyone had to muck in together. At that age, too, before the onset of the more cautious twenties, friendships tended to be more intense, though fleeting – one regret shared by many National Servicemen is that they failed to keep in touch with their mates on their return to civilian life. One advantage of National Service was that it did break down class barriers, albeit temporarily, and during their two years' stint men were frequently surprised to find that they enjoyed friendships with men they might never have met – or indeed liked – in civilian life.

> The comradeship, of course, was unique. Young men from different social backgrounds, with different accents and different attitudes were to become as one, linked by a dislike both for the army which they had been forced to join and for the civilians outside who were not part of that elite fraternity. Those comrades, once such a close-knit band, are now vague faces receding into memory – faces whose names have been long forgotten. Even dog-eared snapshots of twenty-five years ago cannot bring back names that meant so much. But the faces are still there and the images linger on – images of a period which, measured in terms of achievement, is hardly worth remembering, but which, for not entirely explicable reasons, will never be erased.
>
> (Corporal Denis Gane, Royal Corps of Signals)

> No, I wouldn't have missed those National Service days – there were frustrations and difficult times, certainly, but overall I look back on them with a great deal of pleasure. I often wished that I had kept in touch with more of my service colleagues, and perhaps had the occasional reunion, but sadly, all are now only fleeting memories on photographs and in diaries. I often wonder what happened to all those fine people?
>
> (Corporal Mike Burdge, RAF)

On their return to civilian life most National Servicemen also went back to their own social group, and the brief period of 'social levelling' remained in the billet. In any case, the enforced mixture of men from different backgrounds and social classes was really confined to rankers and junior leaders who had to spend all their time in one another's company. For the National Service officers it was rather different. On being commissioned they were quickly admitted into the services' hierarchy and found themselves amongst members of their own social grouping with similar accents and family backgrounds.

> I had been brought up in Canada and the United States and knew no one of my own age in the UK. I was, therefore, thrilled to be made a Guards officer which, in the circle in which I moved, gave me a considerable social cachet and entrée to an exciting social life when, later, I went up to Oxford. The most enduring friends I now have were fellow National Service officers, mainly in my own regiment or others whom I had met through these same men while at university. This, of course, reflects the more class-orientated values of that particular period.
>
> (2nd Lieutenant Simon Coke, 3rd Bn. Coldstream Guards)

The selection of officers has been another area of radical change in the armed forces. The right accent and background are no longer a passport for a young man intent on an easy life, hiding behind conferred rank and burning off his youthful energies in the Mess or on the hunting field. Today, infantry officers, for example, have to spend a period as private soldiers to learn what their men have to put up with: conformity to a rigid hierarchy enforced by blind obedience is now a thing of the past.

Other fondly remembered highlights of National Service life include travel, even though the confinements of many overseas postings restricted such pleasures as sight-seeing or sun-bathing. (National Service was never meant to be a holiday.) Sport, too, stands high on the list of good things to be recalled, and there is hardly an ex-National Serviceman who does not admit that he reached the peak of his physical fitness during basic training. Pride in the service is another legacy, prompting wistful curiosity in the subsequent exploits and career of the regiment, squadron or ship.

> I still get a thrill to see the caubeen and green hackle of the Royal Irish Rangers and to hear their pipes and drums and bugle band. Of course, they haven't got the 160 paces per minute dash that we had, but the Royal Green Jackets come near it. I have sometimes wondered how different I'd have been without the discipline of National Service. I mean, what did a Teddy Boy graduate to?
>
> (Rifleman George Savage, 1st Bn. Royal Ulster Rifles)

Discipline remains the corner-stone of service life, even in today's more relaxed and meritocratic armed forces. Colonel Blimp has passed away and most officers are glad to see the back of him, but curiously the absence of yesterday's reliance on 'yessir, nosir' has reinforced the tightness of modern service discipline. This is especially true of soldiers who see action in Northern Ireland, where the platoon corporal is a key figure, frequently more important than the officer in active service situations. The army's recruiting literature of the 1980s makes much of the fact that there has been a sea-change in attitudes and that 'anyone who remembers the old-time Army would be amazed to see how life has changed': nevertheless, it still makes clear that however much attitudes have changed, discipline is still all-important.

> Of course there's still discipline. You can't run an Army without it. Nobody values spit-and-polish for its own sake. These days we expect you to keep your kit, your living quarters and yourself clean and tidy and equipment in good working order. You do what you're told promptly. But that's only commonsense. Our main concern is to make you into an efficient Professional who knows his job and won't let his mates down when the heat is on.

It is an attitude – more delicately phrased, perhaps – with which all National Servicemen would be familiar. Unnecessary bull might have gone with the introduction of sensible materials for uniforms, but basic training remains a tough, no-nonsense and strictly disciplined period, designed to change a civilian into a serviceman in a few weeks. In that respect it is a curious anomaly that although every National Serviceman disliked, with varying degrees of intensity, the weeks of recruit training, there remains in retrospect a commonly-held belief that the experience was beneficial.

> My service gave me self-confidence, taught me comradeship, understanding of my fellow men, discipline and an appreciation of my home and parents. I returned to Caernarvon a very responsible adult. I had come across quite a few hoodlums from the bigger cities, but the Army soon knocked them into shape and they left their National Service far better citizens than when they entered it.
> (Lance-Corporal Griffith Roberts, Royal Corps of Signals)

At the same time, too, those men would admit that their generation was more amenable to obeying orders. Discipline was usually strict at home and school, and National Service, when it arrived, was merely seen as an extension of that discipline. The crime rate for crimes of violence in Britain trebled between 1955 (5,869) and 1964 (15,976), and many alarmed observers linked the increase to the breakdown in national discipline heralded by the end of National Service. Although it has to be admitted that those conscripts who went into the Army as Teddy Boys had ceased to be Teddy Boys at the end of their National Service, there is no evidence to suggest that military standards of discipline were carried over into civilian life. Indeed, the findings of Ferguson and Cunnison's Glasgow research project suggest that National Service was not a factor in preventing violent crime, which they concluded had its origins in poor living conditions and socio-economic changes in the city.

The imposition of discipline, though, is by far the most abiding memory of National Service, and it is on its virtues – or otherwise – that most ex-National Servicemen will beg to differ. Those who regarded it as an essential component in the process of growing up and as a means of social control, will look back on it, if not with affection, then at least with some gratitude.

> I took a real pride in my uniform (battledress with smart black beret and blancoed belt and shining boots and brasses). We were well respected when travelling on trains and buses etc., and this pride made one feel good inside. I found very little cynicism amongst my comrades *at the time*. Most of us *did* feel proud to be part of an army which had only recently won the war. I feel sorry that modern youth cannot experience such feelings.
>
> (Lance-Corporal M. Jones, REME)

Others view the disciplinary regimen of National Service as an imposition which brought nothing but unwanted unhappiness and stress.

> Dwelling upon the more positive aspects, one constantly hears the allegation that 'so-and-so "grew up" in the army'. Well, a young man is going to grow up at a given age no matter whether he's in an office, a factory, the army, or on a boat. When I returned to Glasgow, one erstwhile friend commented in public that 'the army made a man of Iain'. I rejoined, 'It's clear you never went,' and stalked off in a huff . . . One fellow, having volunteered for a three-year stint, in his first week took the initiative, borrowed the humble sum required and bought himself out. Many haw-hawed, saying he would be back in a month as a National Serviceman. But he was a miner. Everyone thought, how dismal a life, how would anyone want that horror, compared to their present one. I worked for two years in the pits in Scotland, and I would. Compared to the Army, the Scottish coal

mines were a warm, profoundly moving and satisfying way to live.
And the pits were still pretty bad.

(Corporal Iain Colquhoun, Corps of Royal Engineers)

No one would deny that sadistic NCOs existed, or that conditions
were often harsh and barbaric, or that National Service could be a
boring waste of time; but the opposite was also true. Usually it
was a matter of luck or it all boiled down to how a man reacted to
the experience – and to how he views it today. Certainly, the
much-vaunted benefits of discipline did not carry over into the
1960s and early 1970s, which were more relaxed, libertarian and
questioning.

It is now almost a quarter of a century since the last National
Serviceman left the nation's armed forces, and the first post-war
conscripts are well into middle life. Hardly surprisingly, many of
their memories tend to be rosy-hued, the distance of time lending
enchantment to their view of National Service.

> Without having revisited the place in thirty years, I still feel part of
> Cornwall in general and Newquay in particular. It was a
> completely new world at an impressionable age, a bit like going to
> university, and the experience was comparable and equally valid. I
> also saw unforgettable things which could not now be seen even by
> a millionaire with time on his hands – the misty coast of Cornwall
> from a Lancaster on a spring morning, the cathedral of Mosta
> before the tourist invasion and the last serving Spitfire climbing
> into an eggshell blue sky over Grand Harbour. Even now, a trivial
> thing can trigger off a complete picture – the smell of asphalt on a
> hot day brings back Wilmslow where the roads and paths were
> being made up that spring, the sound of 'Blue Tango' is Compton
> Bassett on a Wiltshire evening . . .
>
> (SAC David McNeill, RAF Coastal Command)

Nostalgia is a powerful yet curious emotion. On the one hand it
prompts melancholia about the long-lost, irretrievable past: on
the other, it can make that past seem better than it really was. For
every National Serviceman who experienced existential dread
during his period of service, there are others who remember only
the bright days when it always seemed to be summer, the sun
shining, long grass rippling, the bees buzz-buzzing.

> I recall with delight my first excursion into Bedford and walking
> along the River Ouse on a warm Saturday afternoon, or turning a
> corner in Lichfield and seeing for the first time the great facade of
> the cathedral . . . and the thrill, also from Yatesbury, of exploring

> Avebury and the old earthworks on the Marlborough Downs . . .
> and buying a Rudge 'Pathfinder' bike in London (which I still
> have) and touring the south-west and Wales on the weekends from
> Yatesbury. Yes, I really loved National Service . . . it afforded a
> young fellow from a very sheltered environment the opportunity
> to spread his wings and to do the kind of things I'd longed to be
> able to do throughout my childhood and youth.
>
>   (Corporal Charles Abel, RAF)

National Service changed Charles Abel in other more profound
ways. Towards demob it had become clear to him that he wanted
to forswear his chosen career in science and to train instead for
the ministry of the Church of Scotland. Today he is a minister in
Armidale, Australia, and looks back on his National Service as a
'liberating and spiritually enriching experience'. Other National
Servicemen have had similar experiences, especially when a
career or university course had been chosen before their call up.
In that sense National Service gave them a fresh perspective on
life, opened new doors, introduced unusual experiences and
made them feel restless, uneasy with their new-found maturity.

> Although at the time of our National Service we accepted that it
> was a necessity, the disruption it caused at a crucial stage in our
> development was significant. Because I knew that I would have to
> do two years' National Service, I never seriously thought about
> what I wanted as a career, nor about going to university – I had
> qualified for a major county award. On finishing my National
> Service in late October 1953 I had no desire to take up study (the
> academic year had started anyway), so I drifted into clerical work.
> It was nearly ten years before I finally commenced studying and
> eventually qualified as an accountant.
>
>   (Trooper Michael Baker, 2nd Royal Tank Regiment)

Like Charles Abel, Michael Baker lives in Australia and feels
certain that he would not have made the decision to emigrate had
it not been for National Service's broadening of his horizons.

Others, of course, found the transition back to civvy street easy
enough, and picked up their lives where they had left them two
years previously; but there is little doubt that National Service
was a potential cause of social disruption. A man of twenty or
twenty-one with two years of military experience behind him was
a very different person from the eighteen- or nineteen-year-old
fresh out of school or finished with his apprenticeship, tied to his
home and his home town. As Iain Colquhoun remarked, a boy
will grow into a man at a given age whatever the circumstances,
but the fact remains that during the period of National Service

most teenage boys 'grew up' as soldiers, sailors or airmen in the service of their monarch. Since 1963 that option has not been open to the youth of Britain, and it is for that reason that many people, particularly ex-servicemen, would like to see some form of service to the nation introduced for the young people of today.

In its most extreme form, there are advocates who would like to see national military service brought back for the 'good' of modern youth. Crime, hooliganism, football violence, they argue, would be eradicated by putting teenagers into the armed forces: the argument usually emerges when there has been a public outrage, like the violence which disfigured English football grounds in 1985. To their way of thinking, military service is akin to corrective discipline; the belief is that bad manners, vandalism and sloppy dressing would quickly disappear after the short sharp shock of basic training. Fortunately, the notion that National Service should be regarded as therapy for wayward young people belongs to the right-wing fringe and is not taken seriously within the forces themselves. Today the armed forces offer planned careers for young men intent on gaining a professional training: there is no room for backsliders, unwilling recruits or recalcitrant conscripts. In such a professional set-up, NCOs and officers can see no reason why the forces should be considered as a punishment or corrective agency for the nation's social problems.

More serious in its appeal is the argument that a form of community service to the nation could be evolved for young people of eighteen or nineteen. In *The Young Meteors*, his study of young people of the 1960s, Jonathan Aitken proposed that a 'national service for peace' should be inaugurated by the government. This would take the form of community or social service at home or abroad, and would augment the work being carried out by such existing voluntary agencies as Dr Barnardo's or Voluntary Service Overseas. Aitken was twenty-five when he made his case in 1967, and had missed National Service: his argument has continued to find favour in many quarters. Speaking at the University of Aston on 14 January 1984, David Owen, the leader of the Social Democrats Party, argued that a form of community service for young people would give the country a greater sense of shared community, help to eradicate class divisions and encourage young people to assert their rights and responsibilities.

> I believe there are many who between school and higher education would welcome enhanced opportunities to contribute for a year,

and perhaps reinforce this with a further few weeks every year for a period. A potential nurse or medical student might choose to serve in a mentally handicapped hospital or hostel. A potential engineer on an environmental project. Someone going into industry might like to join the armed forces for a year, then continue as a ready reserve. An accounts clerk might well wish to administer a community project for a one- or two-year period.

Owen was not advocating a return to any form of national service; his concept was purely voluntary, and was put forward as a means of enabling young people to contribute to society in a positive fashion, 'to contribute to the health of society as a whole'. Under Margaret Thatcher's Conservative administration several community schemes already exist for young people. These are run by the Manpower Services Commission and include the Community Programme, Voluntary Projects Programme, Opportunities for Volunteering and the Armed Services Youth Training Scheme, all of which are designed for the young unemployed. Consequently, none have been particularly successful, mainly because there is little motivation: the Armed Services Youth Training Scheme gives boys and girls aged 16–18 training in military skills which have a civilian application, but this only lasts a year. Those young people who want to make a career in the armed forces prefer regular entry, and in 1985 only 1,500 of the available 5,000 ASYTS places had been taken up. Another drawback is that many of the 'volunteers' frequently find themselves doing the same kind of time-wasting tasks that disfigured National Service. Because they are considered as palliatives for the young unemployed, any sense of service to the community has quickly departed from these no doubt well-meaning schemes.

Nevertheless, the idea of harnessing the energies and idealism of young people and channelling them into a form of service to the nation has attracted considerable support in the last twenty years. While researching his thesis on National Service and British Society in 1969–70, General Sir Anthony Farrar-Hockley discovered that an average of 50% of his interviewees aged 16–18 favoured the suggestion that National Service be introduced with a choice of community service or military service. When he checked the accuracy of that sample, using further interviews with 500 boys aged 14–18 attending a selection of state and private schools, the results were similar. 'By far the most common reason given for acceptance of conscription,' he noted, 'was "something to do". These words were used over and over

again.' Surprisingly, perhaps, at least 30% favoured the re-introduction of military service for young people.

That same year, 1970, also saw National Service re-emerge as a
topic for discussion in political and military circles. During the
defence debate in March 1970, Sir Fitzroy Maclean, MP, wrote to
The Times arguing that the re-introduction of military conscription would solve any shortage of manpower in Britain's armed
forces: he also pointed out that its implementation would bring
the country back into line with its NATO allies, all of which, bar
Canada, still relied on conscript armed forces. (This argument
resurfaced in 1973 when Britain became a member of the EEC
and it was suggested – though never as a serious proposal – that
the existing member countries might insist that conscription be
re-introduced.) Maclean's letter started a silly season of claim and
counter-claim about the merits of National Service. Those in
favour based their arguments either on the military necessity of
maintaining a large conscript army for service in Europe, or on
the social advantages to be gained by putting youngsters through
a strict code of military discipline. Those against National Service
put their case in the efficiency of Britain's professional armed
forces of the 1970s and in the corresponding wastefulness
produced by the conscript system.

By and large, the military did not want to see a return to
conscription because equipment and training had become too
sophisticated for the short-service recruit, and because they no
longer had a system to cope with a large turnover of recruits.
Voluntary recruitment, too, was not a problem: in other words,
there was no requirement to bring back National Service as it
existed between 1945 and 1963. The only logical military grounds
for the re-introduction of conscription would be as a reserve force
in the shape of a militia or citizens' army, a point made by
Correlli Barnett in a lecture to the Royal United Services
Institute in 1970.

> In contrast to conscription within the framework of a professional
> army, there are modern militias: entirely citizen forces. The
> French Socialist Jean Jaurés advocated a citizen army as an
> effective military alternative to conscription and one which
> avoided the dangers of militarism and of the excessive power of
> the professional military hierarchy within the state.[32]

Barnett went on to point out that the militia had much to offer
British society and was historically acceptable – 'the militia is as
ancient an English institution as the Common Law, and beside the

militia, with a life stretching from the Saxon kings to Edward VII, the regular Army appears very much a novelty.' He concluded that every citizen had an ancient obligation to bear arms in the defence of the state and that some form of part-time military training should be adopted to build up a large reserve force capable of rapid mobilisation. Similar systems are in force in Sweden, Switzerland and Israel. Barnett was a critic of the Sandys' defence doctrine and rejected the idea that nuclear deterrence, or the policy of mutually assured destruction, obviated the need for substantial conventional forces. In his view, Britain's forces of the 1970s were too small to fulfil the nation's NATO responsibilities, and he also argued that military strength could only act as a deterrent to war if it were capable of successfully waging conventional war. As he paraphrased it, Britain still maintained a small 'imperial' type of army to meet her European obligations: the creation of a militia would provide a radical solution to the traditional problem of Britain going to war in Europe with an expeditionary force small in numbers.

To some extent Barnett's criticisms have been met by the strengthening of Britain's reserve forces – at the time of his writing, the government was uncertain how to deal with the Territorial Army which had been transmogrified into three categories of reserve, two earmarked for civil defence and one of specialised units in reserve for the Regular Army. In the early 1980s the Territorial Army, which provides almost 30% of the Army's mobilised strength, was expanded from 70,000 to 86,000 and its structure changed to provide a Territorial division for service with BAOR in time of war or increased tension in Europe. Based in York in peacetime, it is equipped with the most modern military equipment such as Blowpipe missiles and Milan anti-tank weapons. At the same time, a new Home Service Force was established to help in the guarding of important civilian and military installations in time of tension or war, thus releasing Regular Army units for other tasks. The Royal Naval Reserve was also equipped with new types of minesweeper, and the number of ground defence squadrons of the Royal Auxiliary Air Force was increased.

Excellent though these new reserve forces might be, there is a limit to the numbers of men willing to meet the demands of 42 days' training per year, and it is here that a new problem has come into focus. In time of tension in Europe the bulk of the Territorial Army will be committed to backing up 1st British Corps in Germany, thus leaving the country open to attacks on key points vital to national security. Presuming the enemy to be the USSR, and presuming, too, that nuclear weapons will not be used in Europe, Soviet 'spetsnaz' troops (similar to the British SAS and SBS forces) would infiltrate the country causing disruption and committing acts of sabotage: in such circumstances neither the Regular Army nor the TA would be able to offer sufficient cover and protection.

That is the scenario envisaged by the Defence Begins at Home Committee, which in 1983 launched a campaign for the creation of a home defence force, a citizens' militia or home guard, whose primary task would be deterrence of enemy incursion and the security of the UK home base. Founded on the ancient principle of 'watch and ward', it would be a volunteer force, properly armed and trained, with the platoons formed on a local basis, their greatest asset being the men's knowledge of the locality. Such a force would only be mobilised if war threatened and its units would be integrated into a central military command structure, thus allaying suspicions that a home defence force could be used by an unscrupulous government in suppression of civil liberties. At the heart of the Committee's proposals, however, was the belief that the creation of a home defence force would be a powerful statement of Britain's resolve:

> There will be no 'phoney' war as in 1939–40, when Britain narrowly managed to get onto a war footing in time to avert invasion; should there be a next time there will be little or no warning, and the whole nation must be prepared to fight from the outset for its survival and for the right to decide its own political destiny (of whatever political hue it chooses) in the decades and centuries to come – free from coercion by any foreign power. In such circumstances we shall have to fight with what we have when war begins; it will be futile to start filling sandbags and trying to master the basic skills of defence as the clock starts to strike midnight. The surest defence is by deterrence, and such defence begins at home.[33]

The 1984 Defence White Paper acknowledged the threat posed by the Soviet 'spetsnaz' forces by extending the Home Service Force of the TA, which acquitted itself well in September 1985 during Operation 'Brave Defender', the biggest home defence exercise ever held in this country. Despite that success, though, the Defence Begins at Home organisation has kept up its pressure for the formation of a light home defence force created on a voluntary basis. Its argument hinges on a belief that any future European war will be conventional – the laying waste of the

western European heartland, with its rich industrial and agricultural resources, is not an enticing proposition to the Soviet
military leadership, they argue; nor is the inevitable prospect of
massive NATO retribution against the Soviet Union. The
organisation claims to have achieved a wide range of popular
support for its proposals; certainly their arguments in favour of a
home defence militia, either by creating a new force or by
extending the TA, are hardly radical. Over the centuries the
danger of invasion has been ever-present and to meet that threat
the militia, with its emphasis on part-time training, has been
regarded as a cheap, effective, and above all constitutionally safe
means of providing a home defence force and a reserve for the
regular forces. In today's terms, such a force would be unpaid,
raised from a wide range of ages and social class, and committed
only to a few hours of training a year. There is no question of it
being a conscript organisation or of any form of National Service
being re-introduced.

Although the idea of a home defence force is still a matter for
debate – and the idea of a citizens' militia refuses to go away – the
notion of bringing back National Service is not, however, a
serious proposition in any of the main political parties. Politically,
it would be difficult to adopt, expensive to reconstitute and
unpopular with young people. Quite simply, there is no need for
it – and the various proposals for home defence forces or militias
are seen entirely as voluntary measures.

From the point of view of service to the community, some form
of 'national service' by young people remains a fashionable
alternative to military service. Britain has a great tradition of
voluntary service, whether it be in a local society helping
handicapped children or in the national and global work
undertaken by Oxfam. Without the help of full- or part-time
volunteers many organisations would cease to function on their
present scale. Various governments have tinkered with the idea
of providing schemes for voluntary community work, but all too
often these have been regarded by young people as a means of
occupying idle hands. Unless the work can be seen to be of use to
society, and unless it can be built into the existing professional
infrastructure of the social services, then any such scheme is
condemned to failure. Nevertheless, those in favour of some form
of national community service argue that past problems and
present difficulties should not be allowed to stand in the way of an
idea that has considerable, if unfocused support. Unemployment,
the run-down of the welfare state, inner-city deprivation: these

are only some of the problems young volunteers could tackle, working under the leadership of the professional agencies. An added attraction is that such work could enable young people to feel that they were making a valuable contribution to society – an element which was often missing from National Service.

How, then, does National Service stand historically in relation to the idea that service to the nation fulfilled a social function? Contrary to popular belief, National Service was never regarded by the services or the politicians as a means of making young people better citizens. In some people's minds that might have emerged as a by-product, but it was never a military priority. The notion that a spell in the armed forces was good for character development or beneficial to the nation as a whole seems mainly to have arisen once National Service had come to an end. At the time, those young men regarded their National Service as a military duty to be performed regardless of their personal inclinations.

From a military point of view, though, National Service was a success. It might not have bolstered the nation's reserve forces in the way it was originally intended, but it did provide the country with large armed forces at a time when it needed them most. The defence of western Europe, the covering of the withdrawal from Empire, the successful waging of counter-insurgency wars would have created unacceptable strains on the Regular forces had it not been for the presence of the National Servicemen. In relieving those strains, National Service also gave a generation of young British men a unique shared experience: serving their country's armed forces as conscript soldiers, sailors and airmen in time of relative peace.

> In retrospect, one forgets the real horrors, the five-mile bashes, crawling through mud with thunderflashes exploding, exercises with live ammunition on Dartmoor, night exercises in North Wales, drill parades when one's hands literally froze on your rifle. At least they made good stories afterwards. And I remember the camaraderie, of all being in the shit together.
>
> But the bull and the boredom were the worst. If it were clear that one was needed to do a useful job, OK, one would do it however unpleasant. But bull for bull's sake, or whiling away the hours waiting for something (or nothing?) to happen . . .
> (Lieutenant Alexander Dunbar, 1st Bn. Queen's Own Cameron Highlanders)
>
> It was a very happy time of my life, with good friends made more easily than at any time before or since. With very few exceptions everyone got along very well together and I experienced much

generosity and kindness. The harsher the conditions, the greater
the spirit, and very few complained about conscription, even
though everybody claimed to have had a better paid job in civvy
street than I had!

(Sergeant Peter Kilmister, Flying Training Command, RAF)

It was a quick growing-up course and taught me how to look after
myself. I learned tact and diplomacy, too, and an ability to mix
with others from different social backgrounds. Looking back, one
rarely remembers the bad times: it was an experience I feel
privileged to have undergone. We just accepted the knocks.

(Writer William Nuttall, Royal Navy)

For those who were called up as civilians to do an eighteen-
month or two-year stint in the armed forces, there is a
commonality of experience some thirty or forty years later:
memories of long-forgotten values, of laughable, even ridiculous
incidents, of the sad trivia of human failings, of danger in
combat, of the detritus of the everyday life of the British
serviceman. Some undoubtedly enjoyed their acquaintanceship
with the forces, learned a trade, passed their driving tests or
travelled abroad for the first time in their lives. Some gained
commissions and became temporary officers and gentlemen.
Others just liked service life and adapted themselves to its arcane
rules and regulations. Even given memory's tendency to see the
past in a generous light, they can still conjure up thoughts of
togetherness, of physical and mental maturity, even of such old-
fashioned virtues as character training and development. Others
have recollections which are less bland, remembering only the
coarsening and belittling incidents: the bullying NCOs, the long
days doing nothing in damp billets, the revulsion of bayonet drill,
the indifferent food and the loss of liberty, the tedium and futility
of endless drill and bull and counting the days to demob.

However much their opinions might diverge today, though,
they are drawn together by a common bond. All the National
Servicemen were in their late teens or early twenties when they
were compelled to don uniforms: it was a time when they were
supposed to be enjoying the best years of their lives.

NOTES

Chapter One: OUR GUARDS AND GARRISONS

1 (p. 3 et seq.) The reminiscences of Rifleman Harris, Bombardier Alexander and John Shipp are taken from T. H. McGuffie (ed.), *Rank and File*. London: Hutchinson, 1954

2 (p. 5) William Skill's story is from H. G. Thursfield (ed.), *Five Naval Journals*. London: Naval Record Society, 1952

3 (p. 10) George Coppard, *With a Machine Gun to Cambrai*. London: HMSO, 1969, p. 1

4 (p. 11) John Tucker, *Johnny Get Your Gun*. London: William Kimber, 1978, p. 11

5 (p. 14) Rupert Hart-Davis (ed.), *Siegfried Sassoon Diaries 1915-1918*. London: Faber and Faber, 1983, p. 282

6 (p. 18–19) Richard Hillary, *The Last Enemy*. London: Macmillan, 1942, pp. 28–9

7 (p. 20) R. M. Wingfield, *The Only Way Out: An Infantryman's Autobiography of the North-West Europe Campaign, August 1944 to February 1945*. London: Hutchinson, 1955, pp. 18–19

Chapter Two: YOU'RE IN THE ARMY NOW

8 (p. 32) Julian Thompson, *No Picnic: 3 Commando Brigade in The South Atlantic, 1982*. London: Leo Cooper, 1985, pp. 19–26

9 (p. 35) Compton Mackenzie, *On Moral Courage*. London: Chatto and Windus, 1962, p. 153

Chapter Four: OFFICERS AND GENTLEMEN

10 (p. 106) Edmund Ions, *A Call to Arms: Interlude with the Military*. Newton Abbot: David & Charles, 1972, pp. 248–249

Chapter Five: EVEN THE BAD TIMES WERE GOOD

11 (p. 118) Major-General F. M. Richardson, *Fighting Spirit: A Study of Psychological Factors in War*. London: Leo Cooper, 1978, pp. 131–133

Chapter Six: IS YOUR JOURNEY REALLY NECESSARY?

12 (p. 144) Trevor Royle, *James and Jim: A Biography of James Kennaway*. Edinburgh: Mainstream, 1983, p. 80
13 (p. 154) Royle, p. 81

Chapter Seven: THE NATIONAL SERVICEMEN'S WARS: MALAYA AND KOREA

14 (p. 165) From General Horrocks's Introduction to Guthrie Moir, *The Suffolk Regiment*. London: Leo Cooper, 1969
15 (p. 167) A. F. Campbell, 'Jungle Patrol', *Blackwood's Magazine*, November 1952
16 (p. 170) 2nd Lieutenant Comyn's report is quoted from Christopher Sinclair-Stevenson, *The Life of a Regiment, The History of the Gordon Highlanders from 1945 to 1970*, vol. VI. London: Leo Cooper, 1974, p. 42
17 (p. 179) 2nd Lieutenant Wightwick's action and his medal citation are quoted from John Baynes, *The History of the Cameronians (Scottish Rifles), The Close of Empire, 1948–1968*, vol. IV. London: Cassell, 1971, pp. 66–67
18 (p. 186) Colonel Jeffrey's remarks are quoted from William Moore, *The Durham Light Infantry*. London: Leo Cooper, 1975, p. 70 and p. 71
19 (p. 189) Ions, p. 162
20 (p. 191–2) The description of 2nd Lieutenant Purves's action is quoted from *The Borderers' Chronicle*, December 1951
21 (p. 193) The description of 2nd Lieutenant Orr's action is quoted from *The Iron Duke*, April 1953
22 (p. 198) General Kendrew's words are quoted from A. J. Barker, *Fortune Favours the Brave: The Hook, Korea, 1953*. London: Cassell, 1974, p. ix

Chapter Eight: NO MORE SOLDIERING FOR ME

23 (p. 201) *The Red Hackle*, January 1954
24 (p. 203) War Office Papers, WO 216/411, Public Record Office
25 (p. 212) George Forty, *Called Up: A National Service Scrapbook*. London: Ian Allan, 1980, p. 11

Chapter Nine: THE END OF AN OLD SONG

26 (p. 227) Ministry of Labour and National Service Papers, LAB 6/413, Public Record Office
27 (p. 228) WO 32/14692
28 (p. 234) *The Oxfordshire and Buckinghamshire Light Infantry Chronicle*, vol. LVII, 1956
29 (p. 235) Stewart Menaul, *Countdown: Britain's Strategic Nuclear Forces*. London: Robert Hale, p. 74
30 (p. 237 et seq.) Information from the Campaign for Nuclear Disarmament, London
31 (p. 241) Ions, p. 94

Chapter Ten: SUMMER SOLDIERS AND SUNSHINE PATRIOTS

32 (p. 259) Correlli Barnett, 'The British Armed Forces in Transition', *Journal of the Royal United Services Institute*, June 1970
33 (p. 261) *Defence Begins at Home*. London: Inner Sound, 1983, p. 7

FURTHER READING AND SOURCES

In an attempt to keep notes and references to a minimum, the source of quotations has been placed, wherever possible, within the text. Other references are given by their page numbers in the Notes.

The principal sources on post-war National Service are to be found in the following papers and publications.

PUBLIC AND PARLIAMENTARY PAPERS

Admiralty Papers
Air Ministry Papers
Ministry of Labour and National Service Papers
War Office Papers
House of Commons Select Committee on Estimates. Third Report, Session 1952–53, *The Call-Up, Posting and Movement of National Servicemen* (HC 132), Departmental Replies (HC 295), 1953
Ministry of Defence. *National Service* (Cmnd. 9608), 1955
Ministry of Labour and National Service, *Call-Up of Men to the Forces, 1957–1960* (Cmnd. 175), 1957
Ministry of Labour and National Service. *Report on the Enquiry into the Effects of National Service on the Education of Young Men*, 1955
War Office. *Report of the Committee on the Employment of National Servicemen in the United Kingdom* (Cmnd. 35), 1956

REGIMENTAL PUBLICATIONS

The Borderers' Chronicle
The Covenanter
The Die-Hard
The Iron Duke
The Oxfordshire and Buckinghamshire Light Infantry Chronicle

The Red Hackle
The Thin Red Line
Baynes, John, *The History of the Cameronians (Scottish Rifles): The Close of Empire, 1948–1968,* vol. IV. London: Cassell, 1971
Carew, Tim, *The Glorious Glosters: A Short History of the Gloucestershire Regiment, 1945–1970.* London: Leo Cooper, 1970
Crichton, Richard, *The Coldstream Guards, 1946–1970.* Bungay, Suffolk: Richard Clay (The Chaucer Press), 1972
Fitzroy, O., *Men of Valour: The Third Volume of the History of the King's Royal Irish Hussars, 1927–1958* (privately published)
Foster, R. C. G., *History of the Queen's Royal Regiment, 1948–1959,* vol. IX. Aldershot: Gale and Polden, 1961
Malcolm, G. I., *The Argylls in Korea.* Edinburgh: Nelson, 1952
Moir, Guthrie, *The Suffolk Regiment.* London: Leo Cooper, 1969
Sinclair-Stevenson, Christopher, *The Life of a Regiment: The History of the Gordon Highlanders, 1945–1970,* vol. VI. London: Leo Cooper, 1974
Whitehead, Kenneth, *The History of the Somerset Light Infantry 1946–1960.* London: William Clowes for the S.L.I., 1961

BOOKS

Ascoli, David, *A Companion to the British Army, 1660–1983.* London: Harrap, 1983
Barnett, Correlli, *Britain and Her Army, 1509–1970.* London: Allen Lane, The Penguin Press, 1970
Bartlett, C. J., *The Long Retreat: A Short History of British Defence Policy.* London: Macmillan, 1972
Baxter, D., *Two Years To Do.* London: Elek, 1959
Baynes, J. C. M., *The Soldier in Modern Society.* London: Eyre Methuen, 1972
Beveridge, T. B., *A Guide for the National Serviceman in the Army.* London: Phoenix, 1953
Blaxland, Gregory, *The Regiments of the British Army, 1945–1970.* London: William Kimber, 1971
Chambers, P. and Landreth, A., *Called Up: The Personal Experiences of Sixteen National Servicemen.* London: Allan Wingate, 1955
Clutterbuck, R. L., *The Long, Long War.* London: Cassell, 1967
Crawford, Oliver, *The Door Marked Malaya.* London: Rupert Hart-Davies, 1958
Davey, Philip, *British Defence Policy East of Suez.* London: OUP for the Royal Institute of International Affairs, 1973
Eden, Sir Anthony, *Full Circle.* London: Cassell, 1960
Farrar-Hockley, Anthony, *The Edge of the Sword.* London: Frederick Muller, 1954
Foot, M. R. D., *Soldiers in Uniform: Military Manpower in Modern*

Societies (Studies in International Security No. 3). London: Weidenfeld and Nicolson for the Institute for Strategic Studies, 1961

Ferguson, T. and Cunnison, J., *In their early Twenties: A Study of Glasgow Youth.* London: OUP for The Nuffield Foundation, 1956

Forty, George, *Called Up: A National Service Scrapbook.* London: Ian Allan, 1980

Gorer, Geoffrey, *Exploring English Character.* London: The Cresset Press, 1955

Hayes, Denis, *Challenge of Conscience: The Story of the Conscientious Objectors, 1939–1949.* London: Allen and Unwin, 1949

Henniker, M. C. A., *Life in the Army Today.* London: Cassell, 1957

Hoggart, Richard, *The Uses of Literacy.* London: Chatto and Windus, 1957

Hollands, D. J., *The Dead, The Dying and The Damned.* London: Cassell, 1956

Holmes, Richard, *Firing Line.* London: Jonathan Cape, 1985

Ions, Edmund, *A Call to Arms: Interlude with the Military.* Newton Abbot: David & Charles, 1972

Johnson, B. S., *All Bull: The National Servicemen.* London: Quartet, 1973

Linklater, Eric, *Our Men in Korea.* London: HMSO, 1952

Lodge, David, *Ginger, You're Barmy.* London: MacGibbon and Kee, 1962

Marshall, S. L. A., *The Military History of the Korean War.* New York: Franklin Watts, 1963

Marwick, Arthur, *British History Since 1945.* London: Penguin, 1982

Montgomery, Field Marshal, *The Memoirs of Field Marshal Montgomery.* London: Collins, 1958

O'Ballance, Edgar, *Malaya: The Counter-Insurgent War.* London: Faber and Faber, 1966

Paget, Julian, *Counter-Insurgency Campaigning.* London: Faber and Faber, 1967

Raven, Simon, *The Sabre Squadron.* London: Anthony Blond, 1966

Rawlings, J. D. R., *The History of the Royal Air Force.* London: The Temple Press, 1984

Rees, David, *Korea: The Limited War.* London: Macmillan, 1964

Richardson, F. M., *Fighting Spirit: A Study of Psychological Factors in War.* London: Leo Cooper, 1978

Sillitoe, Alan, *Key to the Door.* London: W. H. Allen, 1961

Sinclair, Andrew, *The Breaking of Bumbo.* London: Faber and Faber, 1959

Snyder, W. P., *The Politics of British Defence Policy.* Ohio: Columbus University Press, 1964

Stanhope, Henry, *The Soldiers: An Anatomy of the British Army.* London: Hamish Hamilton, 1979

Thomas, Leslie, *The Virgin Soldiers.* London: Constable, 1966

Wingfield, R. M., *The Only Way Out.* London: Hutchinson, 1955

ARTICLES

Barclay, Brig. C. N., 'National Service: A Survey', *Brassey's Annual*, 1956

Barnett, Correlli, 'The British Armed Forces in Transition', *Journal of the Royal United Service Institution*, June 1970

Burcher, Major J. A. C., 'The Training of National Servicemen', *Army Quarterly*, April 1955

Crawford, Major W. K. B., 'Training the National Service Officer at Eaton Hall', *Journal of the Royal United Service Institution*, February 1951

Hudson, Major E. R. B., 'New Style National Service', *Army Quarterly*, July 1951

Lanning, Flt. Lt. G. E., 'National Service – the Education Officer's Part', *Journal of the Royal United Service Institution*, 1950

Lee, Major F. L., 'Compulsory Service in the Armed Forces', *Brassey's Annual*, 1954

Lloyd, Maj. Gen. C., 'Integration of National Service with the Country's Economic Future', *Journal of the Royal United Service Institution*, 1955

Low, Brig. A. R. W., 'Army Manpower: The Case against Wishful Thinkers', *Army Quarterly*, 1949

Martel, Lt. Gen. Sir Gifford, 'The Case Against Conscription', *Army Quarterly*, 1949; 'National Service', *Army Quarterly*, 1950

Radcliffe, Lt. Col. R. A. C., 'The National Serviceman and Industry', *Army Quarterly*, 1952

Raitt, Captain R. I., 'The George Knight Clowes Memorial Essay, 1961', *Army Quarterly*, October 1961

Tinker, Lt. Col. E. H., 'National Service Without Tears', *Army Quarterly*, April 1950

ACKNOWLEGEMENTS

I wish to acknowledge my debt to all of the following National Servicemen without whose valuable assistance this book could never have been written.

Corporal Charles Abel
263 Squadron, Royal Air Force
1953–1955
Armidale, Australia

Sergeant Alan A. Aldous
Royal Corps of Signals
1951–1953
Ipswich

A. B. James H. Austin
Royal Navy
1949–1951
Guildford

Trooper Michael P. Baker
2nd Royal Tank Regiment
Royal Armoured Corps
1951–1953
North Ryde, NSW, Australia

Lance-Corporal Charles Baxter
14/20th King's Hussars
1955–1957
Penicuik, Midlothian

Piper Drew Bennett
2nd Bn., The Scots Guards

1955–1959
Auchtermuchty, Fife

Pilot Officer C. H. Berthelot
Royal Air Force
1948–1950
Badnellan, Sutherland

Squadron Leader Dennis L. Bird
Royal Air Force
1949–1968
Shoreham, Sussex

Corporal N. R. Brockie
Army Catering Corps
1958–1960
Newport-on-Tay, Fife

Major W. R. R. Bruce
4th/5th Bn., The Black Watch
1946–1960
Caversham, Berks

Corporal Mike Burdge
Headquarters 62 Group, Royal
   Air Force
1954–1957
Cheltenham

Private R. H. Burford
1st Bn., The Duke of Edinburgh's
    Royal Regiment (Berkshire
    and Wiltshire)
1957–1959
South Harting, Hants

SAC J. Malcolm Burrill
Royal Air Force
1953–1955
Blackpool

Private Alan Byers
1st Bn., The Border Regiment
1953–1955
Carlisle

Corporal Tony Carter
'C' Coy, 27 Command
    Workshops, REME
1949–1951
Wootton Bassett, Wilts

Signalman James R. Christie
Royal Corps of Signals
3rd Infantry Division
1955–1957
Monifieth, Dundee

2nd Lieutenant Simon Coke
3rd Bn., Coldstream Guards
1950–1951
Edinburgh

Corporal Iain Colquhoun
Senior Railway Traffic Office,
    Royal Engineers
1953–1955
Culver City, California, USA

Private J. D. Colvin
Royal Army Service Corps
1949–1951
Newbridge, Midlothian

SAC Alexander Copland
2 FRU, Royal Air Force

1955–1957
Kilwinning, Ayrshire

Sergeant R. Darbyshire
220 Squadron, Royal Air Force
    Coastal Command
1951–1953
Orrell, Lancs

Private Terence Davenport
Army Medical Equipment Depot,
    MELF 16, Royal Army
    Medical Corps
1950–1952
Sutton Coldfield

Corporal Peter Davies
BMH Nicosia, Royal Army
    Medical Corps
1958–1960
Gloucester

LAC Byron T. Denning
Aircraft Torpedo Development
    Unit, Royal Air Force
1948–1950
Ebbw Vale, Gwent

Corporal Jack Devlin
Royal Air Force
1950–1952
Glasgow

LAC D. A. Dingwall
16 MU Stafford, Royal Air Force
1955–1958
Elgin, Moray

SAC John Dinning
Royal Air Force
1955–1957
Worthing, Sussex

Lance-Corporal Bob Downie
9 Base Ammunition Depot,
    MELF 10, Royal Army
    Ordnance Corps

1952–1954
Aberdeen

Lance-Corporal R. Dulson
1st Bn., The Cheshire Regiment
1951–1953
Madeley, Crewe

Lieutenant Alexander Dunbar
1st Bn., Queen's Own Cameron
  Highlanders
1947–1949
Elgin, Moray

2nd Lieutenant A. R. Dunbar
1st Bn., Queen's Own Cameron
  Highlanders (attached 1st Bn.,
  The Gordon Highlanders)
1945–1948
Duffus, Elgin

2nd Lieutenant Ian Duncan
No. 9 Training Regiment, Royal
  Engineers
1953–1955
Preston

2nd Lieutenant A. A. Faucheux
Royal Army Pay Corps
1955–1957
Henley-on-Thames

Signalman W. Findlay
Royal Corps of Signals
1954–1956
Glasgow

Lance-Corporal Arthur Franks
1st Bn., West Yorkshire Regiment
1951–1953
Blackpool

Sapper Frank Gaff
No. 1 Engineers Stores Depot,
  Royal Engineers
1953–1955
Guildford, Surrey

Corporal Denis Gane
4 (Ind) Signals Squadron, Royal
  Corps of Signals
1960–1962
Cwmbran, Gwent

Craftsman Donald Greaves
No. 4 Training Regiment, Royal
  Electrical and Mechanical
  Engineers
1955–1957
Aldbourne, Marlborough

Stores Assistant Robert V.
  Greenshields
HMS *Warrior*, Royal Navy
1948–1950
Arcadia, California, USA

Corporal Frank Hill
Royal Engineers
1947–1949
Guildford, Surrey

Private Robert Hood
Royal Army Medical Corps
1947–1949
Thurso

Corporal John Gordon Inglis
33 LAA Squadron, Royal Air
  Force Regiment
1951–1953
Scunthorpe

Private J. M. Inglis
No. 9 Training Regiment, Royal
  Engineers
1955–1957
Inverness

Lance-Corporal M. Jones
HQ REME, Arborfield, Royal
  Electrical and Mechanical
  Engineers
1948–1950
Cheltenham

Pilot Officer Peter S. Jones
Royal Air Force
1956–1957
Guildford, Surrey

Signalman R. G. Jones
3 R Force, MELF, Royal Corps of
    Signals
1953–1955
Coventry

Gunner Jack Kerr
Royal Regiment of Artillery
1953–1955
Dundee

Corporal W. L. Kerr
1st Bn., Royal Scots Fusiliers
1949–1951
Stranraer

Sergeant Peter Kilmister
RAF School of Gunnery, Royal
    Air Force
1951–1953
Mossbank, Shetland

Corporal Jim Laird
1st Bn., The Black Watch
1951–1953
Glasgow

Private Charles Lubelski
1st Bn., West Yorkshire Regiment
1953–1955
Bushey, Herts

Gunner Ernest Macdonald
58 Medium Regiment, Royal
    Regiment of Artillery
1953–1955
Alness, Sutherland

Writer John G. McIlvean
HMS *Cochrane*, Royal Navy
1949–1951
Mauchline, Ayrshire

Gunner Gregor F. McIntosh
12 LAA Regiment, Royal
    Regiment of Artillery
1959–1961
Edinburgh

Lieutenant Ian Macleod
546 Bomb Disposal Unit, Royal
    Engineers
1950–1952
Kettering, Northants

2nd Lieutenant A. D. S.
    MacMillan
1st Bn., The Royal Scots, attached
    1st Bn., King's Own Scottish
    Borderers
1955–1957
Edinburgh

Corporal David McMurray
Royal Army Service Corps
1947–1949
Glasgow

SAC David McNeill
Royal Air Force Coastal
    Command
1952–1954
Larkhall, Lanarks

LAC Derek Morgan
MEAF 15, Royal Air Force
1950–1952
Hornchurch, Essex

2nd Lieutenant R. M. Morgan
1st Bn., The Gordon Highlanders
1953–1955
Edinburgh

SAC Graham Mottershaw
Royal Air Force
1950–1951
Stafford

SAC D. J. Munro
Royal Air Force
1958–1960
Livingston, West Lothian

SAC John Murphy
280 Signals Unit, Cape Gata,
    Royal Air Force
1958–1960
South Queensferry, Lothian

Writer William Nuttall
Royal Navy
1953–1955
Bolton, Lancs

Corporal Bryan Nutter
16 MU, Stafford, Royal Air Force
1950–1952
Poulton-le-Fylde, Lancs

AC1 James O'Donoghue
Royal Air Force
1961–1962
Dundee

Driver David Peterman
Royal Army Service Corps
1957–1959
London

Corporal C. W. Phelps
1st Bn., The Gordon Highlanders
1949–1951
Hoddesdon, Herts

Staff Sergeant D. F. Phillips-
    Turner
Royal Army Ordnance Corps
1950–1972
Twickenham

Corporal Derek Pilkington
Royal Army Pay Corps
1956–1958
Romford, Essex

Sergeant P. A. Preston
Royal Army Education Corps
1950–1951
Worthing, Sussex

AC1 David Price
Royal Air Force
1946–1948
Pontypool, Gwent

Lance-Corporal E. J. Priestley
Royal Corps of Signals
1946–1948
Edinburgh

LAC Frank Punchaby
MEAF 15, Royal Air Force
1951–1953
Bolton, Lancs

2nd Lieutenant J. M. H. Radford
1st Bn., The Queen's Royal
    Regiment
1955–1957
Ash Green, Surrey

Lance-Sergeant Alan Rattray
2nd Bn., The Scots Guards
1957–1960
Burghead, Moray

Private David Rees
1st Bn., The Royal Welch
    Fusiliers
1948–1953
Cwmbran, Gwent

SAC Gordon M. Reid
Royal Air Force
1953–1955
Aberdeen

Corporal Malcolm Richards
Medical Directorate
    Headquarters, BAOR, Royal
    Army Medical Corps
1956–1958
Grangemouth

Private Alexander Robb
1st Bn., The Seaforth Highlanders
1947–1949
Aberdeen

Lance-Corporal Griffith Roberts
Air Formation Signals Unit,
    Amman, Royal Corps of
    Signals
1952–1954
Caernarvon, Gwynedd

Rifleman George Savage
1st Bn., Royal Ulster Rifles
1952–1954
Luton

Gunner John Shepherd
Royal Regiment of Artillery
1950–1952
Voe, Shetland

Private William Skinner
1st Bn., The Seaforth Highlanders
1950–1952
Aberdeen

Private P. G. Smith
Regimental Pay Office, Wrexham,
    Royal Army Pay Corps
1959–1961
Rugeley, Staffs

Signalman P. H. Smith
602 Signals Troop, Royal Corps of
    Signals
1959–1961
Halifax, West Yorkshire

Sergeant T. J. Smith
57 HAA Regiment (RA), Royal
    Electrical and Mechanical
    Engineers
1958–1960
Lechlade, Glos

Craftsman Norman Stewart
Royal Electrical and Mechanical
    Engineers
1949–1950
London, Ontario, Canada

Corporal Derek Stoddard
Royal Army Service Corps
1947–1949
Stoke-on-Trent

Sergeant Richard Storey
RAC Training Brigade, Royal
    Army Educational Corps
1959–1961
Kenilworth, Warwicks

Corporal M. H. Taylor
Royal Air Force
1947–1949
East Oakley, Hampshire

Gunner Martyn Thomas
63rd HAA Regiment, Royal
    Regiment of Artillery
1948–1949
Bodmin, Cornwall

Craftsman Frank Thompson
Royal Electrical and Mechanical
    Engineers
1949–1951
Stornoway, Isle of Lewis

LAC B. J. Tipping
16 MU, Stafford, Royal Air Force
1951–1953
Newcastle, Staffs

LAC James Tod
No. 1 School of Recruit Training,
    Royal Air Force
1950–1952
Renfrew

2nd Lieutenant Patrick Tolfree
58th Medium Regiment, Royal

Regiment of Artillery
1951–1953
Stockport, Cheshire

SAC Donald Turner
207 Squadron, Royal Air Force
1954–1956
Killin, Perthshire

Sergeant-Dispenser III Thomas
    Varty
77th British Ambulance Train,
    Royal Army Medical Corps
1946–1948
Isle of Sheppey, Kent

Private J. W. Webb
Royal Army Medical Corps
1953–1955
Stoke-on-Trent

Lieutenant H. Max White
4th Hussars, Royal Army Medical
    Corps
1947–1949
Bromsgrove, Worcestershire

Trooper Brian Wilkinson
11th Hussars, Royal Armoured
    Corps
1953–1955
Pontypridd, Gwent

Corporal D. M. Williams
Royal Corps of Signals
1945–1948
Chippenham, Wilts

Lance-Corporal Jack Withers
Corps of Royal Military Police,
    7th Armoured Division
1955–1957
Glasgow

2nd Lieutenant R. J. Wyatt
Royal Electrical and Mechanical
    Engineers
1952–1954
Wokingham, Berks

Craftsman A. Yule
3 AA Group Workshops,
    Gosford, Royal Electrical
    and Mechanical Engineers
1949–1951
Aberdeen

The men are listed alphabetically together with their National Service unit and rank, and their present whereabouts.

INDEX